The Rodrigo Chronicles

THE RODRIGO CHRONICLES

Conversations about America and Race

Richard Delgado

New York University Press
New York and London

NEW YORK UNIVERSITY PRESS
New York and London

Library of Congress Cataloging-in-Publication Data
Delgado, Richard.
    The Rodrigo chronicles : conversations about America and race /
Richard Delgado.
        p.   cm.
    Includes bibliographical references.
    ISBN 0-8147-1863-9
    1. Afro-Americans—Civil rights.   2. Civil rights—United States.
3. United States—Race relations.   4. Racism.   I. Title.
E185.615.D45   1995
323.1'11969073—dc20   94-48155
                                 CIP

New York University Press books are printed on acid-free paper,
and their binding materials are chosen for strength and durability.

Manufactured in the United States of America

10   9   8   7   6   5   4   3   2   1

When we feel we are loved by the person we love, we love more, and nothing inflames our love so much as to know we are loved by the person we love, and being loved more makes the other love more too. When we think about the person we love, we love him more until we are nothing but one burning flame of love.
　　　　　—Ernesto Cardenal, "Love," in *Vida en el Amor* (1974)

Contents

Acknowledgments

I wish to thank Jean Stefancic for her inspiration and encouragement; Bonnie Kae Grover for her unflagging research assistance; and Peter Johnson, for technical support during the final stages of this book's production. Special thanks go to Derrick Bell, who graciously lent me some of his personae along with his moral support. Harriet Cummings, Devona Futch, Lash LaRue, Michael Olivas, Kelly Robinson, Erich Schwiesow, Louise Teitz, and Gerald Torres contributed to one or more Chronicles. Marge Brunner, Kim Clay, Anne Guthrie, Cynthia Shafer, and Kay Wilkie prepared the manuscript with precision and intelligence.

My gratitude also goes to my editor Niko Pfund and the New York University Press, and to the Rockefeller Foundation Scholar-in-Residence Program in Bellagio, Italy, where much of Rodrigo's Seventh Chronicle was written.

I am grateful to the following journals for permission to reprint or adapt essays that first appeared in their pages: *Yale Law Journal*, for *Rodrigo's Chronicle* [101 YALE L.J. 1357 (1992)]; *Michigan Law Review* for *Rodrigo's Second Chronicle: The Economics and Politics of Race* [91 MICH. L. REV. 1183 (1993)]; *California Law Review* for *Rodrigo's Third Chronicle: Care, Competition, and the Redemptive Tragedy of Race* [81 CAL. L. REV. 387 (1993)]; *Stanford Law Review* for *Rodrigo's Fourth Chronicle: Neutrality and Stasis in Antidiscrimination Law* [45 STAN. L. REV. 1133 (1993)] and

Rodrigo's Fifth Chronicle: Civitas, Civil Wrongs, and the Politics of Denial [45 STAN. L. REV. 1581 (1993)]; *NYU Law Review* for *Rodrigo's Sixth Chronicle: Intersections, Essences, and the Dilemma of Social Reform* [68 NYU L. REV. 639 (1993)]; *UCLA Law Review* for *Rodrigo's Seventh Chronicle: Race, Democracy, and the State* [41 UCLA L. REV. 721 (1994)]; *Virginia Law Review* for *Rodrigo's Eighth Chronicle: Black Crime, White Fears—On the Social Construction of Threat* [80 VA. L. REV. 503 (1994)]; and *Southern California Law Review* for *Rodrigo's Final Chronicle: Cultural Power, the Law Reviews, and the Attack on Narrative Jurisprudence* (forthcoming).

Foreword

In the Native American tradition, to assume the role of Storyteller is to take on a very weighty vocation. The shared life of a people as a community is defined by an intricate web of connections: kinship and blood, marriage and friendship, alliance and solidarity. In the Indian way, the Storyteller is the one who bears the heavy responsibility for maintaining all of these connections. Sacred stories and profane ones; stories of the clan, the camps, the hunts, the loves, the feuds, the names given and the nameless ones banished from the tribe for some unspeakable crime; trickster stories and ghost stories—the Storyteller shares all of these so that the next generation will recall these narrative links between generations. We recall the memories of our grandmothers and grandfathers, and their grandmothers and grandfathers, through the stories told by the Storyteller.

To be a Storyteller, then, is to assume the awesome burden of remembrance for a people, and to perform this paramount role with laughter and tears, joy and sadness, melancholy and passion, as the occasion demands. The Storyteller never wholly belongs to himself or herself. The Storyteller is the one who sacrifices everything in the tellings and retellings of the stories belonging to the tribe.

There is an art to being a Storyteller, but there is great skill as well. The good Storytellers, the ones who are most listened to and trusted in the tribe, will always use their imagination to make the story fit the occasion. Whether the story gets the "facts" right is really not all that important. An Indian Storyteller is much more interested in the "truth" contained in a story. And a great Storyteller always makes that "truth" in the story fit the needs of the moment. That is what Aunt Susie and Aunt Alice, two Storytellers extraordinaire, did, Laguna Pueblo writer Leslie Marmom Silko tells us in her appropriately titled autobiography, *Storyteller*. They "would tell me stories they had told me before but with changes in details or descriptions. . . . There were even stories about the different versions of stories and how they imagined these different versions came to be."

Here is the hard part about being a Storyteller. "We are what we imagine," the great Native American Storyteller of our time, N. Scott Momaday, tells us. "Our very existence consists in our imagination of ourselves." To be a Storyteller is to transcend the ordinary ways we have of imagining ourselves and our world. To be a Storyteller, a really good Storyteller, you have to go beyond yourself, you have to be a daring guide, a seer even; you take others where you and they have never thought of going. You must take the old stories, the really good ones, and make them better. Nobody listens to someone who tells the same story in the same way all the time. You must make it new, like a song of yourself, of your people, of your community. That is what it means to be a Great Indigenous American Storyteller. You must tell and retell the stories that are really important, the true ones, the ones that really challenge your imagination and the imaginations of your audiences. It is hard work to be a Storyteller, but a great Storyteller relishes this type of hard work because ultimately, it is just play, just gaming, just telling stories.

The Christian Bible, that great compilation of meta-stories of the Western narrative tradition, says that a false prophet is one who tells the people what they want to hear. A great Storyteller, in the Native American tradition, tells the people what they do not expect to hear. A Storyteller, in this sense, is always a prophet.

Richard Delgado is just such a great Storyteller. He could pass as an indigenous American Storyteller, but then, we are all indigenous Americans now. We are all native sons and daughters. It's just that some of us are still outsiders in our native land.

Delgado's stories are many things, but mostly they are outsider stories. They help us imagine the outside in America, a place where some of us have never been and some of us have always been, and where a few of us, like Rodrigo, shift-shape, like the trickster, asking the hard questions, the bedeviling questions, without answers, questions about what it means to be outside, what it means to be inside, and what it means to be in-between in America.

A good story should always remind us of other good stories. When I read *The Rodrigo Chronicles*, I am reminded of a favorite story of mine, told to me by an Indian elder who could see that I needed a certain kind of story on this particular occasion. "When I was growing up, I had to walk down this wash, which was the path to my school," this elder told me. "One day, two big white boys jumped out in front of me, and told me to empty my pockets. 'Indians shouldn't have money,' they said, and they took my lunch money. It wasn't much, but it was all I had, and I went hungry that day."

"What happened then?" I asked the elder, as I found myself being drawn into his story. "Oh, nothing much. I didn't tell my grandmother, who was taking care of me then. I didn't want to worry her. But the next day, I was walking down that same path to school, and those two white boys jumped out at me again."

"What happened this time," I asked. "This time," the elder said, "they asked me to empty my pockets, but I had hid my lunch money in my shoes. They got real mad when I showed them my empty pockets. To punish me, they took my jacket along with my money. It was the only jacket I had, and I went around cold that day."

"Surely you did something then?" I asked. "What could I do?" he said. "They were bigger than me, and I didn't want to worry my grandmother, who was watching me while my mother was off working in Phoenix. I thought, 'Maybe now, they've got what they want, they'll leave me alone.' "

"Did they?" I asked. "No, the next day, they stopped me in the path, and decided to beat me up. They took my money, my shirt off my back, even my shoes. I cried awhile, and went back to my grandmother's house. 'Grandmother,' I said, 'these white boys, for the past three days, have taken my lunch money, my jacket, the shirt off my back and the shoes off my feet. What should I do? Every time I walk down that path, they wait for me.' My grandmother looked at me. I was a small boy, she knew I couldn't fight those boys waiting for me on that path and come out of it better off than when I came in. 'Grandson,' she said quietly to me, 'for now, you need to think about taking a different path.' "

The Rodrigo Chronicles are about the most important story there is in America, the story of different races of peoples confronting each other on the different paths of American contemporary life. These confrontations occur in the classrooms, in the streets, in the boardrooms, in the courts of America.

Rodrigo walks down many of these paths. Sometimes he is the incessant questioner, at other times, the neophyte waif, the hyper-educated intellectual, the mercurial critic. He is all these and more, but no matter what path he is on he always keeps us interested in his projects and schemes. He keeps us questioning the answers he develops to the questions he asks. He keeps us imagining what kind of human being this many-faceted character Rodrigo is.

How you read this book will depend on how you imagine yourself—on the outside, on the inside, in-between. If you read it with the clouds covering your eyes, as the Indians say, so that the Sun which shines truth on all peoples cannot reveal itself to you, if you read it as someone who already knows the endings he or she wants to hear, you will probably not read much of it at all. But if you imagine yourself as a person who listens seriously to the stories told by others, if you are patient and an engaged listener and understand that a story creates a magic which unfolds according to its own scheme of time and things, then you will find many useful things.

You will find stories that make you ask questions about the economics and politics of race in America, about civil rights and civil wrongs, about antidiscrimination law aand social reform. Some of these stories you will want to retell; you will change them in the retellings, of course, to make their truth fit the occasion, and perhaps in time you will forget where the stories even came from. This insidious ability of a good Storyteller—to create a story so important that we appropriate it and dispense it as our own, and then conveniently forget its source—requires both art and skill. All great Storytellers strive to make themselves disappear. Only their stories live on. That is why, in the Native American tradition, to be a Storyteller is to sacrifice everything.

When I was growing up, my Lumbee elders would often look at me sternly and ask me in an almost accusatory fashion, "What have you done for your people today?" There was really only one right answer to this question, as I now realize. "Today, I have told the stories of my people, through my deeds and my thoughts. Today, I have assumed the heavy burden of being the Storyteller, the one who sustains the tribe. Today, I have made the sacrifice."

Our lives are the stories we are ultimately responsible for telling, and the richness of the stories we tell will be a reflection of the richness of the lives we live. It is a rich person who has stories to give away that others want to hear and take to heart as their own. Delgado is one of the richest Storytellers we have in America today.

We listen seriously to the stories told by others in order to make their stories a part of our lives, to give our lives that richness and depth which only stories can provide. If you imagine yourself as a Storyteller, you will listen closely to these stories, these chronicles of Rodrigo; you will retell them many times, to yourself and to your children, and to your children's children. We are all Rodrigo, we are all Storytellers.

ROBERT A. WILLIAMS, JR.

Introduction

Who is Rodrigo? Where did he come from? And what is a law professor doing writing fiction, anyway?

To a large extent, the reader curious about these matters will find answers in the dialogs themselves. The first and second Chronicles, for example, tell about the personal history of my exuberant young alter ego, Rodrigo—who his father and mother are, where he was educated, how he came to spend his teen and college years in Italy, and what he wants to do in life. In the third Chronicle, the reader learns about "Giannina," his companion and soulmate; in the fourth, sixth, and seventh, about his struggle to become a law professor like his mentor and straight man, the narrator of this book. Throughout, the reader learns quite a bit about Critical Race Theory (with as little jargon as possible), how two typical intellectuals of color talk to each other, what they think about inconsequential things like food, personal security, and coffee, and about quite consequential things like racial justice, economic fairness, the black left, the rise of the black right, and black crime. In the first, second, fifth, and seventh Chronicles, the reader listens in as Rodrigo and the professor discuss legal scholarship and some of the ideas and currents that professors, particularly the young (which, the professor admits, does not include him), have been discussing around the nation, including the legal storytelling movement itself.

Rodrigo is not the first black narrator and storyteller. Before him there was his sister, Geneva Crenshaw, the African-American superlawyer of Derrick Bell's *Civil Rights Chronicles* and 1987 book, *And We Are Not Saved*. Indeed, this is a good place for me to mention how grateful I am to Professor Bell for his permission to borrow Geneva's persona and develop her family tree a little further, as I have done.

Bell's book and this one are parts of the legal storytelling movement, which sprang up a few years ago and which, in turn, builds on a legacy of storytelling by outsiders going all the way back to the slave narratives and even before. These early tellers of tales used stories to test and challenge reality, to construct a counter-reality, to hearten and support each other, and to probe, mock, displace, jar, or reconstruct the dominant tale or narrative— for example, about their own laziness, lack of intelligence, or deservingness to share in life's bounty. Many of today's legal storytellers—writers like Derrick Bell, Mari Matsuda, Milner Ball, Patricia Williams, and myself— write for many of the same reasons. To be sure, much of our work is classically legal, densely footnoted, hardly intelligible to the ordinary reader. But much is readily accessible, and the reader who finds Rodrigo compelling, engaging, a good read, will not have to search hard to find more.

The events of *The Rodrigo Chronicles* form an integrated whole, with characters, a plot, and intellectual discussions that build on chapters that came before. Thus, the best way to read this book is sequentially. Nevertheless, the reader with limited time or with particular interests may wish to pick and choose. Most of the Chronicles are about race, sex, and class, matters that are very much on my two protagonists' minds. The reader interested in feminism may wish to note particularly chapter 6; the reader interested in law school and legal pedagogy, chapters 1 and 5.

The reader interested in economic conditions in the West, the rise of global markets and competition, and what this means for minorities in the U.S. will wish to read chapters 1 and 2. The reader intrigued by economics and the question of why the free market does not drive out discrimination may wish to note particularly chapter 2. Chapter 3 is the most hopeful; chapter 4, the bleakest. Chapter 8, on black crime, may strike many readers as the most audacious, as Rodrigo, who has been out of the country for more than ten years and sees our society with new eyes, puts forward a striking theory: White crime, not black, is the major problem in U.S. society today.

I hope the reader finds Rodrigo as engaging and challenging as I did as author. He came into my life at a time when I was in transition, just as law—indeed Western civilization generally—is in transition today. In reflecting on these cultural and personal currents, it began to dawn on me that Geneva must have a brother, that he must be part black, part Latin, and that he must have much to say about all the matters that trouble me and my countrymen. Within a few days, I knew that he would be interested in the West's predicament, the cultural wars now raging over multiculturalism, affirmative action, and the legal canon.

Writing in a fever, I produced Rodrigo's first Chronicle in just a few weeks, edited him, added footnotes (with the help of my computer-literate research assistants) and mailed him off to *Yale Law Journal* where a talented editor, James Forman, Jr., pushed me to flesh him out even more, then when he was satisfied I had done all I could do, edited him, brushed him up, and made him shine.

A final word: The professor, like Rodrigo, is not an actual person, but a composite of many individuals I have known, and should not be identified with any single one. As I have drawn him, the professor is a man of color teaching at a major law school in the same city where Rodrigo will eventually land, and is in the late stages of his career. Like Rodrigo, the professor is a civil rights scholar and activist but, unlike the young man, has suffered scars and disappointments from years in the trenches. He needs Rodrigo's impetuous energy as much as Rodrigo needs his caution and counsel.

To place the opening scene, imagine my office, a small, somewhat dark place packed with books and littered with the too-many projects I have undertaken—a letter of recommendation for this student, a request for an annotated bibliography for that journal, the notes for a talk at an upcoming conference I too hastily agreed to give six months ago, blue books to be graded, boxes to be unpacked. It is late in the afternoon, and my energy level is at low ebb.

As though by magic, a tall figure appears in my doorway. . . .

1

RODRIGO'S FIRST CHRONICLE

Introduction: Enter Rodrigo

"Excuse me, Professor, I'm Rodrigo Crenshaw. I believe we have an appointment."

Startled, I put down the book I was reading[1] and glanced quickly first at my visitor, then at my desk calendar. The tall, rangy man standing in my doorway was of indeterminate age—somewhere between twenty and forty—and, for that matter, ethnicity. His tightly curled hair and olive complexion suggested that he might be African-American. But he could also be Latino, perhaps Mexican, Puerto Rican, or any one of the many Central American nationalities that have been applying in larger numbers to my law school in recent years.

"Come in," I said. "I think I remember a message from you, but I seem not to have entered it into my appointment book. Please excuse all this confusion," I added, pointing to the pile of papers and boxes that had littered my office floor since my recent move. I wondered: Was he an undergraduate seeking admission? A faculty candidate of color like the many who seek my advice about entering academia? I searched my memory without success.

"Please sit down," I said. "What can I do for you?"

"I'm Geneva Crenshaw's brother.[2] I want to talk to you about the LSAT, as well as the procedure for obtaining an appointment as a law professor at an American university."

1

As though sensing my surprise, my visitor explained: "Shortly after Geneva's accident, I moved to Italy with my father, Lorenzo, who was in the Army. After he retired, we remained in Italy, where he worked as a civilian at the same base where he had been serving. I finished high school at the base, then attended an Italian university, earning my law degree last June. I've applied for the LL.M. program at a number of U.S. law schools, including your own. I want to talk to you about the LSAT, which all the schools want me to take, and which, believe it or not, I've never taken. I'd also like to discuss my chances of landing a teaching position after I earn the degree."

I reflected a moment, then said: "Your situation is somewhat unusual. But I'll do my best. I didn't know Geneva had a brother."

"We're only half-siblings," he explained, "and separated by nearly twenty years. But I've kept in touch as best I could, and I'm grateful to you for bringing her message to the attention of your friends. She has a rather acerbic manner, as you know. But she respects you and your work enormously."

"Your sister is a remarkable woman," I said. "I have learned at least as much from her as she from me."

Small Talk: Rodrigo Worries about the LSAT

I continued, "You said you are going to be taking the LSAT. What are your concerns about that?"

"The usual," he replied, "including that I don't see why I should have to take it at all. I graduated second in my class at a law school even older than yours.[3] I should think it would be obvious to anyone that I can read a case or make a legal argument. But I'm more than a little worried about the cultural bias people tell me the test contains. I'm proficient in English, as you can tell. But I've been away from the United States for nearly ten years; I'm afraid some of the questions may assume information I lack simply because I've taken half my schooling outside the culture."[4]

"I've made the same argument myself in the case of minorities in the United States," I said. "But it goes nowhere. They say the test is not biased because it predicts law school grades, which always seemed like a non sequitur to me.[5] I didn't realize that we required the test for foreign law graduates." I paused, then added, "Maybe they think it provides a check against grades, which might vary from one system to another."

"Yet in each system," Rodrigo countered levelly, "those grades reflect, in most cases, broader and more pervasive forms of cultural power, including the backgrounds and advantages of those who earn them. They also correspond to the law firm jobs and prestigious government positions the students will hold after they graduate. Identifying the LSAT as a predictor of grades, or even of later job performance, tells us only that this narrow test will identify people who thrive in particular types of environments—the ones, of course, that rely on the test to do a certain type of screening."

Not bad, I thought—I hoped he would come to my law school. But instead I asked: "So, what are you going to do? If you skip the test, you can kiss your LL.M. good-bye."

"I know, I know," he said. "If I have to take the test, I will. I bought one of those practice books. I'm sure I'll do OK—although I can't help thinking the whole thing is a waste of time."

"I agree—on both scores," I added.

Rodrigo and the Professor Discuss the Law School Hiring Market

"But the main reason I'm here is to ask you about the law school hiring market. I've heard it's extremely tight. But I'm also worried about something else. Geneva said it's becoming saturated with minority professors. I think she used the term 'tipping point' and mentioned an experience she had recently at a school where she was teaching.[6] She produced several good candidates of color but couldn't get her colleagues to take them seriously because the school already had six minority professors and was thought to be in danger of losing its character as a white-dominated institution. Is this happening at other places?"

"Too few!" I replied. "Most of them profess to be searching desperately for candidates of color."

"Profess?" Rodrigo's eyebrows arched.

"Those that say they are looking the hardest complain the loudest that the pool is too small. And, of course, if they start with that assumption, that is what they are likely to find, whether it's true or not."[7]

"How can that be?" Rodrigo asked. "There must be many lawyers of color like Geneva and me with excellent grades, practical experience, and so on. Why are the schools having such trouble finding us?"

"It works something like this," I said, reaching for a much-thumbed reprint.[8] "Every law school appointments committee starts out in October looking for a candidate with stellar credentials—a super-graduate with top grades from one of the top law schools, a law review editorship, a Supreme Court clerkship, and just the right amount of experience at the right firm. This individual should be humane, compassionate, and wise. Ideally, she or he should have published a classic Note in the law review."

"I have some of those things, but not all," Rodrigo noted with a trace of anxiety. "Do the schools actually find and hire people like that?"

"No, not at all," I replied. "They're looking for mythic figures, of which there are very few. To be sure, if they do find one who is black or Hispanic, they'll hire him or her in a flash—as they would, of course, if the person were white. But the AALS's own figures show that the pool of those actually hired, black or white, is much less prepossessing than that. Only about a third served on the law review, and half that figure were elected to Order of the Coif. Only a small percentage published anything at all."[9]

"So they obviously lower their standards at some point."

"Precisely. Although the committee members all begin the hiring season with these paragons in mind, by February they have managed to hire few, if any, of them. Several show up for interviews, only to turn down offers. So, now it's February and the dean is pressuring them to find someone to teach the UCC course and Trusts and Estates. Although by then there are few candidates left who were Supreme Court clerks and at the top of their classes at Harvard or Yale, there are several a notch below that—who graduated high, but not from a top school, or went to a top school but did not graduate at the head of their class. Still, the committee members know that these people are intellectually able and can do the job. They know this either from personal experience—someone on the committee practiced, clerked, or went to law school with one of them—or from someone they trust. Harry told Bill that Smith is really smart and will be a fine teacher. And so it works out— Smith is hired and goes on to have a fine career."

"I see what you're saying," Rodrigo said. "Those hired according to the relaxed, informal criteria schools use in February when they are under pressure are always white—right?"

"Exactly," I said. "With the result that majority-race candidates have two chances of being hired, while we have just one. They can be hired early in the season, just as we can, by being mythic figures—by satisfying the ostensible criteria, the superstar ones you hear about. But they can also be hired by word of mouth, under the relaxed criteria that are employed late in the game."

"A sort of affirmative action for whites," Rodrigo observed.

"You *are* Geneva's brother! You may be twenty years younger, but something of her rubbed off on you."

"We've always kept in touch. I must also confess, Professor, I've been reading your stuff and that of your colleagues in the Critical Race Theory movement.[10] It's fairly popular in Europe; many Italian law students read and discuss it."

"I'm flattered. But I wish the news were better. The trouble is that the patterns I mentioned are self-perpetuating. When the all-white appointments committee hires the white professor late in the year, it doesn't trouble them at all—although it should."

"It wouldn't feel like an exception," Rodrigo interjected, "because business as usual never does. One of our own intellectuals said something similar during a period of hard times for him."[11]

"To be sure," I quickly added, "once in a great while a law school will bend the rules and hire a professor of color who falls slightly short of the nominal criteria, who is just shy of Paul Freund or Thurgood Marshall in attainments and promise. And when they do so, the hiring *will* seem like an exception. They will congratulate themselves for bending down to lift up one of the downtrodden. The conservatives among them will complain that something unethical has been done—a great injustice to whites."[12]

"From my studies, it appears that those in the majority always see merit as God-given, fixed, and eternal," Rodrigo responded.

"And of course they are the ones who have it, while affirmative action is necessary for us who lack it," I replied.

"Yet your account of the two avenues for whites paints a different picture. I'm sure you've had the experience, Professor, of trying to get your colleagues to hire one of us."

"Many times," I replied. "They're some of the most predictably frustrating moments in my career. Every year the same thing happens. They say they are looking for candidates with qualifications A, B, and C. I produce a hungry, hard-driving candidate of color with credentials A, B, and C, and they say, 'Well, there's really also qualification D, which your candidate does not have. So, we cannot hire him after all.' Then I produce a candidate who possesses credentials A, B, C, and D, and they say, 'We also meant E.' Or, 'We meant something different by B from what you understood.'"

"So, the criteria regress until it dawns on you they are really talking about themselves—the criteria will fit only candidates who are like them, i.e., white."

"Exactly," I said. "Although every now and then I try a different approach—namely pointing out that many of their most highly valued colleagues are also glaringly deficient in one or more of the criteria. Professor Jones hasn't published anything in twenty years. Professor Smith is such a lackadaisical teacher that none but the unwary take his classes, and so on."

"And what happens when you point this out?"

"They always have some excuse. Jones wrote the leading article on contingent remainders in 1949 and is obviously germinating an equally impressive one, which accounts for his silence. Fifteen years ago, Smith, the notorious teacher, sat on a prestigious commission. And so on. It turns out there is a whole set of defenses available to their colleagues to justify their current positions—but not for us."

"Merit sounds like white people's affirmative action!" Rodrigo exclaimed. "A way of keeping their own deficiencies neatly hidden while assuring that only people like them get in."

"I've often thought that myself," I said.

Rodrigo was silent for a time. Then: "I wonder how they'll see me? I'm black, and my family is middle class. But I went to one of the great universities of the world."

"My guess is that one of them will hire you. And as with the rest of us, when it does so it will make sure that you know—and that the students do, too—what a huge favor it has done by extending an offer to you."

Rodrigo was silent for a long time. Then he mused, "Ironic, but I suppose that's the price I have to pay for wanting to return to the States."

"Ironic?" I questioned. "How so? Tragic, unjust, wrong are what come to mind, mine at least. What is the irony that you see?"

"The irony is that those who most need our help are those who most resist getting it."

In Which Rodrigo Begins to Seem a Little Demented

"I'm not sure I follow you."

"Let's start with something familiar—academic publishing. A recent article pointed out that nearly three-fourths of articles on equality or civil rights published in the leading journals during the last five years were written by women or minorities.[13] Ten years ago, the situation was reversed: minorities were beginning to publish, but their work was largely ignored.[14] The same is true in other areas as well. Critical legal studies and other modernist and postmodern approaches to law are virtually the norm in the top reviews. Formalism has run its course."[15]

"Perhaps," I said. "You don't see many articles in the classic vein today. In fact, I haven't seen one of those plodding, case-crunching, 150-page blockbusters with six hundred footnotes in a top journal for a while."

"No one believes that way of writing is useful anymore. Some are writing chronicles.[16] Others are writing about storytelling in the law,[17] narrative theory,[18] or 'voice' scholarship.[19] The feminists are writing about changing the terms of legal discourse and putting women at the center.[20] Even mainstream writers—the serious ones, at any rate—have moved beyond mere doctrinal analysis to political theory, legal history, and interdisciplinary analysis. There is a whole new emphasis on legal culture, perspective, and on what some call 'positionality,'[21] as well as a renewed focus on the sociopolitical dimension of judging and legal reasoning."[22]

"I'm not up on all these postmodern approaches, Rodrigo," I said quickly, "although I have read your countryman who, as you say, got into trouble with the authorities.[23] I find his work quite helpful. And I gather that the current ferment in American law is one of the reasons why you are thinking of returning here for your graduate degree?"

"In part. But I was mainly responding to your question about irony. However progressive certain mainstream scholars may be in their writing and analysis, the institutions they control still exclude and oppress minorities by manipulating the status quo and refusing to challenge their own informal expectations. The irony is that the old, dying order is resisting the new, rather than welcoming it with open arms."

Hmm. I thought of the words of a Bob Dylan song,[24] but instead asked: "And just who, or what, do you think this new order is, Rodrigo?"

"Well, let me put it this way," Rodrigo explained. "You've heard, I assume, of double consciousness?"

"Of course. It's W. E. B. Du Bois's term.[25] It refers to the propensity of excluded people to see the world in terms of two perspectives at the same time—that of the majority race, according to which they are demonized, despised, and reviled, and their own, in which they are normal. Lately, some—particularly feminists of color—have invented the term 'multiple consciousness' to describe their experience."[26]

"And you know that many members of minority groups speak two languages, grow up in two cultures?"

"Of course, especially our Hispanic brothers and sisters; for them, bilingualism is as much an article of faith as, say, Martin Luther King and his writings are for African-Americans."

"And so," Rodrigo continued, "who has the advantage in mastering and applying critical social thought? Who tends to think of everything in two or more ways at the same time? Who is a postmodernist virtually as a condition of his or her being?"

"I suppose you are going to say us—people of color."

Rodrigo hesitated. "Remember that I have been sitting in Italian law libraries all these years, reading and learning about legal movements in the United States secondhand. I suppose it looks different to you here."

"It has scarcely been a bed of roses," I replied dryly.[27] "The old order, as you put it, has not welcomed the new voices with any great warmth, although I must agree that the law reviews seem much more open to them than my faculty colleagues. And your notion that it is we—persons of color—who have the edge in mastering critical analysis would strike most of them as preposterous. If double consciousness turns out to be an advantage, they'll either deny it exists or insist that they can have it, too. Aren't you just trying to invert the hierarchy, placing at the top a group that until now has occupied the bottom—and isn't this just as wrong as what the others have been doing to us?"

Rodrigo paused. "I see your point. But maybe this way of looking at things seems harsh only because it is so unfamiliar. In my circles everyone talks about the decline of Western thought, so finding evidence of it in law and legal scholarship doesn't seem so strange. I'm surprised it does to you. Are you familiar with the term 'false consciousness?'"[28]

"Yes, of course," I said (with some irritation—the impudent pup!). "It's a mechanism whereby oppressed people take on the consciousness of the oppressor group, adjusting to and becoming parties to their own oppression. And I suppose you think I'm laboring under some form of it?"

"Not you, Professor. Far from it. But when you rebuked me a moment ago, I wondered if you weren't in effect counseling me to internalize the views of the majority group about such things as hierarchy and the definition of a 'troublemaker.'"[29]

"Perhaps," I admitted. "But my main concern is for you and your prospects. If you want to succeed in your LL.M. studies, not to mention landing a professorship at a U.S. law school, perhaps you had better 'cool it' for a while. Criticizing mainstream scholarship is one thing; everyone expects that from young firebrands like you. But this business about a more general 'decline of the West'—that's out of our field, frowned on as flaky rhetoric, and nearly impossible to support with evidence. Even if you did have evidence to support your claims, no one would want to listen to you."

"Yes, I suppose so," admitted Rodrigo. "It's not the story you usually hear. If I had told you that I'm returning to the United States because it's the best country on earth, with rosy prospects, a high quality of life, and the fairest political system for minorities, your countrymen would accept that without question. No one would think of asking me for documentation, even though that is surely as much an empirical claim as its opposite."

"You have a point," I said. "The dominant story always seems true and unexceptionable, not in need of proof. I've written about that myself, along with others.[30] And you and I discussed a case of it earlier when we talked about minority hiring. But tell me more about your thoughts on the West."

"Well, as I mentioned, my program of studies at Bologna centered on the history of Western culture. I'm mainly interested in the rise of Northern European thought and its contribution to our current predicament. During my early work I had hoped to extend my analysis to law and legal thought."

"I think I know what you will say about legal thought and scholarship. Tell me more about the big picture—how you see Northern European thought."

"I've been studying its rise in the late Middle Ages and decline beginning a few decades ago. I'm interested in what causes cultures to evolve, then go into eclipse. American society, even more than its European counterparts, is in the early stages of dissolution and crisis. It's like a wave that is just starting to crest. As you know, waves travel unimpeded across thousands of miles of ocean. When they approach the shore, they rise up for a short time, then crest and lose their energy. Western culture, particularly in this country, is approaching that stage. Which explains, in part, why I am back."

I had already switched off my telephone. Now, hearing my secretary's footsteps, I stepped out into the hallway to ask her to cancel my appointments for the rest of the afternoon. I had a feeling I wanted to hear what this strange young thinker had to say undisturbed. When I returned, I saw Rodrigo eyeing my computer inquiringly.

Returning his gaze to me, Rodrigo went on: "I'm sure all the things I'm going to say have occurred to you. Northern Europeans have been on top for a relatively short period—a mere wink in the eye of history. And during that time they have accomplished little—except causing a significant number of deaths and the disruption of a number of more peaceful cultures, which they conquered, enslaved, exterminated, or relocated on their way to empire. Their principal advantages were linear thought, which lent itself to the development and production of weapons and other industrial technologies, and a kind of messianic self-image according to which they were justified in dominating other nations and groups. But now, as you can see," Rodrigo gestured in the direction of the window and the murky air outside, "Saxon-Teuton culture has arrived at a terminus, demonstrated its own absurdity."

"I'm not sure I follow you. Linear thought, as you call it, has surely conferred many benefits.[31] And is it really on its last legs? Aside from smoggy air, Western culture looks firmly in control to me."

"So does a wave, even when it's cresting—and you know what happens shortly thereafter. Turn on your computer, Professor," Rodrigo said, pointing at my new terminal. "Let me show you a few things."

For the next ten minutes, Rodrigo led me on a tour of articles and books on the West's economic and political condition. His fingers fairly danced over the keys of my computer. Accessing data bases I didn't even know existed, he showed me treatises on the theory of cultural cyclicity, articles and editorials from the *Economist, Corriere della Sera,* the *Wall Street Journal,* and other leading newspapers, all on our declining economic position; material from the *Statistical Abstract* and other sources on our increasing crime rate, rapidly dwindling fossil fuels, loss of markets, and switch from a production- to a service-based economy with high unemployment, an increasingly restless underclass, and increasing rates of drug addiction, suicide, and infant mortality. It was a sobering display of technical virtuosity. I had the feeling he had done this before and wondered how he had come by this proficiency while in Italy.

Rodrigo finally turned off the computer[32] and looked at me inquiringly. "A bibliography alone will not persuade me," I said. "But let's suppose for the sake of argument that you have made a prima facie case, at least with respect to our economic problems and to issues of race and the underclass. I suppose you have a theory on how we got into this predicament?"

"I do," Rodrigo said with that combination of brashness and modesty that

I find so charming in the young. "As I mentioned a moment ago, it has to do with linear thought—the hallmark of the West. When developed, it conferred a great initial advantage. Because of it, the culture was able to spawn, early on, classical physics, which, with the aid of a few borrowings here and there, like gunpowder from the Chinese, quickly enabled it to develop impressive armies. And, because it was basically a ruthless, restless culture, it quickly dominated others that lay in its path. It eradicated ones that resisted, enslaved others, and removed the Indians, all in the name of progress.[33] It opened up and mined new territories—here and elsewhere—as soon as they became available and extracted all the available mineral wealth so rapidly that fossil fuels and other mineral goods are now running out, as you and your colleagues have pointed out."

"But you are indicting just one civilization. Haven't all groups acted similarly? Nonlinear societies are accomplishing at least as much environmental destruction as Western societies are capable of. And what about Genghis Khan, Cortez, Columbus, the cruelties of the Chinese dynasties? The Turkish genocide of the Armenians, the war machine that was ancient Rome?"

"Sure. But at least these other groups limited their own imperial impulses at some point."

"Hah! With a little help from their friends," I retorted.

"Anyway," continued Rodrigo, "these groups produced valuable art, music, or literature along the way. Northern Europeans have produced next to nothing—little sculpture, art, or music worth listening to, and only a modest amount of truly great literature.[34] And the few accomplishments they can cite with pride can be traced to the Egyptians, an African culture."[35]

"Rodrigo, you greatly underestimate the dominant culture. Some of them may be derivative and warlike, as you say. Others are not; they are creative and humane. And even the ones you impeach have a kind of dogged ingenuity for which you do not give them credit. They have the staying and adaptive powers to remain on top. For example, when linear physics reached a dead end, as you pointed out, they developed relativity physics. When formalism expired, at least some of them developed Critical Legal Studies, reaching back and drawing on existing strands of thought, such as psychoanalysis, phenomenology, Marxism, and philosophy of science."

"Good point," admitted Rodrigo a little grudgingly, "although I've already pointed out the contributions of Gramsci, a Mediterranean. Fanon and your Critical Race Theory friends are black or brown. And Freud and Einstein are, of course, Jews. Consider, as well, Cervantes, Verdi, Michelangelo, Duke Ellington, the current crop of black writers—non-Saxons all."

"But Northern Europeans, at least in the case of the two Jewish giants," I interrupted.

"True, people move," he countered.

"Don't be flip," I responded. "Since when are the Spanish and Italians exempt from criticism for 'Western' foibles? What about the exploitive capacity of the colonizing conquistadors? Wasn't the rise of commercial city-states in Renaissance Italy a central foundation for subsequent European cultural imperialism? Most ideas of Eurocentric superiority date to the Renaissance and draw on its rationalist, humanist intellectual, and artistic traditions."

"We've had our lapses," Rodrigo conceded. "But theirs are far worse and more systematic." Rodrigo was again eyeing my computer.

Wondering what else he had in mind, I continued: "What about Rembrandt, Mozart, Shakespeare, Milton? And American popular culture—is it not the envy of the rest of the world? What's more, even if some of our Saxon brothers and sisters are doggedly linear, or, as you put it, exploitive of nature and warlike, surely you cannot believe that their behavior is biologically based—that there is something genetic that prevents them from doing anything except invent and manufacture weapons?" Rodrigo's earnest and shrewd retelling of history had intrigued me, although, to be honest, I was alarmed. Was he an Italian Louis Farrakhan?

"The Saxons do all that, plus dig up the earth to extract minerals that are sent to factories that darken the skies, until everything runs out and we find ourselves in the situation where we are now." Then after a pause: "Why do you so strongly resist a biological explanation, Professor? Their own scientists are happy to conjure up and apply them to us.[36] But from one point of view, it is they whose exploits—or rather lack of them—need explaining."

"I'd love to hear your evidence."

"Let me begin this way. Do you remember that famous photo of the finish of the hundred-meter dash at the World Games this past summer? It showed six magnificent athletes straining to break the tape. The first two finished under the world record. All were black."

"I do remember."

"Black athletes dominated most of the events, the shorter ones at any rate. People of color are simply faster and quicker than our white brothers and sisters. Even the marathon has come to be dominated by people of color. And, to anticipate your question, yes I do believe the same holds true in the mental realm. In the ghetto they play 'the dozens'—a game that requires throwaway speed. The dominant group has nothing similar. And take your field, law. Saxons developed the hundred-page, linear, densely footnoted, impeccably crafted article—saying, in most cases, very little. They also brought us the LSAT, which tests the same boring, linear capacities they developed over time and that now exclude the very voices they need for salvation. Yet you, Matsuda, Lawrence, Torres, Peller, and others toss off articles with ridiculous ease—critical thought comes easy for you, hard for them.[37] I can't, of course, prove your friends are genetically inferior; it may be their mindset or culture. But they act like lemmings. They go on building factories until the natural resources run out, thermonuclear weapons when their absurdity is realized and everyone knows they cannot be used, hundred-page law review articles that rehash cases when everyone knows that vein of thought has run dry—and they fail even to sense their own danger. You say they are adaptive. I doubt it."

"Rodrigo," I burst in. "You seriously misread the times. Your ideas on cultural superiority and inferiority will obviously generate resistance, as you yourself concede. Wait till you see how they respond to your hundred-yard dash example; you're sure to find yourself labeled as racist. Maybe we both are—half the time I agree with you. But even the other things you say about the West's predicament and its need for an infusion of new thought—things I strongly agree with—will fall on deaf ears. All the movement is the other way. This is a time of retrenchment. The country is listening to the conservatives, not to people like you and me."

"I know," said Rodrigo. "I've been reading about that retrenchment. We do get *The New York Times* in Italy, even if it comes a few days late."

"And so you must know about conservative writers like Allan Bloom,[38] Thomas Sowell,[39] Glenn Loury,[40] Roger Kimball,[41] Shelby Steele,[42] E. D. Hirsch,[43] and Dinesh D'Souza,[44] and the tremendous reception they have been receiving, both in popular circles and in the academy?"

"Yes. I read D'Souza on the flight over, in fact. Like the others, he has a number of insightful things to say. But he's seriously wrong—and hardly represents the wave of the future, as you fear."

"They certainly represent the present," I grumbled, glancing at the D'Souza book on my desk. "I can't remember a period—except perhaps the late 1950s—when I have seen such resistance to racial reform. The public seems tired of minorities, and the current Administration is little different. The backlash is apparent in the university setting as well: African-American studies departments are underfunded and the exclusionary Eurocentric curriculum is making a comeback."

"But it's ordinary, natural—and will pass," Rodrigo responded. "In troubled times, a people turns to the past, to its own more glorious period. That's why these neoconservative writers are popular—they preach that the culture need not change direction to survive, but only do the things it did before, harder and more energetically."

"What our psychologist friends call 'perseveration,'" I said.

"Exactly. In my studies, I found that most beleaguered people do this, plus search for a scapegoat—a group they can depict as the source of all their troubles."[45]

"An old story," I agreed ruefully. "D'Souza, for example, places most of the blame for colleges' troubles at the doorstep of those demanding minorities who, along with a few deluded white sympathizers, have been broadening the curriculum, instituting Third World courses, hiring minority professors, and recruiting 'unqualified' students of color—all at the expense of academic rigor and standards.[46] He says the barbarians—meaning us—are running the place[47] and urges university administrators to hold the line against what he sees as bullying and a new form of racism."[48]

"Have you ever thought it curious," Rodrigo mused, "how some whites can see themselves as victimized by us—a pristine example of the sort of postmodern move they profess to hate. I suppose if one has been in power a long time, any change seems threatening, offensive, unprincipled, wrong. But reality eventually intervenes. Western culture's predicament runs very deep—every indicator shows it. And, there are straws in the wind, harbingers of hopeful change."

"Rodrigo, I'll say this for you—you've proposed a novel approach to affirmative action. Until now, we've struggled with finding a moral basis for sustaining what looked like breaches of the merit principle, like hiring a less over a more qualified person for racial reasons. But you're saying that white people should welcome nonwhites into their fold as rapidly as possible out of simple self-interest—that is, if they want their society to survive.[49] This is something that they are not accustomed to hearing, to put it mildly. Do you have any support for this assertion?"

"Turn on your computer again, Professor. This won't take but a minute."

I obliged him, and was treated to a second lightning display of technological wizardry as Rodrigo showed me books on Asian business organization,

Eastern mysticism, Japanese schooling, ancient Egyptian origins of modern astronomy and physics, and even on the debt our Founding Fathers owed the Iroquois for the political ideas that shaped our Constitution. He showed me articles on the Japanese computer and automobile industries, the seemingly more successful approach that African and Latino societies have taken to family organization and the treatment of their own aged and destitute, and even the roots of popular American music in black composers and groups.[50]

"It's only a beginning," Rodrigo said, switching off my computer. "I want to make this my life's work. Do you think anyone will listen to me?"

"It's hard to say. I don't know if the times are right. Most Americans believe that their economic problems are just temporary and that they have the best, fairest political system in the world—conveniently forgetting a chapter or two of their own history.[51] But never mind that. Let me ask you instead a personal question: If things are really as bad as you say, why are you thinking of returning? Shouldn't you remain safely in Italy while your native culture self-destructs? When a wave crests, then hits the beach, it creates an immediate commotion. There's a lot of foam, a loud noise, a great expenditure of energy, and sometimes an undertow. I should think someone like you would be at some risk here—particularly if you go around speaking as candidly as you have to me today—notwithstanding our much-vaunted system of free expression."

Rodrigo Explains Why He Has Returned

"I'm back for family reasons. Geneva and my other half-brothers and sisters are here. And since my mother died, I have no other close relatives in Italy. Your decreasing quality of life[52] and high white-collar crime rate[53] gave me pause. And I could be quite comfortable in Italy, now that I've got my military service out of the way. I suppose I thought, as well, that with a little more training I could do something to ease the pain of my native country as it goes through a difficult transition."

"You mean helping America adjust to its new multiracial character, plus its own shrinking share of world markets?" I asked.

"That and more," Rodrigo answered quietly. "The dominant group will need help. All of us will."

"What if they don't see it that way?" I pressed. "Has a dominant group ever given up power gracefully? Has it ever abandoned the modes of thought, military organization, and extractive industries that brought it to power without a struggle? [54] And if so, how are we—I mean those who believe like you—going to conduct such a campaign? I'm afraid they have all the power. You may think truth and history are on your side. But what if they don't go along?"

"They will," Rodrigo replied with conviction, "as soon as they recognize their own dilemma. The early Visigoths destroyed themselves by warring. We can help the current dominant culture avoid a similar fate. [55] We may even have some friends and allies in the majority group—ones who believe as we do. [56] Maybe we can bill our offerings as 'hybrid vigor'—something they already endorse."

"And, once again—what if they refuse? Paradigms change slowly. What if your transformation requires a hundred years?"

"In that case, we can simply use sabotage and what you call terrorism to speed things up. The more advanced, the more technologically complex a society becomes, the more vulnerable it is to disruption. [57] Imagine what a few strategic—and nonviolent—taps on telephone switching stations around the country could do—or a few computer viruses, for that matter. Disruption is economically efficient for the subordinated group. In Italy, the government tried for a time to exclude leftist organizations. A few kidnappings and commando raids, and they were ready for serious negotiation. Something like that could happen here—or do you think I'm wrong, Professor?"

"Rodrigo, I have many doubts about all the things you have said—and particularly this one. If you repeat even half of what you have told me today to your colleagues or students, you will find yourself out of academia on your ear—and probably disbarred to boot."

"I had no idea those were the rules of discourse. On the Continent we discuss these things openly—especially since recent events in Eastern Europe showed that rapid reform is, in fact, possible. Your society certainly perpetrated plenty of terrorism on blacks, Chicanos, and Indians. Nevertheless, if one cannot discuss these things in—how do you put it?—polite company, I'll keep them to myself and for my close friends. I don't want to be seen as having an attitude problem."

Our conversation soon concluded. I had to prepare for a faculty colloquium I was to give at my new school that afternoon, and Rodrigo quickly excused himself, saying he had to get ready for the LSAT—"that dinosaur relic of an outmoded system of thought"—the coming Saturday. But I couldn't shake his image. Here was a man who spoke what he saw. I feared for him. [58]

Exit Rodrigo

I heard from him a few more times in the weeks ahead. He left a message the following Monday saying he had found the LSAT easier than expected and hoped he had done well. About a week later, I received a polite letter saying how much he had enjoyed meeting me and asking whether, in view of our lengthy conversation, I felt I could write letters of recommendation on his behalf to certain LL.M. programs. I called him at Geneva's Greenwich Village apartment where he was staying, and we spoke for nearly half an hour, during which I tried to get a better sense of his professional and personal goals. In particular, I wanted assurance that he would not too openly advocate or prematurely engage in disruptive acts of the sort he had mentioned so casually in my office. Hearing enough to satisfy myself, I wrote four letters of recommendation, each to a different LL.M. program, over the next week.

All my work was wasted. Three weeks later, I received a long letter, on flimsy airmail stationery, written from a city in southern Italy. It read:

Dear Professor:

Thank you for all your efforts on my behalf. As you can see, I am back in Italy, courtesy of your immigration authorities. It seems I made the fundamental error of performing six months of part-time military training in the Italian Army shortly after my twentieth birthday. At the time it seemed a reasonable way of paying back the Italian nation for subsidizing my education at a fine university. Also, I don't know if I told you, but my late mother was an Italian citizen. How all this came to the attention of your authorities, I do not know. Is it possible your office or telephone is being monitored? [59] The immigration officer who conducted my hearing seemed to know a great deal about my political attitudes and interests.

At any rate, I have been informed that I am subject to denaturalization, whatever that means. I have to apply for a U.S. visa like any other foreigner, which could mean a delay of several years. So you will be deprived of further exchanges with me, in person at any rate, for the foreseeable future. I've found decent employment here, but had looked forward to returning to my homeland. I guess there is no reason to assume that a culture bent on demonstrating its own destructive absurdity will interrupt that demonstration for critical remonstrance. Well, as they say, Que sera, sera.

Arrivederci,

Rodrigo

As I walked across Washington Square park that evening I thought: Have we lost a prophet, or a madman? A racist or a savior? One with a message of hope, or of hatred and confusion? All these things at once?

A homeless man, his few possessions stacked neatly on the bench beside him, looked up at me despairingly as I walked past. Rodrigo's image of a wave cresting rose in my consciousness. I wondered if I would see him again.

2

RODRIGO'S SECOND CHRONICLE:
The Economics and Politics of Race

Introduction: Rodrigo's Return

"Rodrigo. My God, you're back!" (Normally, I do not use profanity or take
the name of the Lord in vain. But the familiar lanky figure standing in my
office doorway had given me quite a start.)

My visitor broke into a broad grin. "I needed a while to get my affairs in
order, take care of that immigration problem, and pack. I was admitted to
the LL.M. program of that school uptown. So we'll be neighbors—living in
the same city, at any rate."

"I'm delighted," I stammered, putting down the book I had been reading[1]
and reaching out to shake his hand. "I wrote the INS as soon as I got your
letter. But I didn't expect to see you so soon. This is wonderful news."

"It took a little doing. I received some letters from colleagues of yours who
must have read your account of my predicament. They urged me to return.
But I'd already resolved to do that myself. And here I am—just moved into
my new apartment on upper Riverside last week. My sister Geneva gave me
a hand. You're the first person I've looked up since getting settled."

"You have no idea how glad I am to see you. I was afraid you'd spend the
rest of your life as a café intellectual in sunny Italy. At least my letters of
recommendation to the LL.M. programs weren't wasted. Tell me how you

did it. I talked to some colleagues about your immigration problem; they were stumped." I motioned for him to take a seat in my still cluttered office. "Would you like a cup of coffee?"

"Thanks," Rodrigo replied, casting a glance at my office coffeemaker and supply of beans. "I'm afraid I became addicted to espresso in Italy, where it's practically the national drink."

As I busied myself grinding the beans and setting the timer, Rodrigo launched into his story. "First, I appealed the INS decision, emphasizing the brevity of my service with the Italian army and my reasons for performing it.[2] But the agency was having none of it—they acted as though they had no discretion, which of course you know they do. They kept telling me to reapply, as though I hadn't been born here and had no good reason for being in Italy while I was growing up."

I poured the coffee and asked, "So are you here on a student visa? And if so, how are you going to get a law teaching job later without lying about your intent?"[3]

"That worried me, too, Professor, because as you may know I hate lying."

"So, what did you do?" I asked, indicating the cream and sugar. "Whatever it is, I hope it's legal. You're not one of those undocumented aliens, as our Anglo friends call them, are you?"

"Both, please," he replied. "I used a two-step procedure. As you know, the European Community went into effect recently. Under the basic agreement, a citizen of one member state is entitled to travel freely and settle in any other."

"Sounds sensible to me," I said. "Although I can't help contrasting it to the situation here. If anything, we've been tightening up our own immigration policies in response to growing xenophobia aimed at limiting the influx of outsiders—particularly ones with coloration like yours and mine. It reminds me of those waves of 'nativism' that seem to rise up when our culture is under threat."[4]

"I heard about that. So I planned things carefully. First, I became an Irish national. This was much easier than you might think, since both Italy and Ireland are members of the EC and, as a graduate lawyer, I had no problem proving I wouldn't become a public charge. Within a short time I had my own apartment and paralegal job in Dublin, which by the way has a great literary and intellectual life."

Probably a close call, I thought, for I knew how Rodrigo loved such settings. "And how did you get from Ireland to here?"

"Oh, that part was easy. I enlisted the support of an Irish immigration society located in an eastern U.S. city. I told them I was a lawyer with American forebears, and they agreed to sponsor me. Technically, the route used was a private bill."

"A private bill?" I asked.

"I was surprised, too. But, as they explained, it's fairly routine. A U.S. senator of great prestige and standing, himself of Irish descent, sponsors such bills fairly regularly. He thinks the United States needs more Irish men and women, and his colleagues go along even if that year's quota is filled."[5]

"And I suppose there was nothing in the record to show that you had previously been excluded or that you are a budding racial reformer and the subject of a recent law journal article laying bare your somewhat unflattering analysis of Western culture."

"I think your term for it is 'separation of powers.' The immigration service did learn of my plan and may well have tried to intervene. But they got nowhere, because it's a different arm of government. It's one of the nice features of your—I mean our—political system."[6]

I looked up and found my young interlocutor looking slightly guilty. "What is it?" I asked.

"There's one more thing I ought to tell you. I may have overdone it—but you must understand I really wanted to get back. While in Ireland, I bought a title for a few thousand pounds from some down-at-the-heel member of the English nobility. I wanted to assure favorable consideration by your authorities. It turned out probably to have been unnecessary; my law degree and American ancestry were probably enough."

"So, what are you—Rodrigo, the third duke of Crenshaw?"

"Something like that," Rodrigo muttered, looking down at his feet. "The incongruity has not escaped me."

"I'm just glad you made it back. It's quite a story."

Getting Caught Up: Rodrigo and I Discuss the Economics and Politics of Race

"Aside from Geneva and the folks at the Boston Irish immigration office, you're the only person who's heard it. What are you working on these days?" Rodrigo craned his neck in an effort to read upside down the titles of the books lying on my desk.[7] "The last time we talked you were struggling with black neoconservatism."[8]

"Your memory is good. Now, I'm trying to get a handle on their counterparts, the law-and-economics movement."

"I did notice that footnote in the reprint you sent me. And you guessed right. When we spoke in your office I knew very little about that school of scholarship. It's not well known yet in Italy—there are hardly any books available except the first one by Richard Posner.[9] But there were more in Dublin and, as you can imagine, dozens in the library of my new school. I've been reading everything I could lay my hands on. What motivated you to dive into this stuff?"

"Even at my advanced age, Rodrigo, we're expected to keep abreast. And, as luck would have it, I've been invited to a conference on the economics and politics of racial discrimination. The organizers plan to pair conservative law-and-economics types with racial reformers like me. I think they are hoping some sparks will fly, although frankly I'm not sure we'll have much to say to each other."

"Really?" Rodrigo brightened. (Hah—I thought, maybe I'll learn something. Little do students know how much we get from them. Their enthusiasm and even their sometimes half-baked ideas keep us going and provide the spark necessary to sustain us in an otherwise drab and desolate world.)

"Yes, really," I replied, refilling his coffee cup. "The law-and-economics folks write pages full of formulas and little squiggly signs. They talk about things like transaction costs, speak of racism as a 'taste,' and spend more time showing why governmental efforts to cure it would be 'inefficient' than they do deploring the practice itself. We, on the other hand, treat racism as subordination, not a mistake, much less an idiosyncratic 'taste,' and struggle to understand its connection with culture, history, and the search for psychic and economic advantage."[10]

"I have noticed that gulf between the two groups," Rodrigo agreed. "Some LL.M. students and I were talking about it the other day. Maybe that's one of the things you and the other panelists could talk about at the conference, don't you think?"

Smart kid, I thought. That one idea should be enough to get my speech off and running.

"Maybe you could even tie that difference to the notion of 'positionality' that you see emerging in feminism, Critical Race Theory, and other critical literature.[11] The law-and-economics scholars have a certain background, training, and set of disciplinary assumptions, so naturally they look upon discrimination the way they do. They treat civil rights statutes as a form of tariff because that's how they see the government—as a well-meaning, if clumsy, regulator. That's their slant, their disciplinary bias, their 'positionality.'"

"That's a start," I said, refilling my own coffee cup despite the lateness of the afternoon hour and my doctor's warning to cut down on caffeine. "But where do you go from there? Position, color, and even life experience don't determine all, as our friend Randall Kennedy has been good enough to point out.[12] Tom Sowell, for example, a leading economist of race, is black. And he takes as dim a view of affirmative action as any blueblood East Coase theorist."[13]

Rodrigo looked at me sharply. "Interesting double entendre," he said. "You're right that perspectivism only goes so far." He paused for a moment. "Maybe you could challenge their basic premise that racism is a form of irrationality."[14]

"Good idea," I said. "I had planned to take them to task for failing to take into account the intentional, interest-serving dimension of white-over-black prejudice. Maybe I'll call them 'reductionist.' They're sure to hate that because they all fancy themselves scientists."

"But of course they'll reply that people like you are just as much at fault, with your loose talk about a culture of racism, interest-convergence, hegemony, false consciousness, and other vague and unquantifiable things."

"You're right," I conceded. "I have to show them that their approach is not only reductionist, but wrong."

"That's easy," said Rodrigo with his customary elan. "Why not take their major premise about the market and show that it doesn't explain, much less cure, racism? Show them they need critical thought if they are to understand and deal with that scourge."

"It's not clear to me exactly how to do that, although I definitely would if I could," I said.

"Correct me if I'm wrong, Professor, but don't your law-and-economics colleagues believe that, in the absence of monopoly, the market ought to cure most forms of irrationality?"

"At least some of them do."[15]

"And don't they think of racism as a form of irrationality?"

"They do.[16] But the market obviously doesn't work that way. Consider— the United States has had a free market economy for over two centuries, and racism is as firmly entrenched as ever. The economists reason that an employer or real estate owner who discriminates against African-Americans, gays, or women places himself or herself at a competitive disadvantage. Nonracist landlords or employers will be able to employ or rent to better people—at least if they can get their other workers or tenants to go along. Over time, they should drive out competitors who discriminate, because these others will end up hiring or renting to less qualified whites."

"That's the theory, all right, but you and I know the reality is quite different."

Rodrigo drained his cup. "Remind me later, Professor, to explain why things work just the opposite—why racism tends to increase over time rather than dampen, as the economists say it should. The first step, though, is to explain why competitive pressures don't eliminate racism in the market."

"I think I know what you're going to say," I said. "Competitive pressures don't work because discriminators as a group know that irrational-seeming individual decisions, if followed by all or most whites, create a system of social advantage. I've written about that myself, along with others." [17]

"I know. But, actually, I was going to add something else."

"Please go ahead. I didn't mean to interrupt."

"Racism persists, in part, for the reason you mentioned—simple group self-interest. But there's another dimension, as well. Take employment discrimination. Antiracist hiring decisions are so rare that they make news, and the reason is that it never occurs to individual whites to think that hiring a black could benefit them—that is, the whites."

"But isn't that just regular irrationality, which the economists say will be cleared up once the lagging firms get the message that nonracist ones do better in competition?"

"With due respect, Professor, I think it's different. Look at it this way. You and your friends have written about the social construction of reality, including racial reality, have you not?" [18]

"Others more than I," I grumbled. "Although I'm familiar with that literature, I haven't found it as useful as some have. It seems to me that racism offers such powerful economic and psychological incentives to any group able to get away with it that resorting to fancy theories is unnecessary."

"Maybe so," Rodrigo conceded. "Although I'll just note that you are considered a leading proponent of legal storytelling, one function of which is to deconstruct and displace comfortable, self-serving majoritarian myths and replace them with less sexist and racist views. [19] So in a way you're contributing to the reconstruction of social worlds."

"I know some have said that. But I think of myself as just an ordinary foot soldier. If others want to put an elaborate postmodern gloss on it, that's their privilege. I just don't find it necessary."

"Bear with me for a second," said Rodrigo. I noticed he was furrowing his brow, the first time I'd ever seen him depart from his air of youthful exuberance. "Let's suppose there's a world where all the As hate and disdain all the Bs, whom they consider stupid, lazy, and morally debased. The Bs think of themselves as normal, and of the As that way as well—except for this unlovely trait."

"Sounds a little bit like a society I know," I said.

"And let's suppose, Professor, that the reason the As hold this view of the Bs is not that there is anything wrong with the Bs. Rather, they were brought to their current land in chains to perform menial work, and the As coined an attitude—call it B-inferiority—to justify that practice. Later, they freed the Bs, but the attitude remained because it was advantageous to maintain it. So the As circulate and reinforce stories and myths about B-inferiority at every turn—in children's tales, TV, movies, advertising slogans, and so on. This all creates a stigma-picture or stereotype, so that virtually everyone in the society harbors the attitude to some extent."[20]

"This would obviously benefit the As, who could use the Bs as cheap labor, scapegoats for blue-collar A workers unhappy with their lot, and so on."

"But imagine that a few As are inclined to be rulebreakers and mavericks. Might they not try hiring a few Bs, just to see if it works—just to see if it gave them a competitive advantage?"

"Certainly—if only for menial work in times when the surplus labor supply is exhausted."

"No, I mean at other times, and for regular or high-status jobs."

"It's hard to imagine. I suppose they might," I replied, unsure of where Rodrigo was going.

"But the implication of your thought and that of other postmodernists— forgive me, Professor, if I keep calling you that—is that this is unlikely to happen. The shared construct or stereotype of the Bs makes it unlikely that anyone at all will do this.[21] The person would almost have to stand outside the culture."

"Like yourself."[22]

"Perhaps," Rodrigo brushed off the compliment impatiently. "Another way of looking at it is in terms of knowledge. All the economists say the market won't operate perfectly unless everyone has perfect knowledge.[23] But the stigma-picture that white people hold of blacks operates as a screen. Because of the thousands of stories, jokes, scripts, and narratives they hear, whites can never have that degree of knowledge—even the proverbial ones who boast that they count some of us among their best friends."

"Very funny," I acknowledged. "Although, in one way of looking at it, they do have 'perfect knowledge.' I understand that your favorite authors equate knowledge with power, hold that it is inseparable from social convention and practice.[24] White people in that sense know us perfectly: the universality of the stereotypes, the way in which they are embedded in the very paradigm we require to communicate with and understand each other, means that the market in a way will operate perfectly—that is, with what passes for perfect knowledge."

"And will thus perfectly reinforce racial reality—whites over blacks—all the while maintaining that it is perfectly neutral," Rodrigo added sardonically.[25]

Now *that's* something I can use at the conference, I thought. Worth getting caffeine nerves over.

"We need a good example, or your audience will never get it. What can we use?" Both of us were quiet for a while. I switched the burner on the coffeepot to "Warm."

In Which Rodrigo Explains Why the Free Market Does Not Cure Racism

"I have an idea," Rodrigo said at last.

"I'd love to hear it."

"Imagine this thought-experiment. It concerns children, another disempowered group."

"Do you mean white children or black children—or any kind?" I asked.

"Any kind. Imagine a farm state, say Minnesota, decides to license children to drive vehicles. A lot of children are needed to drive cars, tractors, etc., around the farm, something they now can do perfectly legally as long as they stay on private property."

"Okay," I said. "And why do they decide to let them drive on the roads, which I assume your licensing scheme allows them to do?"

"Two reasons. Sometimes the young drivers need to take the tractor or car on a public road for a short distance to get from one part of the family farm to another."

"So, to get from the front ten to back twenty acres, they can now drive on County Road 112."

"Right—that's the practical reason. But the other one is empirical. Let's suppose the legislature conducts studies to show that young children between the ages of ten and thirteen are likely to prove quite safe drivers. Psychologists testify that children of this age are apt to be careful, conscientious, and law-abiding. Males under the age of twenty-one, by contrast, are high-risk drivers. So the state adopts a new licensing scheme in which children can drive between the ages of ten and thirteen, but the males have to give up their licenses when they become young adults."

"A pretty outlandish idea," I said, nevertheless intrigued. "I suppose you think there is some connection between children drivers and race?"

"Yes, as you'll see in a minute. But first we have to suppose that Minnesota's experiment actually works. Things are much more convenient for farm families, plus the ten- to thirteen-year-olds turn out to be the safe drivers the experts thought they would. With teenagers and young males off the roads, the death rate on the highways plummets. Everybody's insurance rates go down fifty percent."

"An intriguing scenario," I allowed. "And what conclusion do you draw from it?"

"This. Would our state's hypothetical program be followed? Would forty-nine other states quickly bring their own licensing schemes in line with Minnesota's?"

"I suppose you are going to say no, but I'm curious why."

"They would all find reasons not to follow the Minnesota experiment, distinguishing their state from that one in some minor respect, when the real reason has to do with the idea of a child."

"I see what you're saying," I said with interest. "The idea of an eleven-year-old hunched over a steering wheel, cheerfully and safely driving a car all by himself or herself, is inconsistent with our social construct of a child. It's out of role, like the idea of women in combat today,[26] or of blacks in the Navy a few years ago."[27]

"Exactly," Rodrigo said. "Society can't accept the notion of children as independent, of having the autonomy and freedom of movement that driving a car on public highways brings. Children are meant to be watched, dependent, small, and helpless. We want them to be that way. So, whatever the evidence disclosed, we'd find ways to ignore or discount it."

Hmmm, I thought. Hadn't I heard of evidence law discussions in a similar vein? I made a mental note to ask a colleague who teaches in that area. The studies I dimly seemed to remember indicated that child eyewitnesses, although actually better than older ones, are still not allowed to testify. The full implication of what Rodrigo had been saying struck me. "So, it's a kind of market failure—no other state would follow the first one's example, just as racist firms would refuse to follow the lead of a nonracist one, even if this meant giving up a competitive edge."

"They won't do it for the same reasons that we won't empower children, let women fight in combat, or accept gays in certain lines of work.[28] These things go against the grain. Racism, sexism, and homophobia are in the cultural paradigm—in the very set of values, ideas, and meanings we rely on to construct, order, and understand the world, as well as communicate with each other about it."[29]

"And since they are in the paradigm, we don't see them, cannot speak against them without seeming and feeling foolish, much less take action to correct them."

"Exactly, and it's a dimension your economists ignore in their focus on the microcosm, on the individual, atomized aspect of human interaction and choice. Because of who they are, their disciplinary bias or 'positionality,' they systematically misperceive the essence of racism."

"Rodrigo, I need some dinner. You set a fast pace and, as fascinating as all this is, I'm not as young as I used to be. Why don't we walk down to the Village for a bite?"

I noticed Rodrigo's quick flash of concern, then added, "Don't worry, I'll pay. This is helping me get ready for my conference. I know what it's like living in the city on a student's budget. You're my guest."

Wherein My Young Friend Stands Law and Economics on Its Head with a Little Assistance from the Sociology of Knowledge

We were comfortably settled in an Italian restaurant that Rodrigo pronounced "good—at least equal to the ones I used to patronize back there. The pasta seems fresh and homemade. And the wine—not bad, although I see it's from California."

"I come here often with colleagues. It's cheap and they let you stay as long as you want. You had been explaining why law and economics does not account for racism's continuing vitality—for the market's failure to make much of a dent in it."

"Posner, Epstein, and others try, but can't. Their approach is too confined. They focus on individual choices, on the microcosm, when the essence of racism and other forms of prejudice is much broader than that. Epstein, for example, speaks of the right to exclude from a circle of friends and associates as standing on the same footing as the right to join such a circle. He speaks of the antidiscrimination laws as forcing individuals into 'undesired interaction,' something whose 'totalitarian implications become clear only when one realizes the . . . steps that must be taken to enforce [them].' Individuals know their own preferences better than anyone else, so any governmental meddling is inefficient and likely to make matters worse.[30] Charles Murray,[31] Thomas Sowell,[32] and even Gary Becker[33] echo some of these conclusions. What they don't seem to realize is that, with race, we don't so much operate irrationally in an otherwise sound world as create a world with irrationality built into its very structure.[34] Once we create a world where race matters, we become unaware of our creation's contingency. Racial generalizations come to seem natural, a sort of baseline, 'the way things are.' What now seems irrational is to hire a black or let one in your law school. These decisions require 'affirmative action' and are thus morally troublesome, as you and I discussed earlier. Individual actions work in concert ineluctably to reinforce the racial status quo. It feels like freedom, like individual choice. Yet the effect is tyranny."

"This has been quite useful," I said. "I hope you don't mind if I steal your ideas. You asked me earlier to remind you to tell me something. I've forgotten what it was—something about the future perhaps?"

Rodrigo was silent for a moment. "Oh, yes. I was discussing this with one of the other LL.M. students, who is from Ghana. It's my thesis that racism gets worse over time, not better—in other words, exactly the opposite of what the law-and-economics scholars tell us."

"I've been pointing that out myself, although possibly for different reasons.[35] And I doubt you'll have any more success than I've had. I'm sure you've noticed, Rodrigo, that it's almost impossible to get most white folks to see that things are getting worse. They love to fasten on the myth of black progress. Tell them twenty dismal statistics about African-American poverty, early death, and despair, and they'll come up with a single cheerful statistic that they heard somewhere that suggests that things are getting better—that today there are more partially sighted Hispanic plumber's apprentices in Ohio than there were twenty-five years ago, more black undergraduates majoring in Naval R.O.T.C. at land grant colleges, or some such thing. But tell me your theory of why the market does not drive out racism but accentuates it."

"It's simple," said Rodrigo, deftly wrapping a long strand of pasta around his fork. "Once you understand that racial differences are social constructs and that racial mythology is intensely interest-promoting yet firmly believed, you see how racism accelerates, feeds on itself. The image becomes reality, which in turn reinforces the image, which seems truer and truer and ultimately beyond refutation."

"Sort of a self-fulfilling prophecy," I offered. To be truthful, I didn't quite get his drift and wanted him to spell it out a little more. Was my blood sugar level low, or was I just not up to following this wunderkind? I took another bite of my fettucini Alfredo.

As though reading my thoughts, Rodrigo added, "Maybe that's a little too elliptical. What I meant was that we have constructed an image of blacks as inferior—as unintelligent, not very ambitious, and so on. Originally, this served transparently majoritarian purposes—justifying slavery first, and later the black codes. But over time, this transparency drops out. Now, we really begin to see blacks, women, children, the way the construct holds. The occasional high-achieving black or woman—or independent self-sufficient child—is disregarded or lauded as an aberration. For their parts, the objects of the stereotype either internalize it or are coerced into their assigned roles. Minorities, in fact, become poor, women domestic, children passive and 'cute.' The image becomes real, true in the sense of beyond refutation. Young children are probably more dependent today than they were a hundred years ago. Women are just as much objectified sexually, if not more so. And so on."

In Which Rodrigo Explains His Neo-Crypto-Theologico Double Feedback Loop

"I'm still not convinced, Rodrigo. Your argument lacks rigor. It may seem plausible to me, but the law-and-economics types on my panel see themselves as hardheaded scientists. Moreover, few of them are familiar, as you and I are, with the day-to-day reality of life as a person of color. They think things are getting better, that all we have to do is let the market operate. You'll need to show them the exact mechanism by which racism tends to worsen, not improve, over time. You can't just offer vague ideas like self-fulfilling prophecies and social constructions that feed on themselves. Your Minnesota example was interesting, but not persuasive in my opinion."

"I don't know how else to show someone who believes all diseases are individual that there is such a thing as social pathology."

Both of us were silent. Rodrigo was furrowing his brow a second time. "Professor, are many of your law-and-economics colleagues religious?" he asked.

The question took me by surprise. "I don't know. Probably. Yes, at least one that I know of is—fairly devoutly so. But what's the relevance of their faith or lack of it?"

"Religion is something beyond empirical proof. Maybe you can build on that to question their faith in microtransactions and analysis as the whole story."

"I don't follow you."

"Well, haven't many religions emphasized miracles, predestination, the notion of a fair and just world, and other manifestations of God's efficacy?"[36]

"Yes, I suppose so," I said.

"And haven't all conquerors from Hammurabi on down invoked religious explanations to justify their conquests and rule over other nations?"

"Of course. Our young friend Robert Williams wrote a brilliant article entitled 'Documents of Barbarism' showing how the early settlers applied European myths of supremacy and Manifest Destiny to justify genocide and plunder of Indian lands.[37] Even the judiciary was complicit in developing a version of this—the Discovery Doctrine, according to which Indian lands might be appropriated by any European person or nation."[38]

"So, can we say that religion, to the extent it speaks to the issue, confirms a culture in what it thinks and does? If society is unjust, if upon looking about them the members see manifest differences between the standards of living, levels of employment, infant mortality rates, and so on, of their group and others—then something must be wrong with those others. They lack character, ambition, the right genes. The social system is fine, because divinely ordained; the fault lies with individual actors like you and me."

"Religion, like any powerful narrative, is canonical," I observed. "Anything that deviates from the narrative or tends to cast doubt upon it is itself put in question. The poverty and despair of communities of color put the fair-world tenet in question. So, the narrative supplies a reason—our fault."

"Are you and I free of that narrative, Professor?"

"I'm not sure," I answered. "They conclude that, because the world is fair yet we are poor and despised, there must be something wrong with us individually, or with our culture or family—we are not among the elect. We, by contrast, having the same belief in a fair world but knowing that we are normal—like everyone else[39]—interpret differences in the distribution of social goods like jobs, longevity, wealth, and happiness as evidence of malevolence or neglect on the part of those in power, or else as basic defects in the social system."

"And so each group interprets the very same reality to reinforce its own beliefs about racial justice," Rodrigo concluded.

"And whites become more and more convinced that blacks and Hispanics are complainers, always conjuring up exaggerated claims of discrimination when all we need to do is go out and work and find the opportunities that are there."

"Your colleague Thomas Sowell says more or less that, and he's black.[40] He says if the Irish, Chinese, and West Indians can make it, so can African-Americans."[41]

"But you said both groups seize on the same evidence to confirm their positions, thus drifting farther and farther apart over time."

"Oh, yes," Rodrigo replied. "People of our persuasion see the same events, the same history, and either give up and withdraw—feeling what's the use— or else clamor, riot, or write pungent law review articles and books like you, Professor.[42] Each group's conduct just reinforces the other's view that the second group is unjust and impossible. Over time, blacks get more militant and whites more complacent, with a little help—on both sides—from the legacy of John Calvin, Charles Darwin, and Adam Smith."

"A double feedback loop with roots in religion and faith in a fair world," I mused.

"Something like that," he said.

"I think I may try this out on my law-and-economics friends. Now that I think about it, many of them are religious—even if they only believe in the Invisible Hand.[43] Maybe I can get them to see that societal discrimination is something more than irrationality and that it's likely to get worse before it gets better."

"Good luck."

A few minutes elapsed while we finished dessert and I summoned the waiter. I gave him my credit card, and as we waited I expressed a concern that had been nagging at me. Choosing my words carefully, I asked my young friend:

"Rodrigo, if this is the picture that the new Critical thought introduces, I'm not sure I or many others will want to see it. Baleful images deepen and rigidify. Racism and sexism increase over time. Compared to that, most of us will take liberalism. Where's the opening for transformation, for hope? Why struggle if things are the way you say? What's the point?"

"Some of those criticisms have been directed at your own work, Professor, as I'm sure you know," Rodrigo replied levelly.[44] "The world is not ordained to be a pleasant place—that's wish fulfillment. One shouldn't pick a philosophy or perspective merely because it makes one feel good."

"Agreed. But where do you go from there? What's the point of struggle? I assume you are back from sunny Italy for a reason. Why did you return to this vale of tears?"

In Which Rodrigo Explains, Why Struggle

"Because, as I mentioned earlier, the United States's—indeed the entire West's—dominant culture is in disarray.[45] Their economy, infrastructure, educational system, cities, and environment are in sharp decline, yet they are stuck—perseverating—digging in and doing harder and with more energy the very things that got them into trouble in the first place.[46] They're listening to the neoconservatives and nativists who tell them they can be great again by being American—thereby turning their backs on the very voices and points of view that might save them, might enable them to break free from deadlock and stagnation."

"But I thought I just heard you say that the potential for basic change, at least on the racial front, is highly limited. If the United States is to save itself, it must incorporate ideas and people from non-Western sources—and yet these are the very sources they've constructed, as you put it, to seem unworthy, ridiculous, lazy, and morally debased." I paused to drive home to Rodrigo the blind alley to which his analysis seemed inexorably to lead.

"There's a way out," Rodrigo said quietly. "They're our stigma-pictures, after all. We made them, we can unmake them. There's no objective inferiority of peoples of color to worry about, no reason why white folks must always be on top, no reason why all persons cannot have equal levels of dignity and respect. As soon as one sees this, one places oneself on the path of liberation. The culture, the practices, the thousand images and roles they've assigned to us, all reinforcing the idea of our inferiority[47]—all these are revealed as contingent, not necessary. We can accept them or not. They can, too. Our approach in this sense is much more liberating—and more subversive—than liberalism. We need not live in a world we do not like, that we did not help create, and then seek minor adjustments and changed positions within that unfairly structured world. We may work for change. If we don't, everything will fail."[48]

"And so, law and economics is . . . "

"A useful way of ordering relations and transactions within a given system, say, Western capitalism—but a poor way of understanding and dealing with broad, systemic distortions built into the very structure of that system. Relying on economic theory to solve problems of race and sex makes about as much sense as reading Gramsci for help with one's household budget."

"Speaking of budgets, how are you managing your finances? This is an awfully expensive city for a student."

"I had saved up some from my year of practice in Rome and Dublin. Geneva was nice enough to help me find a rent-controlled apartment. And I got a loan, like two-thirds of my fellow students. Which reminds me, Professor—my tuition bill's due tomorrow morning. Thanks for the dinner, but I'd better get to my bank before it closes. Good luck at your conference, if I don't see you before then."

I watched his lanky figure disappear from sight, paid the bill and left, ignoring as best I could the stares of a yuppified couple at the next table.[49] As I walked home through the late summer evening, I felt one of those rare surges of happiness over being a teacher. I was happy to have next month's talk largely mapped out, and grateful to Rodrigo for having helped me think it through. What a rare student! With a start I realized that the afternoon's discussion had focused almost entirely on my concerns and, except for the first part, little on his. I hoped his adjustment to American legal education and pedagogy went well, and resolved to call him up after a week or two of classes to see how things were going.

3

RODRIGO'S THIRD CHRONICLE:
Care, Competition, and the Redemptive Tragedy of Race

Introduction: Rodrigo Accounts for His Recent Activities

"Rodrigo, I was just thinking about you." This was not the usual hyperbole busy professors use to flatter their favorite students. Since returning from my talk at the Economics of Race conference, I had been meaning to call Rodrigo to thank him for helping me prepare for it. "How has the term been treating you?"

"Not bad. How was your conference?"

"Good. They're thinking of making a book out of the proceedings. If so, I'll get a chapter out of it. My talk went over well, thanks in part to our conversation."

"You give me too much credit," Rodrigo replied. "I was just a sounding board. But if you have a minute, I need your ear in connection with something I'm working on myself."

"Glad to oblige, though I hope you'll first tell me about your LL.M. program. I feel I had some role in getting you started. How are things uptown?" I asked, motioning him to have a seat on my office couch. "Like some coffee?"

"You know my weakness," Rodrigo replied. "I've been staying up late with two seminar papers, including the one I need to talk to you about."

In Which Rodrigo Explains How He Won a National Essay Competition, Solved the Riddle of the Ages, Yet Got into Trouble with His Seminar Professor

As I busied myself making a pot of espresso on my office coffeemaker, Rodrigo launched into his tale:

"Things are going fine. Your Socratic method takes a little getting used to. But I'm enjoying myself, except for something curious that happened in my Social Legislation seminar. It's taught by a famous professor, someone you probably know. We had to write papers, so I wrote on a problem that I'd been thinking about for a while—namely, how to reconcile socialism and capitalism."

"No small challenge, Rodrigo!" I replied. I was struck by his audacity but, on second thought, was not really surprised. The brash, talented Rodrigo never had seemed to me one to shy away from difficult challenges. "So, you addressed the riddle of the ages, one that has troubled some of the finest political minds of our times?"[1]

"You know that I studied world cultures before returning here.[2] Plus, there has always been great interest in socialism and Marxism among Italian intellectuals. Yet, all my professors here in the U.S. seem deeply committed to free market solutions for everything. It struck me as an area warranting examination. So I resolved to see what I could do."

"And that's what you wrote about for your course paper?"

"Yes, and I won a national essay competition for student writing. The judges loved it. I even received a small cash award, which I gave to my sister to pay her back for some of the moving-in expenses she helped me with."

"Congratulations!" I replied. "Your professor must have been proud." Gesturing toward the shelf, I said, "Cream and sugar?"

"Thanks," said Rodrigo, pouring and stirring with gusto. "As a matter of fact, that's what I'm here to see you about. Patience has never been my strong point, and when I learned of the essay competition, I sent a draft even before showing it to my professor. The deadline was in early November, and I felt confident enough of my analysis that I sent it in."

"And then what happened?"

"I got a phone call announcing the award. But my professor, although happy that I won, wants me to rewrite the paper. He says it's not legal enough. Plus, to do real justice to the topic, he says it really ought to be a book. But, since there's not time for that, he wants me to scale it down. He suggested that my next draft focus on race—on the 'problems of my people,' as he put it."

"Fascinating," I replied. "They are always commenting that we cluster together in cafeterias and so forth, and only want to teach and write about civil rights. Then, when we address something of broad social interest, they want to herd us back into our cubbyholes as quickly as possible. It happens often.[3] You'd think there would be a cumulative embarrassment effect, but apparently not. But tell me what your paper is about—the one that won the prize, I mean."

"As I said, Professor, I set out to reconcile socialism and capitalism, the two principal systems of economic organization in the world. They've long been thought to be in conflict. So I thought that trying to reconcile them would be a good thing to do, especially for a Social Legislation paper."

"Some very good minds have addressed this very problem, Rodrigo," I replied wryly. "If you've pulled it off, you'd be a candidate for the Nobel Prize in law, if there were such a thing, not just first place in a student competition. Tell me about your analysis. Later, we can talk about what your professor wants in the way of a redraft. Incidentally, you shouldn't feel offended that he wants you to submit two drafts. It's a very common requirement in American law school courses."

"I know. He explained that during the first meeting. I just didn't expect the revision would take the direction he suggested—although, as you know, I'm fascinated by problems of race." Rodrigo peered at the jacket of a book lying open on my desk. "I'm reading the same one. It looks like it might be useful for my rewrite."[4]

I refilled Rodrigo's cup and sat back expectantly. Rodrigo loved to talk about books and ideas. And I was especially curious to learn his thoughts about socialism and free market capitalism, since I had just returned from a conference on a related subject.

"How did you decide on your topic?" I asked.

"I was reading about nursing home scandals, including a recent case in which an elderly patient died for lack of care.[5] Another LL.M. student, a friend of mine from Ghana, is writing about the problem of regulating such homes, so the issue was on my mind. It occurred to me that we have no such problem in Italy, nor in any other Mediterranean country I know about. And the same seems to be true of black and Chicano culture here. No matter how poor an elderly person, there is generally someone who will take care of them."

"I know of exceptions," I interjected. "But as a generalization, you may be right. It is mainly our friends of the majority race who seem most concerned about being alone and uncared for in their old age."

"And this got me to thinking, not so much about white versus nonwhite differences, but the problem of care generally. It struck me that the caregiving sector of a society should almost always be socialized, while the productive sector should be relegated to the free market economy."

"A nice, elegant solution," I replied. "But of course the law-and-economists will argue that everything should be governed by the market,[6] including nursing homes. Where, and why, do you draw the line?"

"Let me explain by means of the example I just mentioned," Rodrigo replied, finishing his coffee and looking up animatedly. "The nursing home had hired the minimum number of employees they could get away with under the law. And they were all high school graduates or less. When the elderly patient went into a semi-coma, they were too busy to notice, even though the other patients tried to call his predicament to their attention. Three days later, the family came to visit him and, noticing his condition, called an outside doctor. But it was too late. The grandfather died the next day."

"And the moral you draw from this is . . .?"

"Caregiving and the profit motive are incompatible. The temptation is to cut corners, which is contrary to what's needed. With caregiving, the focus has to be on the individual, not on the profit line. If what you need to dispense is love, compassion, nurturance, then you need to socialize the caregiving enterprise. That way, we all bear the cost of it, and can, if we decide, hire high-quality caregivers."

I sat up with interest. "And since our society is getting older,[7] and none of us knows if he or she will need a caretaker sometime in the future, people can perhaps be made to go along." I am considerably older than Rodrigo and had given more than passing thought to what will happen to me when I enter old age.

"With the productive sector," Rodrigo continued, "it's fine to try to cut corners. A firm that succeeds in reducing the price of a good or service will drive its competitors out, which is good and to be expected. But people are not commodities, not cans of soup. So, with child care, nursing care, primary education, programs for the mentally ill and other dependent populations, we should socialize every one. Some we already do. We should do the same with all the rest, even if it costs more in the short run."

"So, the trick is to draw the right line between the productive sector, which should be governed by aggressive, dog-eat-dog capitalism—the sort of thing our conservative friends love—and the caregiving sector, which should be socialized. Model-fitting, as they say."

"Right. And that's what my original paper was about. I even gave examples of industries and services that we currently socialize, like the Post Office, which it makes no sense to treat that way. They ought to be relegated to the private sector as soon as possible."

"You may not know this, Rodrigo, because you've been living in Italy. But we've actually been coming around to that view. Recently, we've allowed companies like U.P.S. and Federal Express to compete with the Post Office for the delivery of mail and packages. They've become very popular because they're faster and don't charge any more."

"I know. A friend of mine got an express package in Dublin from some friends in America. It got there in only two days; the mail usually takes a week. And when you think of it, it makes sense. There is no reason at all to have the Post Office be a socialized bureaucracy, other than that your Constitution makes some vague reference to one.[8] The clerks are bored and slow. The Post Office can't attract intensely idealistic persons with nurturing skills, since there's little about a letter to love. Nor is there the zest and *elan* associated with competitive enterprise—trying to deliver a service or good cheaper and better than the next business. No wonder complaints about the service run rampant."[9]

"Let's say we do what you suggest, Rodrigo. We commit all the caregiving activities—the ones we can't handle as individuals, at any rate—to the public sector, and socialize them. And we relegate the Post Office, manufacturing, and other productive activities to the competitive sector. Won't this just set up two nations within one, with the idealistic caregivers working at jobs everyone will regard as second class? We already have this to some extent.[10] Won't your plan just exacerbate it?"

"No," Rodrigo replied quickly, "because we'll be free to pay the caregivers a living salary. As you mentioned, this shouldn't be hard to arrange, because with an aging society, everyone fears that they might need to be taken care of some day. But there are additional arguments."

"I'd love to hear them."

"Well, first of all, everyone today is seeing firsthand the economic and psychic consequences of lack of care," Rodrigo gestured toward the book on my desk, "all the things Professor Hacker writes about—increased crime, juvenile delinquency, school dropouts—and more. The case for socializing caregiving today is plainer and more urgent than ever before. Personalized, loving attention to dependent individuals is today a cultural mandate—one that even makes economic sense."

"Then why not leave it to the private sector?"

"Because by its very nature, it is needed by those who can least afford it. We must socialize caregiving if it is to be effective."

"You may have a point, Rodrigo, but I'm still worried about the problem of second-class citizenship. With caregiving a function of the socialized sector and production left to the private side, won't all the caregivers end up being minorities, just like in the bad old days?"

"No, I don't think so," Rodrigo replied. "Many white folks have idealistic impulses, too, and would gladly work taking care of children, the aged, or the disabled if those jobs paid a decent salary. Some of them do now, even with what they get paid. And for the many caregivers who suffer demoralization and 'burn-out,' the better pay and greater prestige that would go with socialization may be the tonic they need to stay with their stressful, demanding jobs longer."[11]

I was silent for a moment while Rodrigo poured himself a second cup of coffee. I marvelled at his youthful constitution. Two cups in the afternoon would have had me awake half the night. "You mentioned there were a number of arguments in favor of your plan. What are the others?"

"One is synergy—interactions between the two sectors. The productive sector would develop technology for high-quality caregiving—for example, monitoring machines, wheelchairs, interactive learning devices for young schoolchildren. They could sell these to the caregiving sector, compensating for the somewhat higher tax bill the productive sector would have to absorb. At the same time, the caregivers, free to give first-rate attention to their charges, should be able to send many of them into the private sector equipped with skills, a high self-image, and good job prospects. Currently, half a generation of inner-city children grows up unemployed or underemployed—if they don't turn into criminals or drug dealers.[12] Concentrated caregiving from an early age will redeem many of them, enable them to become Thomas Edisons, Colin Powells, or Jonas Salks. Our economy would flourish, instead of sinking to the point where it is now barely in the top five in the world.[13] You recall our discussion before, Professor."

"I do. And your ideas have a certain idealistic appeal. Certainly we should try anything rather than succumb to the predicament Andrew Hacker, Studs Terkel, and others describe so starkly.[14] But what about the problem of incentive, of motivation? Wouldn't those in the caregiving sector become lazy and refuse to work hard? Why should they, if they can't be fired, if their businesses can't ever go under?"

"Mothers are not paid, nor are fathers. Do they take frequent coffee breaks, become lazy and bored?"

"No, of course not. But that's because they have ties of blood. Nature equips them to care. Parents—most parents, anyway—have an instinctual love of their children. Why should anyone love other people's children, or an elderly, incontinent retiree in a nursing home?"

Rodrigo was silent for a moment. "Some people do care about others, even in our dog-eat-dog system which values competition and success above everything else. My approach would enable these people to do what they are inclined to do naturally—help others. As things now stand, those who go to work for Legal Aid, the public defender, or do social work with the inner-city poor, become demoralized.[15] Society does not value their work. They are underpaid in relation to what they do—which often exceeds in importance that which a Madison Avenue advertising specialist does in a lifetime of getting people hooked on cigarettes or consumerism."

"But, Rodrigo, if changing bedpans in a nursing home were highly valued, wages would not be what they are. People have little taste for that kind of work. Much of it is so simple, anyone can do it. That's why it's not highly recompensed. Aren't you trying to distort the market, and isn't that always inefficient, as our friends in the law-and-economics movement put it, and, therefore, a bad idea?"

"Good point," Rodrigo conceded. "But tastes are created. They come from somewhere. The same is true of distastes.[16] People shy away from helping professions because they're taught those jobs are low status. Consider your own students. Don't many of them come to law school imbued with idealism, ready to change the world, to represent the poor and the underdogs?"

"Yes, of course. You're like that now, for some reason."

Rodrigo shrugged off the compliment. "And what happens to them over time?"

"You know as well as I do. They change. Law school depicts corporate, big-firm practice as the best, and criminal and poverty law as not nearly so prestigious or challenging. After a year or two, most of the ones who began certain that they wanted to vindicate justice and defend the outcasts start to think of law as a technical game.[17] And the game is more enjoyable when played in a large firm with secretaries, paralegals, office parties, Xerox and fax machines—and, of course, a high salary."

"So, every year you see firsthand, Professor, that tastes and distastes change?"

"Unfortunately so."

"Could not the pattern be reversed? What if law school painted poverty practice as the best, and big-firm practice as repetitious, sterile, mechanical, and lacking in any serious intellectual content?"

"A few of my colleagues will actually say that in unguarded moments," I said.[18] "If they preached it to the students as consistently as they preach the opposite message, we might get a better balance among the fields our graduates go into."

"My point exactly," Rodrigo said quietly.

"Rodrigo, I'm trying to think of all the objections your plan would face so that you'll be prepared. Here's one: Let's suppose you are right that care is best given by someone whose temperament, training, and job description incline him or her to treat the cared-for person individually, without rush or haste."

"Just the opposite of the factory system, in other words," Rodrigo interjected.

"Yes. And let's concede also that none of us knows whether he or she will need that kind of care later in life. Why does it follow that we should therefore socialize the entire caregiving industry? That goes against our national grain. And you must admit it might lead to a certain amount of sandbagging by halfhearted caregivers who are attracted to the helping professions because of the increased salary and prestige that will go along with them. Would not a better solution be to encourage persons to purchase private insurance? If someone feels he or she is likely to need a nursing home, or if young newlyweds think they may have children who may need child care, etc., why not let them protect against those contingencies by buying insurance?"[19]

"Then, if the need arose, they could use the insurance proceeds to buy care—is that the idea, Professor?"

"Something like that. I'm just trying to anticipate what they might say."

"You can't buy love," said Rodrigo levelly.

I couldn't believe what I had just heard, and wondered if Rodrigo knew he was echoing a line from a well-known song.[20] In a moment, I learned the answer.

"It's trite, but true. Marriages based on money fall apart. Primates separated from their mothers by a glass wall die or fail to grow, even if fed and warmed adequately.[21] Patients even in well-run nursing homes die sooner than ones who stay at home.[22] And look at the crime and delinquency rate among the children our society currently neglects. The conservatives are right—you can't solve a problem by throwing money at it.[23] But, if you address it with care and concern, often you can. Yet, in our society, overbalanced toward production values, there is not enough care and love to go around."

"Perhaps volunteerism is the answer, as the Republicans say," I suggested.

"That only goes so far," Rodrigo replied. "Our communal, loving instincts have atrophied from disuse. We are too caught up in a linear, production-oriented mentality. Not to demean it—it was highly useful during the period of colonial and industrial expansion. But now our needs are more diverse, yet we are equipped with all the wrong impulses."

"And I suppose you think other societies have struck a better balance."

"Actually, yes," said Rodrigo, looking slightly uncomfortable. "Although to be truthful, some of them have gone overboard in the other direction, have sacrificed efficiency and productivity for a rather smarmy form of social life based on connection and—what do you call it? Good vibes."

I wondered if Rodrigo might be referring to countries associated with his own ethnic background and heritage. But noticing his discomfort, I decided not to press him too closely.

"I commend you for your honesty. I agree that there is often an inverse relationship between the two faculties. The more productive a society becomes, the more stunted they tend to be in love, affection, spontaneity. But, if a culture goes all out for love and emotion, develops its affective side too much, it may pay a price in efficiency or productivity. What you're saying, then, is that we have to keep them in balance—right?"

"Not quite. The idea is to relegate activities that lie on the caregiving side to intelligent socialist treatment, and ones on the productive side to aggressive laissez faire capitalism. Within each sphere, it's fine to be as unbalanced as one wants. The capitalists in my ideal society could be aggressive and even devoid of human feelings—so long as they did not break the law or interfere with what the more nurturing caregivers were doing on the other side. And so similarly with the caregivers. Oh—and by the way, Professor. To answer your question about sandbagging: Any caregiver caught doing substandard or halfhearted work would simply be fired and sent over to the private sector."

"And you think that a society run along those lines would be efficient?"

"Yes, for two reasons. First there would be a decided trickle-up effect.[24] A vibrant and well-funded helping sector would turn out able workers and reduce the number of delinquents and welfare drags. And the productive sector, realizing it can sell commodities to the caregiving sector—because that sector is now well-financed—would invest heavily in 'human capital' thereby developing powerful new domestic markets it does not have now. And by the way, Professor, yes, I do think that Hispanic and black populations have done a better job at providing care, certainly for their dependent elderly, and probably for children and the mentally ill as well. Your Anglo friends, with all their production expertise, could well look to these sources for models."

"But, I thought that you said earlier that all one would need to do is put out the call and thousands of talented schoolteachers, child-care workers, and the like would come surging forward."

"Some would. But they might need lessons in how to do it."

"Kind of a reverse Peace Corps."

"Something like that," Rodrigo said. "We talked a little about these things before."

"I remember. Give me a second while I throw this out. Want another cup?" Rodrigo shook his head no, and I carried the coffeemaker and pot to the sink outside, where I deposited the grounds and now thick coffee. As I walked back, I reminded myself to ask Rodrigo about the matter that had brought him to my office in the first place.

When I returned, Rodrigo was leafing through the book on my desk, Andrew Hacker's *Two Nations*. I remembered that he had been reading it, too, and so seized on this to ask him about the matter that had been on my mind: "Rodrigo, I sense we're nearly finished talking about your paper—the first version, I mean. Now, I'd like to find out why you have to revise it for your professor. But first, tell me a little more about the prize. How much did you win? Did you get to make a trip to receive your award?"

"Two hundred fifty dollars, but no trip. They sent me the certificate, the check, and a nice award letter by mail. None of this did me much good with my instructor, however. When I told him about the prize, he hardly blinked. He was having appointments with each of his students, one every fifteen minutes. He had a sheet of notes on each draft. The main gist of mine was that this was an interesting idea, but a little unfocused. He urged me to concentrate on the problems of inner-city blacks. I'm supposed to write up what the ideal civil rights policy would be — 'if any,' he said."

"And so, does he want you to build on your insight about socialism and capitalism?"

"I think that's pretty much up to me, but I'm thinking of doing it if I can. There's actually a second essay competition I can enter if I write fast. It's entitled, 'A Civil Rights Policy for the '90s and Beyond,' and is sponsored by a conservative organization. But they make clear that there are no ideological restrictions. Liberals and folks like me are free to apply," Rodrigo said smiling at his own joke. "Since it would be a more or less completely revised paper, I'm pretty sure I could submit it."

"You might check with them first," I suggested. "Best to avoid any hint of scandal. Conservatives can get righteous about the darnedest things."

"Maybe I'll disclose in a footnote how this essay builds on the previous one."

"That should do it," I said. "But before getting into this one, tell me: Were you disappointed when your professor asked you to restructure your article?"

"No, not really," Rodrigo replied cheerfully. "He's a good teacher, even if he didn't warm up to my paper. I think his mindset was that I was going to write about civil rights. It's natural on his part, given who I am. And it's possible I gave him that impression when we met for our initial conference early in the semester. I don't really mind. It's an opportunity to look at some things I've always wanted to read."

I marvelled once again at Rodrigo's good nature in the face of what some would have seen as insufferable paternalism on the professor's part.

As though reading my mind, Rodrigo interjected: "You could see his reaction as an instantiation of the very mechanism I wrote about in the first paper: corruption of taste, disdain for anything smacking of social service. Civil rights has an urgent, social-engineering ring to some members of society's elites. Maybe the professor unconsciously thought all my talk about love, caregiving, and compassion was 'soft,' and that a paper focusing on eliminating ghetto crime would be more like it."

"Who knows?" I said as noncommittally as possible, not wanting to be too harsh on a fellow faculty member. "Tell me your thoughts on revising the paper. Do I get a cut if you win another prize?"

"How about a dinner?"

"You're on. Now let's hear what you are thinking of saying."

Wherein Rodrigo Attempts to Solve the Problems of "His People"

"I'm thinking of linking the new paper to the general theory I outlined in the first one."

"I'm not sure what you mean. I hope you're not going to maintain that all ghetto kids need is a little love."

"Not at all," Rodrigo replied, a little sharply. "Although love does have something to do with it. You see, I think your country—I mean, our country—has its civil rights policy exactly reversed. In terms of the structure I laid out earlier, I mean. We shower love, affection, and indulgent treatment on minority group members who least need it—the middle-class, well-trained, and intellectually able." [25]

"I can definitely think of a few cases," I replied. "In fact, I've written about that myself."

"So we adulate and grease the skids for talented professionals of color—those who would have succeeded without that anyway. And we tell the rest to lift themselves by their bootstraps, get a job, stop being welfare leeches, and so on. [26] We turn a cold shoulder to those who need individualized care and concern, implying that they should take their chances—nil, if the truth were known—in the free market. [27] And we hold close to our bosoms those who are most like us—who do not need the embrace. Blacks at the bottom of the heap get little personalized treatment, unless, of course, they commit crimes. [28] We exclude them from our consciousness as much as possible, while those who are bright, well-educated, and able, we fawn over and promote."

"Like you."

"That remains to be seen. I'm going on the teaching market this winter—if I ever get my paper done, that is."

"It sounds like you have it well in hand. But tell me, what's your solution to the problem you've just identified? Your professor, like most white people, will want to know not just what's wrong with our civil rights approach, but how to fix it. Do you want to bring back massive social programs like in the sixties?"

"It will take a major national effort," Rodrigo conceded. "But it will require both targeting the poor of color with individual care and concern and integrating them into the economy. The essence of being a colonized people is to be both beyond love and excluded from the main avenues of economic well-being."[29]

"I've read that literature. But the American race problem is different somehow," I said. "And harder."

"It is indeed," Rodrigo agreed. "I'm thinking of calling it, 'The Problem of Being Beyond Love.'"

"Beyond love?"

"Yes. And if you'll give me a second to call my roommate, I'll tell you what I mean. May I borrow your phone? We were going to go out for dinner, but I need some more time with you. This is helping me get my thoughts in order. You're a good listener—I like the way you push me."

I gestured toward the telephone, then picked up Hacker's book from my desk. I had been reading it avidly as a welcome relief from the raft of books written by conservatives, which I had read in preparation for the Economics of Race meeting.

"Don't leave," said Rodrigo. "This will just take a minute. It has something to do with the subject of that very book."

As promised, Rodrigo's phone call was brief. I was intrigued to learn that his roommate was named 'Giannina.'

"Beyond Love": In Which Rodrigo Explains What Stands in the Way of Our National Civil Rights Policy

"There," said Rodrigo, putting down the phone. "We're all set for later. How much of that book have you read?"

"I'm just finishing. It presents a pretty dismal picture. Before starting, I sneaked a look at the conclusion to see if the author makes a grand proposal, offers any sort of hope or 'quick fix' at the end. Nothing that I could see. So your work is definitely cut out for you."

"The main task, as I see it, is to deal with the problem of blacks' being, as I call it, 'beyond love.' For the vast majority, our society is prepared to offer neither entree into the economic system nor love and concern. They are excluded both from the economy and from networks of love."

"So the program of enhanced, synergistic, and reinvigorated spheres of love and economic development, which you outlined earlier, would leave them out—i.e., unbenefited."

"I'm afraid so. Something more is required."

"I agree. I and others have written that our current system of white-over-black ascendancy is far from accidental.[30] It benefits whites; indeed, one can see our entire current system of civil rights laws and policies as a sort of homeostat, assuring that the system has exactly the right amount of racism. Not too much, for that would be destabilizing, nor too little, for that would require that whites forfeit important psychic and pecuniary advantages. We have written about interest-convergence, and the way in which periodic ringing victories, like *Brown v. Board of Education*, end up benefiting whites more than blacks, legitimize a basically unfair system, and, when they become too inconvenient, are simply cut back by narrow judicial construction, administrative foot-dragging, or delay."[31]

"I've read that work and agree with it," Rodrigo said quietly. "I hope to build on it. The trick is to offer a solution that recognizes and takes into account the interest-maintaining, homeostatic element of our current approaches to race."

"If you pull *that* off, I'll nominate you for a second Nobel Prize," I said— then immediately regretted it when Rodrigo shot me an appraising look.

"I'm sorry," I said. "I'm on your side. The search for a solution is urgent and important. I'm just a battle-scarred veteran of many defeats. Don't let my jadedness put you off. It's an occupational hazard. Please continue."

As I had hoped, Rodrigo brightened up. "I'm glad. With the upcoming election, there may be a window of opportunity for new approaches, ones that may actually do some good." He paused for a moment, then continued:

"Have you noticed, Professor, how few animals kill members of their own species?"

"I have. Although you should know some sociobiologists are pointing out exceptions. Jane Goodall has shown that the great apes, for example, do sometimes war against and kill each other."[32]

"I didn't mean to make a universal point. But there's some truth in the generalization, don't you think?"

"Yes, of course. And if you mean to apply it to human beings, I suppose it's a valid starting point. We rarely go to war against those whom we see as closely related by blood and tradition. It's easier to demonize and kill members of that other tribe or clan or nation."[33]

"And might not something like that account for our racial predicament? Society has marginalized and excluded African-Americans from the beginning, rendered them the Other in so many settings that even after the enactment of civil rights laws, most Americans cannot think of them as their equals. Hacker points this out as forcefully as anyone.[34] Blacks, especially the black poor, have so few chances, so little interaction with majority society, that they might as well be exiles, outcasts, permanent black sheep who will never be permitted into the fold. Majority society has, in effect, written them off. We might as well erect walls around their communities— as a few neighborhoods have tried to do."[35]

"I remember some of Hacker's figures."

"The man wields numbers and statistics the way a classical composer wields notes and instruments. His voice is calm and temperate. But the picture he renders is devastating. Fully eighty percent of black students in New York attend segregated schools, as do more than half in many other states.[36] Even in schools that are integrated, black and brown students comprise a majority of the slow-learner tracks, so that ostensibly desegregated schools really consist of white and nonwhite classrooms within the same building.[37] Affirmative action has helped many white women and a few middle and professional class blacks.[38] But blacks, especially black men, have made few gains in the job market. During the 1980s, the income of black men rose only from $715 per $1000 of white income to $716 per $1000.[39] The few black families that have made it to middle-class status, defined by a family income of $50,000 or more, generally have two earners.[40] A white family making over that amount is three or four times more likely than a black family to have a single earner, usually a husband making $75,000, and a nonworking spouse.[41] The typical black middle-class family is more likely to consist of a male bus driver earning $32,000 while his wife brings in $28,000 as a teacher or a nurse.[42] There are many black nurses, but few dental hygienists."[43] Rodrigo picked up Hacker's book and read aloud, "While white patients seem willing to be cared for by black nurses, they apparently draw the line at having black fingers in their mouths."

"Of course, our conservative and neoliberal friends will concede these dismal statistics, but maintain that they are the fault of welfare dependency or a culture of poverty,"[44] I asserted.

"Hacker has an answer to that," Rodrigo retorted. "Blacks live in deteriorated neighborhoods, suffer debilitating diseases, live shorter lives, and commit crimes in far greater frequency than do whites.[45] In a few cases, these may be the products of individual choice, laziness, or inertia. But when large numbers of people live this way, the suspicion arises that social forces are responsible. And Hacker says he knows what the forces are: White racism and neglect. Whites, who hold all the cards, simply are unwilling to permit blacks to achieve equality with them." [46]

"What about blacks who achieve wealth and fame? Some do."

"Most are in sports and entertainment, or else on TV. As Hacker points out, the average young black gang member, if he watched TV at all, would be amazed at the number of cardigan-wearing black doctors and lawyers that appear there—all out of proportion to their numbers in real life." [47]

"But don't most black criminals prey on black victims?" I asked.

"Of course. But it's black-on-white crime that society finds terrifying. Blacks have a three-times greater chance of dying from a policeman's bullet than do whites. [48] The prisons are nearly one-half black. [49] And murderers who kill whites are ten times more likely to receive the death sentence than ones who kill blacks." [50]

"His statistics certainly help you establish your case. As a group, African-Americans live in a condition of near-apartheid. Yet few whites will accept any responsibility for our deplorable condition. We're as far removed from national consciousness as I can ever remember. Every one of our needs is on the back burner. It is even permissible, if not fashionable, to blame blacks for their predicament, to view us as the aggressors, to see us as opportunistic whiners who do not want to work."

"I'm rapidly getting that sense," replied Rodrigo, "both from things I read and from the remarks of my fellow students in class. It's been a revelation. Where I came from, I was little more than a curiosity for my skin color. Here, it's practically a badge of identification—although I must confess that a few whites and a professor or two have taken a great interest in me and my ideas. As have you."

"But of course I'm a man of color."

"True. Although you move in a white world. I hope to be like you one day."

"You flatter me too much. Besides, first things first. You need to finish this paper. And what a dilemma you've painted. Black people are desperate, poor, demoralized, and confined to inferior schools and all-black neighborhoods. As soon as a neighborhood becomes more than about eight percent black, all the whites start to leave. [51] What does your scheme for adjusting love and production have to say about that?"

Rodrigo leaned forward. "We need both a new myth and a form of coercion." I sensed that he had thought about this, but he seemed more tentative now than before. So I said encouragingly:

"I love to hear about myths. I write about narratives and stories myself, and believe this is a fruitful line of scholarship.[52] I'd like to hear what you mean by coercion, too."

Rodrigo began: "I'm sure you know about Hobbes and his belief in a commonwealth created through mutual covenants?"[53]

I nodded, so he went on: "It's a powerful image, not so much because it's true in any literal sense—no one makes explicit promises when they are born into the human community—but because of its mythic significance. People in the majority group know that if all, or most of them, obey the law, everyone will be better off. And so they pay their taxes even if they could cheat, stop at red lights in the middle of the night when no one is watching, and so on. The Rule of Law prevails because everyone knows that if we all adhere to society's rules and regulations, we will all benefit. Otherwise, we could decline into savagery, and it would be every person for himself or herself."[54]

"What about the 'free rider' or sociopath who discovers that he or she can gain an edge by disobeying the law?"[55]

"A few do that," Rodrigo replied, "but the myth discourages them by designating them bad. They know that if they're caught, they will earn everyone's disapproval."

"If not be prosecuted criminally," I added.

"That's where coercion comes in—for those who are not adequately socialized in the myth, or who simply succumb to temptation."

"And I gather you're saying that the social compact and force of law are inadequate to protect minority people—to enforce and guarantee the success of our civil rights laws and policies?"

"Precisely. Would you like me to spell it out a little more, Professor?"

"I'm still going strong," I insisted—even though I was definitely feeling the late hour and fast pace. "And it is my line of work. I hope we're not going to make you late for your dinner appointment."

"Giannina said it's okay, but only on condition that I agree to introduce her to you someday. She admires your work enormously."

"Is she a law student like you?"

"I'll let her explain that when you meet her. Perhaps we'll have you over when the term finishes."

"I'd be delighted," I said. "But tell me more about myths and coercion."
Rodrigo glanced briefly at some papers on my desk, then continued.

In Which Rodrigo Explains the New Civil Rights Myth and Form of Coercion

"The basic problem, as your own work suggests, Professor, is that blacks lie outside the social compact.[56] We are, as I call it, beyond love. The majority group has figured out that they don't need us, that it's more profitable to keep us as a ready supply of menial workers and a source of psychic consolation for blue-collar, working-class whites. Outside these uses, we are surplus, annoyances, of concern only insofar as we impinge on society through the occasional violent crime, or have babies, thus increasing the tax burden. They are prepared to write us off, eliminate us from their concern, to accept little from us so long as we demand little in return."

"Some of them are calling for concern, for attention to our needs."[57]

"But they are voices in the wilderness. The average middle-class white, according to Hacker, knows and cares for no blacks, has none living in his or her neighborhood, has his or her children attend schools where few if any of us attend—and is quite satisfied with that state of affairs."

"A bleak indictment," I mused. "But you said you had a solution of some sort."

"More like an approach, more like what one would do if one desired to change things. But of course I admit, as you've written, that any desire to better our dire estate may be missing from society today."

"That may change. If so, what would you do?"

"I would disseminate a new myth. The current one does not work for us. With ordinary laws, white folks know that if everyone follows them, we will all be better off. But with civil rights, the situation is exactly the reverse."

"Racism benefits whites," I chimed in. "They know that as a class they are better off with us marginalized and excluded. So, they don't take their civil rights obligations that seriously."

"Except for a few tokens needed to legitimate the system. Most of us fall outside the clan. Like a species of wild animal, we are entitled to little consideration. It's not that we may be killed at random, but fellow-feeling simply does not extend to us. We are beyond love and concern. Norm-breaking behavior by a member of the majority that breaches the country's professed ideals about brotherhood, equality, and dignity for all confers a benefit on the lawbreaker and his group. That's why even blatant lawbreakers, persons who refuse to rent to or hire qualified ones of us, rarely receive any punishment."[58]

"With ordinary laws, someone who acts in a law-abiding manner, stopping at a red light in the middle of the night, for example, gets to feel good, satisfied, and proud; he believes himself a good citizen. Are you saying that the same isn't true for people who adhere to the civil rights laws?"

"Yes. The good-citizen myth is much weaker, if it exists at all. Enforcement is infrequent and ineffectual. There are all the well-known excuses. The breach was unintentional. It was justified by a business necessity. There was another cause for the rejection. And so on."[59]

"So we need both a better, or at least a different, myth, and a new way of enforcing it."

"It's easier to think of what the new form of coercion would be," said Rodrigo. "And I think it must come from us, not from them, at least initially. I think it would be some form of what your society calls terrorism or sabotage. We might call it self-help, liberation, or something of the sort. But there would need to be some form of redress for flagrant breaches of equal respect. And it would need to be as swift and effective as the penalties society applies to ordinary lawbreakers."

I shuddered. "Rodrigo, it's fine for you to discuss these matters with friends like me, in the privacy of my office. But I must urge you in the strongest terms to keep your ideas to yourself."[60] I looked at the door to see if I had closed it after emptying the coffee; with great relief I saw I had. "Italy may be different, but here the very word 'terrorism' raises hackles. I wouldn't be surprised if your advocacy of such tactics did not have something to do with your earlier troubles with the INS."

"Fine," said Rodrigo, seeming not at all abashed by my heated warning. "Although surely the most perceptive among your white friends know that continued neglect can only cause more violence, more frustration, more uprisings like those in New York and Los Angeles. I'm merely pointing out that at some point, this anger might get channeled."

"A few of us have dared to broach that suggestion.[61] But unlike you, we have tenure. Perhaps you had better backpedal or at least glide over the part about coercion, and go on to the part about myth. White people love myths. All of us do."

"What's needed is a reason—a plausible and inspiring reason—for expanding our circle of sympathies to include groups who are now excluded. Group self-interest, like that which accompanies paying one's taxes or stopping at red lights, doesn't work because with respect to those excluded groups, the majority's incentives point the other way. We need a reason for caring when caring is costly and does not benefit the caregiver in any obvious way. We need a reason for making a group, now situated outside the social compact, a member of it. Current antidiscrimination law applies coercion, ineffectively, to injure the broader group, to deny it benefits, goods it wants. So the myth must take this into account."

"A tall order," I commented dryly.

"True, since with our treatment of minorities—in this area alone—when we break the law we are better off. And the 'free rider,' the deviationist who defiantly breaks the law, who stands up against affirmative action, is cheered as a hero, one who dares to tell the truth, to call spade a spade." [62]

"So to speak." I winced, resolving sometime to let the innocent Rodrigo in on the meaning of the term. [63] "So, unlike with ordinary laws, one can't appeal to the myth of the social compact."

"Only weakly, at best. Blacks lie outside society. They are the Other. We refer to them as 'them,' as 'those people.' Hacker says lying behind this aversion is the sense that African-Americans are an inferior order of being. [64] This is a white society; these others live here at our sufferance. They mustn't get too close, begin living in our neighborhoods, go to school with our children, date our women. African-Americans were brought here for their labor, and an attitude—racism—was developed to justify that practice. Slavery was abolished, but the attitude remained, because society still needed blacks for menial work. After three centuries of this, it's hardly surprising that the dominant group sees blacks as outside their circle of friends and families, outside their sphere of concern. There are, of course, national norms of brotherhood, equality, and so on—as a prime example, the fine words of the Declaration of Independence. But these have little impact. The dreadful conditions of which Hacker speaks are not at all upsetting because they are *their* problem, not ours."

"And the system works," I added glumly. "Discrimination benefits the dominant group."

"That's why many white folk cannot be made to see discrimination the way they do the red light. Obeying the civil rights laws does not make them feel particularly good and virtuous. In acting generously toward a black, they do not see themselves as building a safer, more cohesive community. And the reason is that the black is not part of their community."

"So the virtue myth doesn't work. What is your alternative?"

"This is the final part of my paper, and it's a little hard to explain," Rodrigo said. He paused, as though collecting his thoughts.

"Take your time." I leaned back in my chair and drained the last bit of coffee from my cup.

"There are actually two parts to my plan. First, the implementation would be put in the hands of 'bridge people'[65]—those older folks, often themselves marginal but yet working or respectable, who still live in the neighborhoods and barrios and have a degree of contact with the lost kids of the gangs. They might be the postal clerk, retired serviceman, or porter—people like the 'Mayor of the Block' in the movie *Do the Right Thing*. We would give them MacArthurs and large grants and put them in charge of redeeming their own neighborhoods, especially the least lovable residents who live there—the black kids in the sweatsuits, tennis shoes, and gang insignia—the ones who terrify whites, the ones that whites cannot relate to."

"There is actually a body of emerging writing that says empathy only goes so far, that we cannot identify with or love anyone who is too different from us, cannot resonate to a 'story' too unlike the one we usually hear.[66] So your idea of finding bridge people, people who split the gap between the stable, taxpaying white suburbanite and the alienated ghetto kid, makes sense. But where would the money come from? How would you get middle-class society to give millions of dollars to bridge people for the benefit of welfare mothers and teenage hoodlums?"

"That's the other part," Rodrigo said. "We need to persuade them that burdening themselves to relieve anguish among African-Americans benefits them."

"And how would you do that?"

"We would tell them they should pay because the recipients—people of color—have a secret. The secret is one that they will learn only later, once the programs are in place, and that once disclosed will bring them an incalculable benefit." Rodrigo was speaking softly yet emphatically. "The secret is one they cannot learn until blacks and other outsiders are brought fully inside, are made equal members of society. They will learn it when they have relaxed the barriers, when they have decided, as a group, that blacks and Mexicans and gays and lesbians are no longer beyond love."

"So, by saying 'I love you,' whites will receive this benefit, learn this secret?" I wanted to get Rodrigo to clarify his thoughts before he handed in his paper, with its extraordinary thesis, to a skeptical professor at his law school.

"Yes, something like that. And by it I mean learning to love those who are least like you, those who frighten and put you off. I mean the sixteen-year-old black youths in jogging suits and gang paraphernalia, walking in groups of four and looking mean. I mean loving the unlovable, the ones you now think of as the enemy, the Other, the ones least like you."

"Whites are pragmatic. They'll want to know what the secret is before they agree to love the unloved, pay to redress centuries of neglect and indifference, remedy the deferred maintenance that in a thousand ways we have allowed to build up within populations of color."

I was silent a moment. Then I blurted out: "Rodrigo, the current situation brings benefits to the majority group, as you yourself conceded. You can't seriously think they will give them up in return for a vague 'secret' that they might receive at some undesignated future time. I'm not sure I would go along, and I'm not even white!"

"You give yourself too little credit, Professor. You have already been doing something like that—loving those who are least deserving of love."[67]

I calmed down, sensing Rodrigo's seriousness. I did not want to deter him from telling me more, from exploring the vein he was following.

"Their own culture supplies a host of narratives, reasons we could draw on to support the new myth. It would not be so unlike stories they already subscribe to, ones about receiving a benefit by giving. We could tap these narratives to show why the current policy that relegates African-Americans to a life beyond love is iniquitous and unworthy."

"I hope you're right."

"The effort would be redemptive. As society integrates outsiders, achieves unity, so would the individuals engaged in that task. The social healing would be mirrored by a psychic, individual one."

"Bearing another's burden does sometimes make one feel lighter—particularly if it enables the other to do surprising things. And I suppose you think our white friends will know the reward when they have done enough?"

"Yes," Rodrigo replied. "The benefit will come naturally, in its time. You see, I believe that all are innocent at birth. Children come into the world asking only for health and care. They begin life helpless. Some become corrupted by circumstances. None choose the corrupting conditions that society or outside influences create." Rodrigo was speaking with great animation now. I wondered what recent experiences he might have had with small children, or whether the mysterious Giannina somehow lay behind this near-spiritual tack of his. I had imagined him to be an atheist or agnostic; I resolved to ask him sometime.

He continued: "And some children then change from innocent beings to Them, a tragedy both for them and us. We can perhaps redeem them—and ourselves—by working to reverse the process. In some ways, the greater sin is ours for having allowed ourselves to become slothful, uncaring, unloving, hedonistic to the point where we think the anguish of the inner cities is 'their problem.'"

"So, we are the ones in the jogging suits, after all," I said slowly. "We are the ones in need of redemption."

"A little too harsh, Professor. I prefer to think we all wear the same jogging suit, whether we have bought it in a store or stolen it during a riot, whether we are rich or poor, black or white."

Something made me glance suddenly at my watch. "Rodrigo, this reminds me—I have a date to go jogging with Professor Abercrombie in the Park in five minutes. Fascinating as all this is, I'm afraid I must break it off. Would you like to join us?"

"Thanks, Professor, but Giannina is waiting for me. I'd better take off. So, you think my paper has promise?"

"Yes," I said. "The theological part at the end is a little surprising, coming from you, but I like it. I'm sure your professor will, too."

"I hope so. And keep your fingers crossed that the Federalist Society doesn't reject it out of hand when I send it in."

I had heard strains from the law school chorale group, which was practicing downstairs for its Christmas program.

"Title your last section 'Amazing Grace,'" I suggested.

Rodrigo looked back intently at me as he left my office, his things under his arm. "I think I will," he said.

4

RODRIGO'S FOURTH CHRONICLE: Neutrality and Stasis in Antidiscrimination Law

Introduction: In Which Rodrigo and I Commiserate and Catch up with Developments in Each Other's Lives

I was in my office late one afternoon, puzzling over how to incorporate certain books addressing the role of courts in protecting minority rights into the next edition of my casebook.[1] I was getting nowhere when a familiar lanky figure appeared as though by magic in my doorway.

"Rodrigo!" I exclaimed. "I'm glad to see you. Please come in." I peered at him closely. The usually ebullient Rodrigo stood in my doorway, looking down. "Is something wrong?"

"Well, as a matter of fact, yes. Do you have a minute? I tried phoning first, but you were out."

"Of course," I assured him, gladly pushing the four books aside. "The last time we talked, things were going well for you. You had won that writing prize and were hot on the track of a second paper that sounded intriguing. Has school taken a turn for the worse?"

"Well, yes. And in a way, it has to do with the paper that I am working on."

"I'd like to hear about it. Can I offer you a cup of coffee? I have a new coffeemaker."

"Yes, thanks. Oh—Giannina and I have one of those." Rodrigo examined my new gadget with interest. "We have the smaller version."

As I busied myself measuring the grounds and setting the switches, my visitor inquired: "Does your law school have an annual 'libel show,' Professor?"

"Yes. I think most do. Here, they're called the Follies—a little singing, some bad dancing, and a lot of mockery of the professors.[2] They're a good way for students to let off steam, although the faculty sometimes grumble over the irreverent way they are portrayed."

"We had something similar back in Italy, too. But the one they had at my school this year set a new low. Half the skits were antifemale or antiminority. One made fun of affirmative action; another, of gays and lesbians. A third, perhaps the most tasteless of all, lampooned a gay scholar who had died less than a year earlier of AIDS—even though her one-time lover and young son were in the audience."[3]

"In bad taste, to say the least," I commented. "Did anyone do anything about it?"

"A number of students and several of the faculty complained and signed a petition demanding action. But the administration did nothing. Several faculty members sided with the students who produced the show. They said that, despite the odiousness of some of the ideas expressed, it was free speech."[4]

"Reminds me of the position certain liberal organizations take on the campus hate-speech controversy. They deplore racism and racist remarks but throw up their hands and say there is little we can do because they include speech."[5]

"I know. But that's only the beginning. When the administration refused to take action against those who put on the first production, my group of nearly fifty LL.M. students decided to produce a show of our own. It was a kind of counter-parody. We made fun of the original production, as well as of a number of law school institutions, practices, and sacred cows. Many of us are from foreign countries, so we chose targets that struck us as funny about the U.S. or legal education here."

"And what happened?"

"There was a huge turnout—probably as big as for the original event, even though we didn't serve alcohol. The crowd loved it. We satirized the

Socratic method, recruiting season, casebooks with unanswerable questions, ultraconservative student organizations, and professors who take seven months to grade bluebooks that we write in three hours."

"Sounds inoffensive enough. How did this get you in trouble?"

"One of our skits poked fun at the law school for currying favor with rich alumni. We called the skit "Blood Money" and acted it out to the music of a popular tune. When word got out, one wealthy and well-known donor rescinded his pledge to give the law school $3 million for a new library. The administration was furious. Several of us got letters formally reprimanding us for conduct inimical to the institution. Others of us were told informally that we had better not count on the school's help in getting teaching jobs."

"No small threat," I acknowledged. "If your program is at all like ours, most of the LL.M.s are there because they want to become academics. What's the point of getting the degree if you can't teach later?"

Rodrigo shrugged and then continued, "I couldn't help be struck by the different treatment of the two programs. The first one was raunchy, mean-spirited, and really pretty amateurish. Ours was much more light-hearted and, if I may say so, literate. Giannina helped with the lyrics—as you may know, she's a published playwright."

"No, I didn't know." Actually, I had not yet met Giannina, Rodrigo's companion, and was curious to find out more about her.

"So, the words were really funny. Swiftian, even Voltairean, in their deftness. But it made no difference to the administration. We were all reprimanded, and now I'm not sure I'll be able to get a job."

"Rodrigo, don't worry. You're a top graduate of a major law school, and you have already won a national prize for student writing. You'll do fine."

"I hope so," Rodrigo responded, a little uneasily. "But the whole business got me thinking about neutrality and color blindness in the jurisprudence of race.[6] As you may recall, my second paper—the one I'm writing for that other contest—"

"You mean the one sponsored by the conservative organization?" I interjected.

"Yes, that one. I've been struggling with a way to articulate just what's wrong with neutrality. It seems logical to think that a society that sets out scrupulously to treat blacks and whites alike in every setting—jobs, housing, education, credit, and the like—should have no discrimination. Yet, it obviously doesn't work that way."

"Rodrigo, I know you're widely read. But possibly you don't know that a number of us in the Critical Race Theory movement have been saying just that: Mainstream jurisprudence's neutrality is bogus, a mask, a cover.[7] In feminist theory, Catharine MacKinnon has been saying the same thing—that the law's procedural regularity, its emphasis on 'legality,' serves to conceal and legitimate an antiwoman bias.[8] So, your observation, while trenchant, is not particularly novel, although in light of your recent experience I can see why you are preoccupied with it. Would you like me to refer you to some things to read?" I reached for the four books on the corner of my desk and began mentally composing a short additional reading list that would get Rodrigo started. In a moment, I regretted my offer.

"I've read those," Rodrigo replied levelly. "And I've read you, and Bell, and MacKinnon, and Freeman, and many others on this subject. But I want to go further."

I could feel the blood rushing into the tiny capillaries in my face. I should have known better than to patronize Rodrigo. If not two steps ahead of me, he's almost always at my own level.

"What do you mean, 'go further'?" I asked quickly, in part to cover my own gaffe, but also because I very much wanted to hear his thoughts. Perhaps Rodrigo could help me discover a way to incorporate the four books I had been struggling with into my teaching materials.

"Many Critical Race Theorists condemn neutrality and color blindness as merely maintaining the racial advantage of whites. But, aside from presenting the 'playing field' or 'starting line' analogy, they offer little explanation of why this is so."

"The coffee's almost ready. I assume you have some thoughts about this?"

"I do."

"I'd love to hear them. Let me wash out these cups."

Wherein Rodrigo Explains How Neutral Principles of Constitutional Law Disadvantage Blacks and Other Outsider Groups

When I returned, Rodrigo was leafing through one of the books on my desk.[9]

"I must correct myself," he said. "I haven't read this one. It looks like it's still in manuscript form."

"It is," I confirmed. "The author, Professor Spann, was kind enough to supply me with an advance copy. It's an expansion of his earlier Michigan Law Review article."

"'Pure Politics'?"[10] Rodrigo asked. "I read that article. I thought it was brilliant. He urges black people to abandon their excessive and misplaced reliance on the Supreme Court as an instrument of social progress, and to concentrate instead on 'pure politics'—the employment of mass force and influence through marches and protests, as well as elections and representative government. Is that what his new book is about?"

"That and more."

"And does he explain what it is about the Supreme Court's fascination with neutrality that causes it to hand down one hurtful decision after another?"

"Not in the version of the manuscript that I have."

"That's disappointing," Rodrigo lamented. "None of the good leftist scholars seem to have addressed that question. And the others agree that the courts haven't been able to initiate sweeping social change. But, unlike the folks on the left, they're not upset about that; they think it's the way things should be. In their view, a neutralist, quietist Supreme Court is simply performing its assigned role in our political system."[11]

"So, both sides agree on the effects of neutral jurisprudence. Left and Critical writers view the Supreme Court's failure to do more to benefit people of color with outrage; they consider our system's noble promises of equality a sham.[12] And more conservative judges and writers see the same thing, but celebrate, since, according to them, that's the way courts should behave."[13]

Rodrigo nodded. "Exactly."

As I mulled over Rodrigo's observation, I noticed that my coffeemaker had stopped making noise. "Ready for a cup?" I asked, rising from my chair. Rodrigo nodded enthusiastically. I poured two mugfuls of steaming espresso and handed one to Rodrigo. Sitting back down, I urged Rodrigo, "So tell me what you think causes this situation. In a way, it is paradoxical, isn't it? I mean, if a legal system sincerely sets out to treat a person of color and a white man exactly the same in every situation that counts, in the long run this should produce something like rough equality, shouldn't it?"

"But it's impossible to assume away the short run," Rodrigo countered. "African-Americans and whites live in vastly different circumstances, as we discussed last time. I think the reason for the paradox has to do with the unspoken background against which people make all of these ostensibly neutral decisions."

"In other words," I mused, "are you saying that the various decision-makers—employers, apartment managers, admissions committees, and so on—strive to decide fairly, but carry around subconscious biases that make it impossible to be truly impartial? Charles Lawrence says something like that; he argues that everyone in American society harbors unconscious racism that manifests itself in a myriad of ways."[14]

"I think Lawrence is right, but the problem is broader than that."

"In what way?" I asked, setting down my mug and leaning forward in my chair.

Rodrigo took a deep gulp. "In our society, even a decision-maker with the most pristine racial conscience, one without a trace of prejudice against minorities, would still end up making decisions adverse to candidates of color. It has more to do with the cultural background against which legal criteria are applied than with any sort of overt antiminority conspiracy."

"What do you mean by cultural background? Do you mean our people's exclusion from informal networks, sources of information—that sort of thing?" I had heard this argument before and thought it had some validity.

"That's part of it," Rodrigo replied. "But there's more. Legal and cultural decisions are made against a background of assumptions, interpretations, and implied exceptions, things everyone in our culture understands but that seldom, if ever, get expressed explicitly."[15]

"And I suppose you are going to say that all those assumptions favor whites?"

"Of course. And they have at least as much efficacy as does law on the books."

"Could you give me an example?" I persisted. "It still seems to me that if every relevant decision-maker sets out to treat two individuals, A and B, identically even though one is white and the other black, then we have achieved formal equality. How," I asked with a wry smile, "can a system like this possibly disadvantage minorities?"

"Take a different kind of promise," Rodrigo said, eyeing my coffee machine. The young wunderkind set a fast pace; I was happy to see he needed fuel from time to time, too.

"Like another cup?"

"In a minute. Let's say that a father promises his son a trip to the ice cream parlor if the child cleans up his room. The child says, 'No matter what?' The father answers, 'Sure.' So the child cleans up his room, but the father never ends up taking him out for the ice cream."

"Hmm," I murmured, turning the hypothetical over in my mind. "I suppose the father had an excuse of some sort?" I recalled with no small measure of guilt times in my own life as a parent when I had done something similar.

"Right. The father says, 'You couldn't have thought that I meant that you had three whole days just to clean that little room.' Or, the day after the promise, the local ice cream parlor goes out of business, and the nearest shop is an hour away. Or, the father loses his job. Or, the car develops engine trouble and has to go to the garage, and the only way to get the cone would be for the two to take a $10 cab ride. Or, the child develops a milk allergy. It turns out, then, that the father's promise assumed dozens of conditions, implied exceptions, and unstated excuses. Although the father never spelled these out, he insists the child must have known of them. The same sort of unstated conditions underlie our society's promises of racial equality."

"So, you are saying that just as all the terms of the argument favor the father, mostly white decision-makers construe the interpretive structure in a manner that inevitably favors whites and disadvantages nonwhites in situations like the ones we've been talking about? And they do this, you're saying, not because they're biased, but rather because they're fully acculturated members of society?"

"Exactly!" Rodrigo replied with animation that I didn't think was entirely caused by the high caffeine content of my mocha java beans, obtained from a new supplier. "Imagine an African-American applies for a job on the faculty of an institution like yours. The only other candidate for the position is white. The hiring committee declares its intention to use only scrupulously race-neutral criteria."

"Yet, the white gets the position, right?"

"Yes. Even though the two candidates went to the same law school, got the same grades—you name it—a difference will emerge, one that is not part of the formal, written criteria. One candidate turns out to have a more pleasant demeanor than the other. The white strikes the hiring committee as better at 'small talk.' The white has more seniority, more 'solid' job experience, better 'communication skills,' or a stronger recommendation from a better-known professor. It turns out that the new 'merit' criteria just happen to favor the white applicant. None of these requirements was mentioned in the formal job description circulated or advertised by the employer."

"Yet everyone knows they're there. The formal, 'on the books' rule—the only one explicitly stated—looks magnificently fair: 'Treat blacks and whites exactly the same.' But the cultural backdrop skews the application of the rule, producing discriminatory results," I summarized. "I bet you think this explains why the LL.M. skit got you into trouble, while those students who put on the main event got off unpunished."

"Exactly," Rodrigo replied. "There turned out to be an implied exception to the rule that satires are acceptable.[16] Free speech reigns unless you poke fun at certain things or cause a wealthy alum to put his checkbook away."

"I'm sure he will reconsider once the fuss dies down. Alums love having their names prominently displayed on buildings, classrooms, and lounges throughout the law school. It reminds them of the good old days."

"Even if the law school is changing—if the composition of the student body and faculty is radically different from the way he remembers?"[17] pressed Rodrigo.

"You may have a point. But in all fairness, I think the original skitsters would have earned retribution, too, if their program caused a rich alum to revoke a donation." I stopped, realizing I was uncomfortably close to taking on the role of apologist for the system. Was I losing my own critical edge? I had a birthday coming up, and this had been on my mind for a while.

Rodrigo shot me an appraising look so I backtracked slightly. "I do agree with you that in this case there is a propensity to apply the 'boys will be boys' excuse, and not the other. The school's reaction does seem more than a little harsh."

"Maybe I'll have my friend Ali write a letter asking him to reconsider— the donor, I mean. Ali's a great conciliator and has a gift for words. Maybe he can remind the wealthy philanthropist that the true test of a great law school lies in its ability to withstand vigorous criticism, and that the LL.M. skit simply confirmed his old school's greatness."

"I'm sure it wouldn't hurt your job chances if you and he were successful," I added.

Rodrigo was silent for a while. Then, returning to his critique of neutrality, he continued as follows: "Maybe this is a way to explain it. Imagine that a lawn treatment chemical turns out to be virulently poisonous. The suburbs disappear. Overnight, white people become a minority who must now deal with blacks and other racial minorities from a position of weakness. A long tradition of black subculture holds that one may freely disparage and ridicule anyone who is a 'jerk.'[18] The definition of 'jerk' is a person who is naive, slow at sports, bad at repartee, lacking in street smarts.[19] A whole culture of songs, myths, stories, and the like derides people who fit this description. Let's suppose that unflattering concept just happens to be associated, fairly or unfairly, with people who have light skins. Is there any doubt that in the new regime, white people would come out second-best, even if they were just as talented, smart, deserving, and motivated as members of the new majority group?"[20]

"A vivid example, if a little far-fetched," I replied. "Whites would end up second-best even if blacks set out to treat them fairly, humanely, and evenhandedly. The background assumptions would cause them to lose out in the race for jobs, slots in law school classes, and so on, even if all the rules were color-blind."

I flipped the switch on the coffee warmer to "On." "But let's return to the world at hand. Much of the action these days concerns retributive, not distributive justice. White society has already figured out, to its own satisfaction at least, how to go about distributing jobs and other benefits to blacks— namely, very stintingly. But the attention is now beginning to focus on the remedial aspects of civil rights strategy—on what society should do, in light of its past mistreatment of blacks.[21] How does your 'cultural background' argument work here?"

"In much the same way," Rodrigo confidently replied, rising and walking over to my coffeemaker. "May I?"

"Of course. The sugar and creamer are over there."

Rodrigo poured himself a second cup, while I marveled at his youthful constitution. "If you want decaffeinated, I can brew some," I offered.

Rodrigo made a face and returned to his chair, where he began gulping his steaming-hot high-octane. "Implied exceptions arise in this setting, too. Any remedy for past discrimination must not be too costly to whites.[22] So-called 'innocent' whites may not be made to pay the penalty for past injustices. Decrees may not bind whites who are not members of a class before the court.[23] Discrimination is not redressable unless an intent to discriminate can be proven.[24] Harms are not compensable unless tight chains of causation are shown.[25] Standing rules limit who may complain.[26] And so on."

"So, essentially what you're saying is that the dominant culture has somehow managed to take the sting out of any and all available remedies?" I asked.

"Right," Rodrigo responded.

"You know, Rodrigo," I said thoughtfully, "I think you may be onto something. Many of us have written about the way in which the costs of racial remedies always seem to be placed on blacks—the faces at the bottom of the well. Your insight helps explain why this happens."

Rodrigo drained his cup. "Neutral rules rarely detect many breaches of the principle of nondiscrimination," Rodrigo continued. "And, when breaches are detected, those violations are remedied in as innocuous a way as possible, one that does not significantly disturb the prevailing social order."

"How does partisan politics affect all of this? Do you think it makes much difference whether the conservatives or the liberals are in power?"

"Not much," Rodrigo answered. "Partisan distinctions may be important in other areas, such as economic policy or foreign relations, but they make little difference for minorities. Both liberals and conservatives champion neutrality in antidiscrimination law, as though treating blacks and whites exactly the same will make discrimination go away. But as we have seen, it won't. We fare little better under one regime than the other. For us, political labels are merely deflections from the issues."[27]

"I'm not sure I'd go that far, Rodrigo," I asserted, "even though I agree that neutrality is flawed. Obviously, rules dictating equal treatment of minorities and whites can't redress long-standing discrimination. But you must admit, such rules are better than the old blatantly racist ones.[28] Perhaps they are way stations to something better. Don't you agree?"

"Maybe," Rodrigo replied somewhat skeptically. "Although they increase the risk of complacency. Since minorities and whites are now definitionally equal under the law, we can tell ourselves that that problem is solved. We can even blame the victim. For, if after four decades of scrupulously neutral legal rules, African-Americans and other people of color are still poor, marginalized, and discontent—well, what can be done? The problem cannot be our fault, since we've put in place all these wonderful legal rules that mandate equal treatment. If minorities of color haven't been able to prosper with such rules in place, then the problem must lie with them. They must be shiftless, or immoral, or not very smart."[29]

"I recognize this danger, in fact, have written along somewhat similar lines myself."

"I know," Rodrigo said with an impatience I found almost charming because of his youth. "And even those of good will, those who don't blame us, end up distracted from the reality of minorities' plight by the rhetoric of neutrality, and are led off into another direction. With formal legal equality, *Brown v. Board of Education*,[30] and the principle of nondiscrimination now in everyone's consciousness, the focus shifts to the courts. Everyone asks whether *Brown* was a justified decision, whether it was principled or not. Everyone talks earnestly about the proper judicial role, about whether courts can or should be in the business of propelling legal change."[31]

Rodrigo gestured toward Gerald Rosenberg's *The Hollow Hope,* one of the books on my desk. "There's an example. Instead of writing about blacks and their predicament, everyone writes about courts—on law and the appropriate judicial function. We start out writing about racial wrongs, about racial justice. But, we end up writing about ourselves. It's a neat shift."

"Traditional legal scholarship seems much more concerned with procedure, the way one should go about solving a problem—rather than actually solving it. It's probably a universal human tendency."

"Perhaps so," Rodrigo replied. "The problem is how African-Americans, a group that was brought here in chains, can achieve retributive justice. Yet, we end up talking about legal principles. We endlessly discuss whether some deviation from perfect formal equality is principled, whether some paltry affirmative action program benefiting a handful of African-Americans can be justified.[32] How can we ever hope to achieve justice when these are what we're calling the burning issues of race? Of course, these issues are much more absorbing—not to mention less guilt-inspiring—because they are about us."

"Well, Rodrigo, I must admit I find your analysis intriguing, particularly the way you tie your ideas back to neutrality as the source of the trouble. Is this what you are writing about for your seminar paper: the one you plan to submit to the second competition?"

"Yes. I'm thinking of focusing on the dichotomy between equality of opportunity and equality of results. I'm sure the conservative sponsors will appreciate that."

"Bravo," I responded, with a trace of amusement. "Conservatives love equal opportunity as much as they hate equal results. In their view, the first is principled, neutral, and fair, while the second is unprincipled, result-oriented, and wrong.[33] You will definitely get their attention, particularly if you can manage to present a new angle. Have you thought about how you are going to link it up with your insight about neutrality as a sham guarantee?"

"That's the trick," Rodrigo answered, a bit pensively. "I've got a few ideas, though. Can I tell you about them over dinner?"

"Sounds good," I said. "I'm starved. My doctor told me not to go too long between meals."

"I'll pay this time," Rodrigo offered.

"Don't be ridiculous. I owe you. You've helped me figure out how to incorporate those books into the new edition of my casebook. Plus, I make more money than you."

"An odd definition of neutrality, Professor. Why don't we go Dutch?"

"Okay, okay, if you insist," I conceded.

In Which Rodrigo and I Discuss Equality of Opportunity versus Equality of Results

About an hour later, Rodrigo and I found ourselves comfortably ensconced in a plain but comfortable Mexican restaurant, located in the meat-packing district, that my friend Jose Oliveros had introduced me to the last time he was in town. I was struck that Rodrigo, who had been raised in Italy and only been back in the States a short time, knew to order Dos Equis beer with his meal. After the waiter disappeared with our orders, Rodrigo continued our earlier conversation.

"As I mentioned earlier, I'm thinking of using the two types of equality, equality of opportunity and equality of result, as my principal illustration of the problems with neutrality."

"A good choice. Do you intend to argue that they merge, that they constitute a false dichotomy?" I worried that my young friend might have fallen prey to the influence of the deconstruction movement, whose main goal, so far as I could determine, is to show that polar opposites collapse into each other upon close inspection.[34] I hoped Rodrigo was not going to take me on a tour of Continental theory. I didn't feel up to it—at least before we had a bite to eat. Fortunately, my fears proved groundless.

"No, although I suspect one could do that," Rodrigo replied. "I'm thinking of doing something more along the lines of a social and conceptual inquiry."

Relieved, I prodded: "I've always been struck by the way conservatives favor equality of opportunity over the other kind. If they were genuinely committed to neutrality, you would think that equal results would be the logical way to measure the effectiveness of racial programs. Have you a theory for why conservatives—and many liberals, too—have such an aversion to equality of results?"

"I do," Rodrigo declared, pausing for a moment as the waiter set down our drinks. I resolved merely to sip my own Dos Equis until dinner arrived. I could see the outlines of a new subsection of my book forming, and wanted to remain alert. I made a mental note to figure out some way of giving Rodrigo credit. Maybe an effusive footnote would suffice for now. Later, when he got his first teaching position, I'd take him on as coauthor, I mused. He certainly had more energy than I did these days, and these revisions were becoming increasingly tedious.

As though reading my mind, Rodrigo offered: "You or I might want to do something with this notion sometime. To my knowledge, no one has really addressed it. It is truly amazing, when you think about it, how all the leftists and civil rights activists, like yourself, prefer equality of results, while those of moderate or conservative persuasion prefer equality of opportunity."[35]

"You said you had a theory for this ideological preference?"

"Well, I think it has to do with one's perspective, one's baseline. If you start out from a certain position, a given practice will look neutral. From a different perspective, the same practice will look one-sided, biased, unfair. For example, look at the quota issue. It's no secret that most conservatives dislike quotas for blacks and other minority groups. Such schemes strike them as radically unfair, because they assure that a certain number of minorities get jobs. Imposition of a quota seems nonneutral, because whites are treated differently from nonwhites.[36] Without the quotas, that number would, no doubt, be much smaller. But that, in large part, is because in the absence of quotas the job criteria operate to hire artificially low numbers of black and minority applicants. Genuinely equal treatment will always strike some as unfair. Apparently, only advantage—a tilted playing field or criteria that favor them—seems neutral and normal. So, with any new arrangement we look to see who benefits, who is advantaged or disadvantaged, and pronounce regimes fair or unfair accordingly."

"I'm still not sure I understand why everyone resists equality of result. Is it merely because such an approach is likely to provide more jobs and benefits to minorities?"

"In part, but the mechanism is a little more complicated. Notice how equality of opportunity is a much more nonformal, multifactorial measure than equality of results. The latter kind of equality is starkly simple. You merely compare the number of minorities and whites at a job site, for example. But with equality of opportunity, many things become relevant. This multiplies the opportunity for cultural factors to come into play."

"By cultural factors you mean the host of background assumptions, interpretations, and implied exceptions that we discussed earlier?"

"Yes. Neutrality works best when it is able to call up and rely on as many of these culturally inscribed routines and understandings as possible. These understandings, read into the culture long ago, now seem objective, unchallengeable, and true.[37] I mean things like the merit principle, the idea that informed consent should insulate a doctor from malpractice liability, or the impression that objective standards for consumer warnings are somehow more fair than subjective ones."

"Women have been pointing out something similar in connection with date rape, urging that consent be examined from a more searching perspective than 'What would most men think in this situation?'"[38]

"And I think it's the same general idea. We inscribe our ideas of power, authority, and legitimacy into the culture, and then pretend to consult that culture, meekly and humbly, in search of justice—for rules that are fair and neutral. A neat trick if you can get away with it."

Rodrigo paused, since the waiter had arrived with our food. Realizing that our long conversation had made us hungry, in unspoken agreement we ate for a few moments in silence. Rodrigo attacked his chile relleno with gusto, while I examined my burrito for anything forbidden by my doctor—a list that seemed to get longer and longer each time I visited her.

After his appetite subsided, Rodrigo continued: "So the nonformal nature of equality of opportunity allows members of an empowered group to call upon and invoke the many culturally established routines, practices, and understandings that benefit them."

"Could you give me an example?"

"Sure. Take our earlier one of the law school that can only hire one professor. There are two finalists, a black and a white. The formal job description contains the standard criteria: potential for scholarship, teaching, and public service. The two finalists seem equally qualified in each of those respects. Equality of results would dictate that the black applicant get the job because of the small number of African-Americans on the faculty. That is, the approach would strive for equality, for proportional representation, or some similar measure. But as we discussed before, under equality of opportunity the white will inevitably get the position. Equality of opportunity only guarantees that both will receive initial consideration. And when both candidates are considered, a myriad of factors, some conscious, some unconscious will come into play: inflection, small talk, background, bearing, social class, and the many imponderables that go into evaluating collegiality.[39] Such an approach is exactly the opposite of fair and neutral. Prudent distrust of a decision-maker who judges persons of a different race suggests that formal, structured rules and strictly confined discretion are the key to just such decisions.[40] But that is the opposite of what we have."

"Or take cases of pay increase and promotion," I suggested. "Formal equality says pay and promote minorities the same as whites doing the same work. But, in practice, this formal rule turns out to have exceptions that are applied in accordance with cultural understandings. The white candidate got a higher test score. So, following the rule of equal treatment would be unfair to the white. The next time, the two candidates have exactly the same test score. Again, the white gets the promotion—this time because he or she had more seniority, or a richer job background, or better references. And so it goes."

"In each case," Rodrigo interjected, "society manages to avoid the strict-equality rule. And the reason is the same: Some unstated cultural understanding or premise comes into play. So, the more empowered person whose predecessors were in a position to dictate the cultural terms for these transactions invariably comes out ahead."

"So, equality of opportunity, like merit, really just amounts to affirmative action for whites," I interjected. "It builds in a background of unstated assumptions that confer a consistent advantage in all the competitions that matter. If society were serious about equality, it would abolish this way of doing things and opt for equality of results. But this is something our culture will never do."

"No," Rodrigo added quietly. "It has defined equal opportunity, the approach that permits its members to win, as legal, principled, and just.[41] If one were to devise a system that would, first, produce racially discrepant results, and, second, enable those who manage and benefit from the system to sleep well at night, it would look very much like the present one."

"A serious charge, Rodrigo," I cautioned. "Not every member of the majority group merits that indictment. Some well-wishers and sympathizers want us to succeed. When you go out on the hiring market, you will see that. Perhaps even now, you have found a professor or two of majority race who has adopted and encouraged you, recognized your talent, gone out of his or her way on your behalf."

"Perhaps," Rodrigo conceded. "But not even they fully understand the personal impact of racism.[42] Most sympathetic whites view our current civil rights laws and regulations as adequate. The only thing missing, they believe, is the will to enforce them consistently."

"Isn't there something to that?" I prodded. "Or, what if we simply retooled the current rules to exclude the type of favoritism you mentioned? Then, would you view the system as fair?"

"I'm skeptical," responded Rodrigo. "Such retooling would entail the majority group's agreement to relinquish its advantages. They would have to agree to abide by quite complex rules, nothing as simple as: 'Treat Blacks and Whites the Same.' But, even if they did agree, rules alone cannot remedy racism."

"And why is that?"

"Because of the nature of racism itself. It's a little hard to explain. I'm working on this part of my thesis right now. Would you mind listening and giving me some feedback?"

"I'd be pleased to. I'm certain I'll benefit from discussing it at least as much as you will. Unfortunately, all I've been doing lately is cutting up case reports and reading and summarizing books. Never write a casebook, Rodrigo. It saps your energy and creativity like nothing else."

Since we had finished our dinner, Rodrigo suggested: "Maybe we could talk about it over dessert? I've heard that there's a wonderful bistro not far from here."

"Good idea. Here comes the waiter." I gestured that we would like to pay our bill, and moments later we were walking down the deserted side street, past warehouses and giant tractor-trailers full (I imagined) of sides of beef.

As we walked, Rodrigo began.

Which Treats of Racism's Refractory Nature in the Face of Legal Regulation

"We both observed earlier that many recent authors have pointed out that current laws don't seem able to make much of a dent in minority poverty and despair. Rosenberg, as you recall, says as much. Savage, too, points out how the Court is moving steadily away from any suggestion of social activism. And Spann and Bell seize on these observations to make their pungent points about the pervasiveness of racism. And they're not the only ones."

"True, although many conservatives don't find that particularly troubling; for them, judicial quietism is almost an article of faith. Our friends on the left are outraged, however. Gerry Spann all but accuses the Court of betraying African-Americans' legitimate hopes for decisions that can eliminate the barriers to black achievement and empowerment."[43]

"So, both the left and the right agree that the legal system does little to redress black misery."

"I'm afraid so. Now, you said you're working on an explanation for this sorry state of affairs. Is this in addition to your earlier comments about neutrality's role in concealing and increasing white privilege?"

"Yes. I think that there is something about racism that makes it peculiarly difficult to dismantle through any system of antidiscrimination laws. Racism would exist even if the dominant group treated minorities and whites similarly in all settings. Even if society recognized and canceled out the myriad cultural interpretations and background factors that now give whites an edge and render equal treatment a hollow illusion, I think racism would still remain."

"Rodrigo, I've been accused of undue pessimism about the prospects for racial reform. But it sounds like I soon will have an ally—namely, you! Please explain your theory about the persistence of racism."

"Facially neutral laws cannot redress most racism, because of the cultural background against which such laws operate. But even if we could somehow control for this, formally neutral rules would still fail to redress racism because of certain structural features of the phenomenon itself."

Rodrigo's First Structural Reason for Racism's Persistence: Its Vertical Character

"Rodrigo, slow down a little. My old legs are having trouble keeping up with you." As Rodrigo's speech became more animated, he had been picking up his pace as we walked to the bistro where we planned to have coffee and dessert. I was grateful when Rodrigo slowed.

"Let me start this way. You and others have written about racism's historical character. Everyone knows that blacks were brought here in slave ships. The practice of chattel slavery remained in effect for over two centuries, then was replaced by a system of Jim Crow laws and social practices that continues to this very day. So, racism's roots cannot easily be ignored.[44] Neutral rules cannot do justice to the thickly embedded historical nature of American prejudice. We act today on a set stage. But the rules ignore this. They tell the actor not to favor the white over the black. The only thing the rules take into account is what happens right now. If the actor—say a school board commissioner—can truthfully say, 'I acted as I did for no racial animus,' that is the end of the inquiry. This is obviously not sufficient."

"Why not?"

"Let me try to give you an example." Rodrigo squinted into the late afternoon sun that glanced off the sidewalk. "Imagine a school board needs to establish an attendance boundary. All of the children who live on one side of the boundary will go to one school; those who live on the other side, to another one."

"And you would predict that the board will choose a boundary that maintains segregated housing patterns, with the practical effect of maintaining segregated schools?"

"No. This school board truly wants to do the right thing. Recognizing that some boards have drawn attendance lines reflecting ethnic neighborhoods, this board has no desire to follow suit. Besides, it knows that if it does, the ACLU might bring suit against it. So, instead, they choose an existing freeway as the dividing line, reasoning that such a boundary will make the children's walk safer and shorter."

"What the board ignores," I continued, following the logic of Rodrigo's hypothetical, "is that many years ago the government probably placed the freeway in that location precisely because minority people lived there. In the past, governments frequently placed freeways, dump sites, power substations, and other such undesirable things in minority neighborhoods.[45] If the school board today selects the freeway as the boundary, it gives effect to a past discriminatory practice. It may do this entirely innocently. Indeed, it may have a laudable motive, one nobody could quarrel with, namely making children's walk to school as safe as possible."

"Exactly."

"In other words," I recapped, "neutrality employs a sort of 'freeze-frame' approach, looking only at present factors, when redressing racism requires a longer view."

Rodrigo smiled, "Without that longer view, one misses things, takes action that seems innocuous but that actually hurts minority people. There's a second feature that works in a similar way. Do we have time to discuss it?"

I checked the numbers on the street. "If you can explain it in the course of two blocks. Otherwise, we'll have to continue inside."

"I'll try my best."

Rodrigo's Second Reason: Racism's Concerted, or Horizontal, Aspect

As I had hoped, my ploy caused Rodrigo to slow down. My legs had begun to complain a second time.

"The other feature is that white-over-black domination is a concerted system. Racism derives its efficacy from its insidiousness. Many whites don't realize this. They equate racism with isolated, shocking acts, such as lynchings or burning crosses. Most white folks, even ones of good will, perceive much less racism in the world than there actually is.[46] In part, that is because they see fewer acts of out-and-out racism than minorities do.[47] But it is also because they analogize racism to other misfortunes that befall everyone, regardless of race, like having a flat tire or being cursed by another driver whom one has inadvertently cut off."

"I've noticed that tendency in the controversy over hate speech and university conduct codes," I said. "Many whites fail to realize how often the victim of one insult is the victim of another, similar one. They analogize it to being called a 'fool lady driver,' something that might happen every six months or year, and which rarely threatens an important feature of one's identity. By contrast, persons of color get almost daily reminders of how different they are. Even my friend Professor Oliveros, a light-skinned Hispanic, reports something similar. He says probably half the people he meets ask him where he is from, what kind of name he has, or how he learned to speak English so well."

"The problem involves what you called the 'freeze-frame' approach, Professor. Law focuses on micro-transactions, looking for something outrageous in a single remark. Not finding anything, it denies the existence of the underlying racism. And if you do confine your attention to the here and now in this way, there's not that much difference between 'Back to Africa' and 'Stay in your lane.' Campus racism so unremitting that young minority undergraduates sometimes drop out of college, ends up analogized to a football cheer: 'Boo, Cal.'"

"I know academics who have presented similar arguments," I commented. [48]

"All of us do. This concerted quality of racism enhances its malevolent efficacy, making it an ever-present force even for those of us with high professional status and wealth. It's as though criminal law were to lack any remedy for conspiracy, monopoly, and other offenses of collusion or aggregation, and, instead, dealt with the underlying evils on a case by case basis."

"Or like trying to identify and avoid poisons by examining their atomic structure when it's the behavior of the molecule that gives strychnine its deadly character," I added. "It just doesn't show up at that level."

Stopping at the entrance to the bistro, Rodrigo asked, "Is this the place?"

Summary: In Which Rodrigo Waxes Apocalyptic, Explaining How Everything Works Together to Maintain Racism's Malevolent Efficacy

Entering the dimly lit cafe and looking around, I observed, "Luckily for us, it's not very crowded. Have you been here before?"

"No, but Giannina and I have talked about coming here. I've heard they give free refills, which is great for someone on a student budget. Some of the other LL.M.s come here, even though it's a long ride."

As we settled down at an empty table, I returned to our earlier discussion: "Your professor urged you to try to solve the 'problems of your people,' as he put it. Instead, you seem ready to conclude that those problems are insoluble. Neutral principles of antidiscrimination law cannot redress racism. By defining blacks and whites as equals, neutrality allows society to blame blacks for their predicament. And, if I've understood the last part of your thesis, racism's nature makes it peculiarly resistant to solution through laws like our own. What a bleak vision for someone so young! For a battered old crusader like me, taking that stance is understandable. I think people give me sympathy for being so downbeat, want to rush in, comfort me, and say, 'No, it's not so.' But, for you, what's the point of struggle, what's the point of your working so hard to become a professor and scholar of civil rights, if you have so little hope of things ever getting better?"

"I didn't say that things would never get better, Professor. I merely observed that the law would not make them better. Any neutrality-based legal rule will look depressingly ineffectual to a black or person of color who lives in this society. By the same token, any practice that the majority group perceives as favoring minorities to promote racial justice will appear unprincipled and wrong."

"Like affirmative action?"

"Yes. Our society has been based on racial privilege since its inception.[49] Formal equality today serves the same purpose as the formal inequality of earlier years. It's a little bit like putting a car into neutral once you reach a downhill stretch. It just picks up speed; you don't even need to press the accelerator any more. The difference between society and the car is that most people don't even notice it's going downhill. So, society has trouble seeing the racism in a freeway boundary. Civil rights law has devolved into a system of 'nots'—'Thou shalt not this,' and 'Thou shalt not that'—all centered around the relatively few cases society is prepared to denounce as unquestionable breaches of the principle of neutral treatment."

"Like hiring a white high school dropout over a black Ph.D. and Nobel Prize laureate."

"Something like that. Majority-race persons are safe, so long as they avoid decisions like those. Nothing in the law requires anyone to do more, to lend a helping hand, to try to help blacks find jobs, befriend them, speak to them, make eye contact with them, help them fix a flat when they are stranded on the highway, help them feel like full persons. The law just says, 'Don't set quotas. Don't discriminate.' How can a system like that change anything?"

"It seems the only positive duties are concerned with capitalism—paying taxes, registering for the draft, and so on," I observed sardonically.

The waiter arrived, briefly interrupting our conversation to take our order. I was glad for the break. Rodrigo ordered a strawberry torte and espresso. Mindful of my doctor's orders and the late hour, I asked for a lemon biscuit and decaffeinated coffee.

As the waiter disappeared, Rodrigo continued: "The negative character of antidiscrimination laws, along with their inability to deal with the concerted and culturally rooted quality of racism, mean that neutral law can't do much. Moreover, neutrality prevents white folks from seeing how their own system advantages them, indeed it enables their more aggressive elements to blame minorities for their plight."

The waiter served our coffee. "Given the nature and prevalence of the cultural background, conservatives and moderates adore neutral rules of a nonformal character, like those providing for equality of opportunity. Actually, nothing is intrinsically wrong with neutral rules." I looked up with surprise. "They could be written and applied from minorities' perspective, in which case they would do a great deal to redress racism.[50] But the rules that minorities would enact, and which would strike them as fair, would appear one-sided and biased to whites. And whites will use their social power to label such rules unconstitutional, unprincipled, bad."

"So, do you mean to say that neutrality always fails to redress racism in practice? If it is applied against a background of minority cultural assumptions, it is not politically feasible; if it is applied in the current manner, against a background of white cultural premises, it fails to achieve retributive justice for minorities and may even makes matters worse."

"Much worse," Rodrigo nodded. "Whites simultaneously get to blame the victim, feel relieved of any responsibility for the victim's plight, and congratulate themselves on their fair-mindedness. It's no surprise that under the present legal regime of neutrality, the gap between whites and blacks in life expectancy, income, total wealth, educational attainment, infant mortality, and virtually every other indicator of social well-being has remained roughly the same.[51] Of course, there has been some improvement. After all, only a few generations ago blacks were formally enslaved. But the economic, social, and political gap between whites and blacks manages to remain almost identical decade after decade."

"This harsh reality pains and embarrasses white liberals, most of whom don't understand why this disparity continues. But, I think it's fair to say that it no longer seems to bother the conservatives. They embrace the idea that the courts cannot and should not function as a mechanism for propelling social change. As we've seen, for them social reform is purely a legislative function. Or better yet, from us they expect bootstrapping efforts, economic development, getting a job, tending to our families, and so on."

"I've been reading some of those books, too," Rodrigo said. "But I think the conservatives overlook something when they maintain that the courts have no efficacy, and that they can and should do little in the area of civil rights."

The waiter brought our desserts. Hungry again from our brisk walk and animated discussion, I immediately attacked my lemon biscuit. Looking up, I challenged Rodrigo: "I'll bite. What are they overlooking?"

"Very funny," he replied. "What conservatives overlook is that our system of cautious, incremental, negatively-phrased, neutral civil rights laws is in fact quite efficacious."

"It is?" I nearly spilled my decaffeinated cappuccino. "In what way?"

"The system works very well. It is just that its successes serve a different goal. For example, Gerald Rosenberg's book is full of tables, charts, and historical analyses, all demonstrating that Supreme Court decisions have not brought about changes, for women's or minorities' rights, that were not already underway.[52] He shows that *Roe v. Wade*[53] did not increase access to abortion[54] and reveals that *Brown v. Board of Education*[55] did not increase the numbers of black schoolchildren attending desegregated schools.[56] But he mistakenly concludes that the civil rights laws have no effect."

"I suppose you are going to say that their effect is too subtle to measure, that it lies in a symbolic dimension that will take years to make itself felt?"

"No, not at all," Rodrigo replied. "Rather, civil rights laws efficiently and smoothly replicate social reality, particularly black-white power relations. They are a little like the thermostat in your home or office. They assure that there is just the right amount of racism. Too much would be destabilizing— the victims would rebel. Too little would forfeit important pecuniary and psychic advantages for those in power. So, the existing system of race-remedies law does, in fact, grant minorities an occasional victory, an occasional *Brown v. Board of Education*. Every now and then, a bigot who burns a cross or beats a black youth will be convicted. Particularly in areas where concessions are not too costly, like voting rights,[57] or media licensing,[58] the courts will grant us an occasional breakthrough."

"One of the authors we mentioned, David Savage, points out in his book, *Turning Right*, that the Rehnquist Court, even in a period of civil rights retrenchment, has granted blacks victories in occasional cases."[59]

"I believe that you and others in the Critical Race Theory movement have a term for this?" Rodrigo prompted.

"Contradiction-closing cases."[60]

"That's it," Rodrigo replied. "I used to think that this notion verged on tautology. But now I think there might be something to it. What else explains such decisions as *Metro Broadcasting, Inc. v. FCC* or *United States v. Fordice* in an era in which the Court methodically has been eviscerating civil rights protection for minorities and women by imposing new burdens of proof, narrowing standing to sue for class-based relief, and requiring tight claims of causation?"

"Under your theory, then," I reviewed, motioning the waiter to bring the check, "courts are doing their job. Many of us just misconceive what that job is. Civil rights proponents still believe that the courts want to stamp out racial unfairness, that the optimal amount of racism in society is zero. But it's not. It's a properly low level, maintained by means of neutral rules that reach little conduct of significance, administered and interpreted by judges whose experiences ill equip them to understand the nature of the problem and who dispense victories as parsimoniously as possible. Is that your thesis?"

"Yes, and I think it operates at the level of cultural assumptions, which is, after all, its beauty. There is no conscious conspiracy. Liberal whites are often as blithely ignorant of the workings of the system, as needlessly indignant as the most rock-ribbed conservative extolling the virtues of our system of individual achievement, where every person rises or falls on her merits."

"Spann is indignant, too."

"Like others on the left, he began by believing—or at least hoping—that the system means what it says when it issues those golden promises of equality. It's a little like the law of gravity. Rosenberg says civil rights law has failed because the position of women and minorities has not improved much as a result of constitutional adjudication.[61] But that's like arguing that the law of gravity has failed because not everything has fallen. In fact, gravity holds everything neatly in balance, the sun, the moon, the stars, and the planets. In that respect it is quite successful, as is our civil rights system."

"So law works," I said, slowly grasping the enormity of what Rodrigo had just articulated. "But it operates to preserve racial advantage, to maintain the status quo."

"Like the law of gravity," Rodrigo repeated, draining the last drop of espresso from his cup.

Conclusion

We soon parted. After watching my energetic young friend stride along the sidewalk in the direction of his law school several miles away, I began my slow walk back to my apartment and yet another session with the casebook. As I walked, I reflected on our conversation. If culture determines our interpretation of legal texts and rules, and if racism is woven so deeply into our cultural fabric that we hardly notice it, then how can civil rights laws ever hope to eradicate racism in our culture? What did Rodrigo mean when he said there might be cause for hope, but not through law? Perhaps he meant that cultural change might occur, possibly through some form of direct action, and that would make legal change possible. I cursed my fate as a casebook writer for having removed me, if only temporarily, from some of the drama being played out on the pages of the law reviews. I resolved to get together again with Rodrigo soon. I wanted to hear how his second essay fared in the competition he had mentioned. But even more importantly, I wanted to know whether he saw any way out of the cultural trap whose gloomy outlines he had so remorselessly sketched for my benefit.

5

RODRIGO'S FIFTH CHRONICLE:
Civitas, Civil Wrongs, and the Politics of Denial

I was staring glumly out my office window, awaiting the arrival of my secretary with a large stack of bluebooks, when I heard a polite cough at my door. I looked up and saw Rodrigo's familiar face.

"Professor?"

"Rodrigo!" I exclaimed. "It's been a while. Come in. I've been thinking of you lately, and here you are. To what do I owe the pleasure of this visit?"

"Are you free, Professor? I don't want to interrupt if you're busy."

"Not at all. They're administering my last exam even as we speak. Any minute now, they'll deliver 107 bluebooks. I'm in no hurry to start. What's on your mind? Did you finish that paper we talked about?"[1]

"I did. I'm still waiting to hear from the judges. The professor liked it and gave me a decent grade, but I'm afraid the conservative society that is sponsoring the competition may not know what to make of it. I expect they'll like some aspects of it; others they're sure to find too radical."

"If they're as smart as I think, they'll realize that neoconservative and Critical Race thought overlap in a surprising number of ways.[2] Now how about you? Are you finished for the term?"

"I took my last exam on Friday. I'll stick around for most of the break, although Giannina and I may visit Dad in Florida for a few days.[3] In the meantime, I'm reading up on legal pedagogy for my study group and a committee report I'm writing for school."

"I didn't know you were in a study group," I remarked. "What kind is it?"

"Oh, some of the LL.M.s and a few of the regular students get together every few weeks at someone's apartment. Whoever hosts the next session gets to select the readings. Legal theory, mostly. We read a number of your articles before we stopped for exams."

Rodrigo peered at a book half-hidden under the papers on my desk. "I'm reading that one right now."

The book the observant Rodrigo referred to was *Anarchy and Elegance*,[4] which I was reading in anticipation of my appearance as a panelist at the law school where its author, Chris Goodrich, studied for a year in a special program for journalists and writers.[5] The conference at which I was to speak was entitled "The Making of a Lawyer", and was organized by the school's student association.

"What do you think of it?" I asked. "I'm speaking at Goodrich's school next term and thought I'd read his book for background. My panel is on legal education, and my role is a small one—that of respondent."

"To whom?" Rodrigo asked.

"A well-known civic republican. I haven't seen his paper. He'll probably argue that law school should do more training in social responsibility and civic virtue.[6] I'm not sure what I'll say. Who could disagree with the idea that we should strive to be more ethical, more community oriented, more concerned with each other than we are today? I suppose the sponsors want me to address whether dialog, love, and so on will cure racism. But several of us have written about that already."[7]

"I know," Rodrigo said. "But the more general point—about *civitas* and legal training—is intriguing, and in a way dovetails with issues of racial justice. Goodrich addresses that, did you notice?"

I searched my memory, but fortunately the irrepressible Rodrigo continued: "In the early pages, Goodrich writes that law school had an intensely normative, almost other-worldly quality, particularly in the opening day speeches. All term long, only one of his professors offered real-world training, and he did so in such a cold, mechanical manner that many of Goodrich's fellow students were put off. The other professors emphasized social policy, theory, and so on, but neglected the realities of the legal profession."[8]

"I think students almost everywhere complain that legal training is not practical enough, that the faculty don't pay enough attention to the nitty-gritty details of lawyering. Is it the same at your school?"

"The regular students grumble all the time. My friend Ali told one of them it's a corporate-capitalist plot to render them unfit for anything but large-firm practice. He showed her an essay by Duncan Kennedy.[9] But most of us in the LL.M. program don't find the approach particularly disturbing. Most of us love theory. Maybe it's because we're foreign born or educated. Where we come from, the professors teach mainly by lecture. It's even more theoretical than here. They expect you to get practical experience later, in an apprenticeship or on the job."

"What your U.S.-born colleagues may not realize is that clinical training is expensive. Many law schools can't afford it, so they teach by means of large lecture classes and the Socratic method."[10]

"Yes, but even so," Rodrigo frowned, "that doesn't explain the disjunction between real life and law school teaching that many students complain of."

"I assume you have a theory?" I asked. Rodrigo, a future teacher, was probably thinking about matters of pedagogy. As his sometime-mentor I thought it behooved me to listen and, perhaps, offer him advice.

"Well, some thoughts, anyway."

"I'd love to hear them."

"And I'd love your reactions. I'm interested in the way law is taught and its relationship to broader intellectual and cultural currents. As you know, I'm hitting the job market soon. I'm sure the interviewers will ask me about my views on teaching. I'm hoping to have something coherent to say."

I made a mental note to urge Rodrigo not to range too far afield, to offer too controversial a theory, during his all-important job interviews. But my brash, talented young friend always had something interesting to say. Besides, I thought, if the "broader intellectual currents" he had just mentioned include civic republicanism, the discussion might well help me prepare for my upcoming conference.

"What connection do you see? But, before we start, can I offer you a cup of coffee?"

"Of course," replied Rodrigo eagerly. "The kind you made before was great."

"I have both regular and decaf. My doctor ordered me to cut down. I assume you want the high-octane kind?"

"Yes, please."

I adjusted the dials on my office coffeemaker, added beans and water, then sat back expectantly. As I hoped, Rodrigo soon began.

The Owl of Minerva: In Which Rodrigo Explains Why Legal Education Is Becoming More Aspirational and High-Flown

"Have you heard of the Owl of Minerva, Professor?"

I ransacked my memory. Rodrigo, educated at the University of Bologna, seemed to have read everything.[11] At length I asked: "Is it a phrase from Hegel?"

"By his translator and editor, actually. It's from his preface to *Philosophy of Right*. The full phrase is, 'The Owl of Minerva spreads its wings only with the falling of the dusk.'"[12]

"Ah, yes," I said. "It refers to the way that philosophy always comes too late, when the world is already slipping into dusk. We achieve wisdom about something only when it is fading, is passing into history."

"The phrase has been coming into my mind a lot lately," Rodrigo said, "in connection with the critique of normativity, in which a group of young Crits maintain that the brand of highly prescriptive discourse you see in the law reviews these days serves many functions, not all of them particularly noble.[13] It occurred to me that one of these functions may be denial— postponing the realization that our situation has indeed deteriorated—that the Owl of Minerva has flown."

"And you think this has something to do with the students' complaints about the overly abstract quality of law teaching?"

"Not so much with abstraction in general, but with the normative quality of it: all the talk of a lawyer's role, the profession's ideals, wise social policy, things of that sort, when what the students want to learn is the down-to-earth details of lawyering."

"And you think this is connected with broader cultural conditions?"

"I do. There's a general pattern today in the West of trying to get beyond Self.[14] In law school that translates into high-flown, highly theoretical teaching. But you see it elsewhere, too."

"In legal theory, I think you said."

"Yes, especially in this new movement called civic republicanism." I pricked up my ears, remembering my date with the famous revivalist only six weeks hence. "It has parallels in philosophy,[15] social theory,[16] and political science.[17] Everyone is becoming more aspirational, just as Western society's troubles are becoming more and more plain.[18] Many writers are reviving Aristotle, as clear-cut a case of Hegel's maxim as there ever has been."

"An interesting hypothesis. I hope you'll fill in the details."

"I'll try. But I must confess, the students' lament poses a problem for me that I've not yet resolved. I love legal theory, as you know. Yet, I agree that there is something wrong with the way law is taught. How to balance things is the trick, and how to explain all this succinctly to an appointments committee at a school where I would like to teach."

"You may not need to enter such treacherous waters, Rodrigo," I counseled. "Already you've won a national prize for student writing. You're getting an LL.M. from a top school—not to mention having graduated second in your class at the oldest law school in the world." I was hoping Rodrigo would soft-pedal some of his more radical ideas in discussions with appointments committees. The critique of normativity I thought particularly likely to get him in trouble. Many found it corrosive, even nihilist, although I could see why it appealed to this young *enfant terrible.*

"But that's not to say you shouldn't talk about these things with me or your friends. You also mentioned a committee at your school."

"Oh, yes. I'm on a joint student-faculty committee to review the curriculum. It was established this year, in part because all the grumbling in the student body seems to be coming to a head. I'm the LL.M. representative. My friend Ali is the alternate."

The coffee machine had stopped gurgling. "Ready for a cup?" I asked. "You said regular, right?"

Rodrigo slurped his steaming hot coffee with gusto. "You make the best espresso I've had since leaving Italy, Professor. Where were we?"

"You were going to tell me how all the currents you mentioned are related. Aristotle, too, I think."

"Oh, yes. They all have to do with trying to get beyond Self. And this is happening in many disciplines more or less at the same time. Moreover, this is occurring as part of a historical cycle, just as our culture is starting to decline. The civic republicans are arguing that we need more virtue in law, just as our society is fragmenting. They argue for deliberation and consensus, just as those things are becoming impossible."[19]

"The author whose panel I'm on writes about all those things. Since the panel is on legal education, I'm pretty sure he'll urge law schools to teach more courses on ethics, examine the role of the lawyer, call for more discussions of social policy, and so on."

"All quite aspirational and elevating," Rodrigo added.

"And, if I understand you correctly, exactly the opposite of what the students want and society needs."

"True. The students want engagement, want to get beyond Self, just as the faculty do. But their approach is different. They want to learn technique, client counseling, black-letter law. The faculty want more theory, more ethics, more attention to the Good."

I was silent for a moment before deciding to play devil's advocate: "Well, Rodrigo, what's wrong with that? Shouldn't we teach students to be more than technicians and hired guns? Shouldn't we teach them to identify with professional ideals and the broader social good? Isn't the rest just hack work, grinding out pleadings—sort of like automobile mechanics but with careful spelling?"

"I don't think so. The Aristotelian revival, civic republicanism in its various forms, and *civitas* in the law—you need to look at all of them in perspective to see the function they serve: namely, denial. Each is a mechanism for avoiding the painful reality of decline."

"Not long ago, Rodrigo, you portrayed aspects of the rise of neoconservatism in terms of perseveration, of doing the same thing repeatedly when social conditions call for a new direction.[20] You said that when threatened, we often respond by doing what worked before, even though that conduct has ceased to bring us the desired results. Is your Owl of Minerva mechanism an aspect of the same thing?"

"The two are related, but not the same. In perseveration, the culture digs in, pretends that bad things aren't happening. It tries to hearken back to its own golden era. Sometimes it looks for scapegoats—outsiders of some sort— to blame for its current troubles. But this other mechanism is a little different. With denial, we avert our gaze from something known to exist. With normativity, we fix our gaze on a point in space—above the particular mess in the real world we wish to avoid because it's so distressing."[21]

"I could use an example."

"I'll give one in a minute. But first let me explain how neat the mechanism is. If you fix your attention on higher things, dwell in realms of abstraction and normativity, you can avoid taking practical action. It's much easier and more enjoyable to say that the West should not be slipping, that the legal profession should not be in such a mess, and so on. You get to discuss what ought to be, not what is and what to do about it. You also get to blame someone, because if things are bad, there must be a cause."

"So, the new normativity is different from perseveration."

"Yes. Perseveration, basically, is for conservatives. Normativity is for moderate leftists, including many of your and my friends."

"But they come down to the same thing—is that what you are saying?"

"Both disable us from appreciating our dilemma, from responding to it directly. Both shift blame. Both enable us to avoid coming to terms with a profession or society in disarray. It's another respect in which the left and the right converge, as you mentioned earlier, Professor. But it's a convergence of the moderate left and moderate right, both using similar avoidance strategies, and with the same effect—things get worse, the poor get poorer, those excluded from society are further cast out."

"The left will not like what you are saying, Rodrigo. Our liberal friends have a positive self-image."

"So do conservatives."

"But liberals think of themselves as the nice guys, the ones with a heart. And they do, in fact, care about us. The civic republicans, for example, deplore the marginalization of minority groups.[22] Our exclusion from life's bounty, from full membership in the human community, is an affront to their ideal of *civitas*."

"I realize that. And I'll be careful not to overstate. But it seems to me that one function of normativity and all the talk of community is to build consensus and solidarity.[23] Things are deteriorating. So, we respond by pulling together, by arranging to live with others in a kind of bubble. Someone who comes along and says the solidarity is pathological can easily expect trouble. History is replete with examples."

I was silent for a moment. Then: "Rodrigo, fascinating as I find all this, you set a fast pace. I do want to hear about society as bubbles, civic republicanism as a response to social decline, and legal pedagogy. I'm beginning to get a glimpse of how all these things fit together. But I haven't eaten in several hours and am beginning to wear down. Why don't we take a short break? Our own LL.M.s are having an end-of-the-term party downstairs. I just heard a couple of them heading down the stairway. We could go down, have a bite to eat, and maybe I'll introduce you to some of your opposite numbers here."

At the mention of food, Rodrigo brightened up, then hesitated.

"We'll come right back. I really want to hear your ideas."

"You're my best sounding board, Professor."

"And you, mine. Don't worry. I'm not going to try to escape. I've got plenty of time, and although you may not realize it, I get at least as much out of our discussions as you do. In particular, I need to figure out something halfway intelligent to say about legal education, *civitas*, and the republican revival for my talk next month."

"Then let's go."

In Which Rodrigo Treats of How Law's Reaction to Its Own Discontents Mirrors Aristotelianism, a Certain Owl, and the Many Good Folks Who Substitute Dialog for Social Action

Thirty minutes later, as we rode the elevator back to my office balancing cheese, crackers, and little paper cups of white wine, I reflected on how I had once again misjudged Rodrigo. When he came to my door an hour earlier, I expected to have one of those nice, avuncular conversations a senior professor has two or three times a year with a favorite protégé. I would give Rodrigo tips on how to handle himself during his employment interviews, pointers on how to conduct his first class, and inquire politely into his first venture with student-faculty governance. Instead, we were discussing Hegel, legal theory, and cultural analysis.

My reverie didn't last long. As we rounded the corner and entered my office, I spied a familiar sight: a 14-inch-high pile of bluebooks perched ominously on the center of my desk where my secretary must have deposited them while we were at the reception downstairs.

"Looks like you have work to do," Rodrigo commented.

"It's both the best and the worst part of teaching, Rodrigo. You get to see what your students have learned. Some answers amaze and astonish you. You'll wonder who the unknown genius is behind the number on the cover. Other bluebooks are off the mark. You wonder how you could have mis-taught someone so badly."

"That's another thing students complain about. Not only is law school too theoretical and abstract, but students feel they get little opportunity for feedback. Few professors give midterms, so the single exam at the end of the course is the only feedback you get. And some professors—not you, Professor, I'm sure you're very good about this—take forever to hand in their grades."

"It is a lot of work," I added feebly, not wanting to excuse the conduct of some of my colleagues who routinely return their grades three months after final exams. "But this brings us back to law teaching. You're on the curriculum committee, Rodrigo, and have to write a report recommending changes in the way law is taught. And, in just a few months, you are going traveling. You're going to face appointments committees and faculties who will want to know your approach to teaching. Let's focus on that for a bit. What are you going to say in your report to the committee?"

"Ali is going to help me draft it. We know what we are going to recommend, but we need a theory, a way to crystallize our thoughts so the report has a structure out of which our suggestions flow naturally."

"Otherwise," I interjected, "the faculty will dismiss it as urging an anti-intellectual, know-nothing approach to law school."

"As I mentioned earlier, that's one of the seductive things about the current highly aspirational, super-normative approach. It enables you to think of yourself as taking the high road, as being an idealist. In fact, we're the ones—the student grumblers, I mean—who are the idealists."

"In wanting practical, skills-oriented training?"

"Yes. The other kind is a deflection, a way of seeing nothing while wrapping up one's nihilistic visions in an aura of seeming-goodness and social concern. In normal times, when things were stable, law was not taught this way. Legal training was less prescriptive, more experiential. A hundred years ago, apprenticeships were common. It's the same phenomenon at work in each of the areas we were talking about earlier. Law is a microcosm of society. If, as we discussed earlier, Western civilization is entering a period of decline, then the Owl of Minerva will spread its wings, right on schedule. Our political leaders will talk to us about our collective greatness and rediscovering our American identity.[24] Philosophers will resurrect Aristotle and talk of civic virtue.[25] And law professors will focus their eyes on the mountain tops, preaching policy, ethics, and the role of the good lawyer exactly at a time when legal practice is cutthroat; no one makes partner; senior lawyers complain that law is not nearly as enjoyable as it once was and that law is now a business not a profession; the bar is divided over the distribution of attorneys, advertising, and use of paralegals; and the public's esteem for lawyers is at its lowest point ever."[26]

"And so your cure is concreteness?"

Rodrigo looked at me sharply, so I quickly rephrased: "I mean, if things are so bad, isn't there a case for ethics, for trying to find out how and where we went astray?"

"Of course," Rodrigo conceded. "But when I said the complainers in the student bodies are the idealists, I meant in a different sense. They have yet to learn the deflection strategy. They still want to fix things. Some of them entered law school imbued with the desire to help the unfortunate, to be public interest and legal services attorneys, to represent prisoners, battered women, the poor and hungry.[27] But law school teaches them that there is a 'grander' mission than this somewhere, and that the whole task is to find it."

"I have noticed that shift in my students. Many of them come to law school aiming to serve the poor. Over three years, they change. Goodrich notes the same thing. But I don't see the connection you are trying to make. Students surely don't lose their ideals because we lecture them constantly about law on a higher level?"

"They do," Rodrigo said firmly. "I know it sounds paradoxical. I couldn't even get Ali to see it at first, and as I think I mentioned, he's a Marxist. Normativity, the many platitudes and bromides of what passes as legal ethics, all the grand sonorous phrases with which your fellow professors fill the classroom air—no offense to you, Professor—have as their natural and intended effect the building of solidarity.[28] We call it professionalism. It's a certain mindset or way of seeing ourselves as lawyers in our society, with all its problems. And, that's the whole point of it. If you focus your gaze on the higher reaches, you avoid dealing with the pain below. If you can get everyone else to look and speak the same way, you build solidarity. You can almost persuade yourself that all is well, that we have not lost our former greatness. You can believe, a little longer, that law is still a gentleman's profession, with no serious blemishes. You can believe that there is nothing seriously wrong with the way law is taught and practiced, or the way legal services are delivered and distributed."

"But the public doesn't see us that way. I suppose you're going to say that this is because they are outside our bubble."

"Exactly," Rodrigo exclaimed, with an alacrity that led me to believe that, for once, I had managed to point out something implicit in his own thinking that enabled him to take it a step further. "And it's the same with those other things. All the bubbles are slowly sinking, wafting down to the ground where they will meet their inevitable fate. But within each, there is a group that steadfastly believes its bubble is quite safe, that it is indeed the greatest bubble there is. It goes about preaching daily how virtuous, lofty, fair, and just it is. This postpones the day of reckoning a while longer."

"A special form of perseveration," I observed.

"More like procrastination," Rodrigo added. "An especially sweet, enjoyable kind, something we all do together that makes us feel good."

"For a little while."

"It may be a period of years. Aristotle, for example, wrote just as the Greek nation-states were falling apart.[29] If Hegel's observation is right—and I think it is—Aristotle was a classic case of the Owl of Minerva, of an intensely normative writer who preached wisdom, unity, and civic responsibility just when it was beginning to be too late."

I was astonished. Aristotle, the great author of the Nichomachean Ethics and Politics, engaged in the politics of denial? As though sensing my thought, Rodrigo continued:

"Sure. And don't worry. I won't tell this to everyone I meet. But Aristotle really was the wrong voice for his age. He spread his wings, but things had already changed, had already moved on."[30]

"I'm not sure I follow you. I'd like to hear more, especially if you plan to tie it to the current Aristotelian revival and subject of my upcoming panel."

"I'll try," Rodrigo said. "Aristotle's work did unite, maybe even inspire, Greek society; that is, at least its aristocratic, white-male elite. But it was exactly the wrong prescription for his times. It is even more wrong for ours."

"Do you mean that our problem is that our society needs to find ways of incorporating immigrants and outsiders, of dealing with our problems with racism and sexism? The civic republicans are already conscious of that."[31]

"I know," Rodrigo replied. "But serious problems remain. Take, for example, Aristotle's famous doctrine of the Golden Mean.[32] Every one reveres that, but a moment's reflection shows that it is completely wrong for our times. A hundred years ago, it would have served some useful purpose. Then, we were in an age of unchecked development, in which we mined the hillsides, dammed the rivers, laid the forests to waste, and killed or relocated the Indians. Moderation would have been a good philosophy to have had back then. But it came too late, just as it did for ancient Greece. Today, the challenge is not for the U.S. to go on doing what it has been doing all along, but moderately and judiciously. Our bubble is drifting downward. We need to arrest the fall, but we won't discover how to do this through the discourse of moderation."

"What about the other elements civic republicanism has borrowed from Aristotle, such as deliberation by the citizenry?"[33]

"It's the same thing. Deliberation, solidarity, the search for consensus are reactions to cultural decline. They're another aspect of the Owl spreading its wings. And just like the Golden Mean, they lead us off in the wrong direction."

"Some of us in Critical Race Theory have been taking the republicans to task for their faith in dialog as a solution to all our social ills."[34]

"I've read that literature," Rodrigo said, "and agree with it. If one's bubble is sinking—one's society in trouble, one's profession in tatters—one needs to talk with someone other than oneself and one's friends. That talk will be circular, reassuring, empty, and 'inscribed,' as the critics of normativity put it.[35] It doesn't get you out of your bubble. And keeping you there is exactly its function. What's needed is not dialog with each other, but with 'Those Others.' We need to reach outside our bubble. From within it, we don't see the rate of descent. We don't see that the bubble closes in on itself. For that, one needs to consult someone who lives and exists outside our bubble."

"So, if the legal academy really wants to improve its pedagogy, its curriculum, it should confer with students, or with the bar?"

"That would be a start. And we should really listen to what they say. We should also talk with ordinary folks, with the consumers of legal services. We should talk with prisoners, the poor, and other underserved groups."

"Get outside our bubble, so to speak," I observed.

"The exact way we—I mean the law professoriate . . ."

"It'll soon include you," I interjected.

"The exact way we will do that still remains to be filled in. Ali and I have a few commonsense ideas. So did Chris Goodrich in his absorbing book.[36] But you're the one with years of experience, Professor. Do you have the time to go on a little further? I could run some of them past you. I like the way you push me. And I've got a few ideas on civic republicanism that might help you at your lecture."

"I'd love any help I can get. But before going on, would you like another cup of coffee? You're going strong, I can see. But at my age, I've learned I do better if I pace myself. Even though it's just the decaffeinated kind these days, a little pick-me-up helps keep me going."

"I'd love another cup." Rodrigo looked at his watch. "Oh, it's not too late. Make it regular."

In Which Rodrigo Talks about Bubbles, Deflection, and the Futility of Normative Discourse

While we waited for our coffee, I asked, "Would you like a sliced bagel to go with your brie? I have a new refrigerator."

"I wondered what that was. Did you have it last time?" Rodrigo asked, motioning toward the compact refrigerator in the corner of my office.

"No, I got it just the other day. I don't know if I told you, but I was lucky enough to get a permanent appointment here following my semester's visit. So, I'm moving in. One of the first things I got was this mini-fridge. It's perfect for snacks. My doctor told me to have a lot of small meals as I go through the day."

"Thanks," said Rodrigo, spreading a wedge of cheese on his bagel. "I get hungry from intellectual conversation myself. Giannina keeps remarking how much I eat for such a skinny guy."

"Speaking of hunger, is there a food drive going on at your school?"

"Yes, organized by the students. At your place, too?"

"Yes. There are a lot of homeless folks around here. The students collect cans and other nonperishables. It's interesting that in both schools, the drives are sponsored by students, not the faculty."

"Just as my thesis would predict," Rodrigo replied. "Those who talk normatively the most are least likely to take practical steps to better the plight of their fellow humans."[37]

"Touché," I said wryly, recalling with more than a trace of guilt that I had meant to bring in a bag of surplus food from my apartment in response to a flyer from the student anti-hunger organization, but had never gotten around to doing so.

"I think it works like this," Rodrigo said. "Remember all the talk about subsistence rights that went on during the mid-nineteen-seventies and eighties?"[38]

"I do," I said, wondering how Rodrigo knew all this—he must have been a teenager completing high school at the base in Italy where his father was serving at that time. "Charles Black and other progressive scholars and activists were hoping to establish a fundamental right to housing, food, medical care, education, and other basic needs.[39] They made a number of powerful arguments, but got nowhere."

"And you don't hear those arguments much any more, do you?" Rodrigo asked. I shook my head, and he continued: "I think I know why. It has to do with normative discourse, and it explains why students and others who are only half 'professionalized,' as they say, tend to be the ones who organize food drives."

"Please go on," I urged. I was intrigued, not merely because I had just upbraided myself for neglecting the hungry during the Christmas season, but because I had been wondering recently about the connection between charity and political philosophies, both of the left and of the right.

"As we were saying, I think one of the functions of normative discourse is to abstract problems, to translate them into something else. A subsistence claim—'I'm hungry'—is answered by: 'All right, I'll talk with you about your hunger.'"

"That's civic republicanism," I said.

"But there are other variations," Rodrigo continued. "For example: 'Hunger is bad. Its persistence must mean there is something wrong with society.'"

That strikes close to home, I thought.

"That's the left. The moderate right has its version, too—'Well, let's talk about your responsibility to solve your own problem, to get a job, take care of your family, and so forth.' Or—'Let's improve the economy generally, so there will be more jobs for all.'"

"So," I summarized. "We start with a simple human-needs claim: 'I'm hungry.' And this gets translated, swept up into various forms through standard normative dialog."

"Which we repeat over and over with our friends. We begin talking about you and your hunger. But five minutes later we're talking about me, my conscience, my favorite normative notions, my lack of responsibility, my prescriptions for social change, what the world would be like if my kind of lawyer was in charge. A neat shift, all facilitated by normative discourse."

"Now I see better what you mean by 'deflection,'" I said. "But I wonder if you're not being too harsh on the legal academy. Don't you think that rationalization and abstraction are universal human tendencies? Surely you're not saying that great thinkers—you mentioned Aristotle earlier— were guilty of ducking hard issues, like hunger and the maldistribution of social resources?"

"I'm not the one who invented the 'Owl of Minerva' metaphor," Rodrigo replied, a little defensively.

"Maybe that's what the Crits mean when they say normative discourse is inscribed, circular, solipsistic,"[40] I offered.

"They're right about that. It shifts attention from the way the world is to my own situation. Now we can talk and discuss my virtue for having listened to you, or your frailty for having allowed yourself to become hungry, or society's shortcomings for being structured so as to have hungry, unemployed people, and so on. In ancient Greece, they began discussing civic virtue in earnest only when their society was on the verge of collapse. Our culture is doing that now. All the great novelists—Tolstoy, Melville, Dostoyevski—have characters who increase their religiosity, their normativity, in times of trouble."

"But, Rodrigo," I interjected, "maybe the whole thing is less sinister than you think. What if the mechanism is not perseveration but preservation? Just as the medieval monks labored to preserve wisdom in the dark ages, maybe the civic republicans are trying to preserve the best of Western civilization for future times. Perhaps that accounts for the inscribed quality you and others note. Maybe wisdom comes with the Owl of Minerva not so much to save the current civilization, as to improve what comes next. Perhaps we are entering a new dark age, and the current *normativos* are our monks."

"I don't think preservation best captures what we see. I still think avoidance and denial are the most accurate terms. But even if all we are observing is an effort to preserve the past, one would have to question whether the patterns being preserved are worth preserving. And in my opinion, dealing with hunger by abstraction, or with a legal profession in disarray by means of elegant classroom sermons, is unlikely to prove useful in any future society."

"If these patterns are near-universal, instinctive, and inscribed, Rodrigo, why are you able to see them? How are we able to identify and talk about them? Why are they not invisible, like air?"

"You and I see these things because we are outsiders. You are a man of color. I was raised in Italy. In some sense we are both outside the bubble. As outsiders, we can see the curvature and the downward drift, as those inside cannot."

"But, Rodrigo, if as you say we are lost in the wilderness, shouldn't we do anything to find our way out?"

"Talking in circles will not do us much good. Nor will doing over and over again, with more and more energy, what in former times brought greatness."

"So, what should we do?"

"That's a normative question."

"But it's a question you'll have to face, Rodrigo, if only to write your report on how to fix legal education at your school. And, if you tell appointments committees that legal pedagogy is too normative, too ethereal, they'll want to know what you propose as its substitute. Law, like life, is concerned with action. That's why people get impatient with the Crits and accuse them of nihilism. We don't offer answers. But in life, there must be answers. Every minute, we are concerned with some practical query or other: Should I have another cup of coffee? Should I tell Rodrigo to conceal his Critical brilliance in the interests of getting a job? One needs to answer such questions fifty times a day. I wonder if you're not being too hard on practitioners of normative discourse. Aren't they just trying to help us with guidelines for practical queries like these?"

"Yes, but their thinking is too conventional. Conventional answers— what sociologists of knowledge call 'normal science'—work only during normal times.[41] In each of the arenas we have been discussing, the difficulties are too serious, too basic for the sort of answers we get by talking with each other. That just takes you round and round in circles, does nothing about the bubble, about the discourse paradigm that is itself slowly sinking, slowly becoming obsolete."

"What do you propose to put in its place?"

"I'll tell you, but this part of my thesis is not fully worked out."

"That's my favorite kind. Like another cup of coffee?"

Rodrigo quickly glanced at his watch. "One more," he said.

In Which Rodrigo Explains How to Get Outside One's Bubble and Why Aristotle Is Not the Right Role Model for Our Times

As I returned from throwing out the old coffee and busied myself fixing a new batch, Rodrigo began:

"What I propose would build on civic republicanism's central insight, but go a step further."

"How do you mean?"

"Let me put it this way. I think we need more Socrates and less Aristotle. We need it in political thought, in law school teaching, and other areas as well. And I'm not referring to the rather tame practice you call the Socratic method, in which a professor asks simple scripted questions about distinguishing this case from that, about whether a particular question ought to be resolved by reference to this formulaic policy principle or that. When the students complain, it's not because the law school classroom asks questions, makes demands on them. Rather it's the sameness and predictability of those questions, which never seem to get anywhere."

"Civic republicanism does try to get somewhere. It grapples with things like racism and the unfair distribution of social resources."

"But it only goes so far. I was talking about this with Ali and Giannina the other day. We agreed the civic republicans are right when they say politics should consist of more than log rolling and balancing interests.[42] We should struggle to decide which preexisting desires are worthy, are most in keeping with our idea of *civitas*. That, I think, is a valid insight. It has real critical bite."

"I've heard it said that intellectuals love this vision of politics because it affords them a central role, rewards them for something they do well, namely, arguing.[43] Well-read, articulate people are just the ones whose ideas are likely to hold sway, whose notions of the best social arrangements are likely to win out in the end."

"Touché, Professor—although I'd note that, despite your radically Critical stance, your own ideas have not been without effect. But let me explain how civic republicanism's program needs refining. Cass Sunstein says we should not accept preexisting preferences as given, as exogenous to politics. Instead, they should be made the subject of it. We should all struggle to determine what we should want as a people."

"A commendable insight, especially if the preferences that they propose to reexamine include ones like racism."

"You've made that your life's work, Professor. But, as you know, one can't stop with merely condemning racism as unworthy of a nation founded on equality and equal respect. That's liberalism's program—declaring over and over that all men and women are equal, while proposing mostly ineffectual laws that reiterate that ideal."

"And it's that approach which Critical Race Theory tries to go beyond," I said. "But I'm curious how you think even the talented Sunstein has fallen short. And do you think we in Critical Race Theory have some retooling to do as well?"

"Let's begin this way. Sunstein and the other civic republicans say we should reexamine preferences, that political life should not consist merely in treating them as givens, then mechanically adding and subtracting them to determine what to do.[44] Yet, they accept dialog as it is, without subjecting it to the searching examination they afford preferences. But language and discourse—dialog of all sorts—prefigure the answers one reaches, at least unless one is very, very careful.[45] And to answer your question, yes, Professor, I have the sense that you and your fellow race-Crits are careful about language, at least sometimes. I'd cite Patricia Williams as an example. And a number of you have been questioning the dialogic premise, the notion that merely talking to one another will increase empathy, reduce racism and other systemic social ills, and lead to a better world."[46]

"I think I know what you mean by prefiguring. But could you explain how the republicans ignore it? This may be something I can use next month, if you don't mind my borrowing your ideas."

"Not at all. You've helped me in innumerable ways. By prefiguring I mean that the terms, metaphors, pictures, and language one uses often determine the result of a discussion or inquiry. Even when they don't, the cultural background against which words are used will. Statutory interpretation is a good example.[47] Or, to use an area in which we both are writing— race remedies—a perfectly neutral law such as: 'Treat whites and blacks the same in such and such area,' will inexorably cause whites to come out ahead."

"So, you mean that the terms and conventions of discourse reflect cultural power, meanings, and understandings established long ago and that now seem natural, fair, neutral: the way things are."

"Speech is paradigm-dependent. But racism is a part of the paradigm. It's hard to get people to see that. They think we mean physical power, or money. If that were the problem, the solution would be simply to make sure that minorities and other disempowered groups have access to microphones, the media, PACs, and so on."

"So the problem isn't just the speaker's efficacy. It also includes the listener, who just won't listen to minorities. Is that what you're saying?"

"That's part of it. We have little credibility because terrible images have been disseminated about us for hundreds of years, about our lack of intelligence, immorality, ugliness, unscrupulousness, and so on.[48] So, when we talk or write about race, we are often written off as partial, as self-interested. Whereas when a white person says something about race or affirmative action, everyone snaps to attention. Women complain of similar disregard for their views."[49]

"But you said that's only part of it."

"The conventions of discourse are another problem—all the unstated expectations about how the speaker is supposed to stand, how he should express himself, what intonation patterns he should use. All these conventions favor white folks, who are trained in such mannerisms until they come naturally. But the main difficulty is the one I mentioned before, about the meanings of terms and the way they favor preexisting power and prestige. Their meanings always render us one-down, yet seem neutral and fair to everyone."

Suddenly I sat upright. "I see what you're saying. Sunstein and the other civil republicans tell us we should not accept preferences as exogenous, as givens. Rather we should critique them—group critique, to be sure. But they do not ask the same questions about dialog, about critique itself. He ignores the inscribed, homeostatic, maintaining quality of much dialog. And so, we remain in our bubbles instead of breaking free of them."

From his expression, I could see that Rodrigo once again enjoyed my use of his metaphor. But he soon made clear that he had other matters than flattery on his mind. "There seems to be a case, Professor, for disavowing dialog. Predictable normative discussion only deepens outgroups' predicament. The strong will win; the weak will lose, and not for any lack of effective advocacy, articulateness, or brilliance. And, because civic virtue, an honorific term, will attach to the resulting consensus, we will be much worse off. Racial disadvantage will harden; stereotypes strengthen. They will become harder to dispel because they will be more consensual, seem more like the truth. Uncritical discussion will increase the disadvantage of the most disadvantaged."

"A Rawlesian would disapprove," I said.

"I hope so," he continued. "But the odd thing is that it will also deepen the predicament of the powerful, at least in times like ours, even though they think they are winning all the arguments—for example, about affirmative action."

"I think I know what you are going to say," I interjected. "The familiar arguments, laden as they are with terms and meanings that favor the powerful, resulting time after time in the same predictable conclusions, seemingly reinforcing their position, nevertheless injure them deeply as well. For by maintaining the status quo, they prevent us from seeing when our situation needs changing. They prevent us from seeing that we are encapsulated in small, self-limiting bubbles. We run round and round, like hamsters, within our cages: law school, social theory, political discourse. Normativity enables us to believe our bubble is the best, most principled, most just, without any serious defects. And all the while we are slipping further and further downward. I bet that's why you liked *Anarchy and Elegance.*"

Rodrigo looked up, smiling. "The author, Goodrich, was an outsider. He never allowed himself to be fully socialized, never gave in to the prevailing law school ethos and pedagogy. He saw those things as a nonlawyer, and it's that perspective that enabled him to be such a powerful critic."

"And do you think that's true in general—that social reform relies on the perspective of the outsider, the heretic who lives outside the culture and thus sees and is in a position to articulate its defects?"

"Yes. And that's why I think Socrates was in fact a greater historical figure than Aristotle, because he challenged orthodoxy and was, in that sense, more 'Critical.' Our time needs his type more than it needs neo-Aristotelians, classifiers, consolidators, who take us round and round well-trod tracks, addressing yesterday's problems, reminding us of what we should have done a hundred years ago. Systemic social evils require radical reform, yet those inside the various bubbles cannot see the trouble they're in. Formalistic, vaguely inspiring discourse makes it that much harder—even though in less troubled times conventional *civitas* can actually do some good."

"I take it you are talking about orthodox prescriptions, like 'A lawyer should avoid conflict of interest and not be an advocate in his or her own cause?'"

"Right. Or that 'Society should strive to maximize both social welfare and an economic system based on profits and individual initiative.' Those were useful prescripts earlier, but are less so today."

"And outsiders can help us attain the vision we need, acquire the reflexivity that can save us and our bubbles from their usual fates?"

"That's the direction to look toward, at any rate," Rodrigo replied firmly. "Multiple consciousness can see warpings, skewings in our own system before we, inside that system, have a glimmering of what's wrong.[50] Excellence in microadjustments, in moderation around a central mean, will hardly help a system in real distress."

"It's like moving chairs around the deck of the sinking *Titanic*," I said. "But to play devil's advocate, how do I know your approach will help? Maybe the *Titanic* will sink no matter what."

"It already has helped to some extent. Outsiders' demands have spurred the system to refine and strengthen First Amendment law,[51] regularize due process in school disciplinary cases,[52] and make the workplace fairer for everyone, not just minorities.[53] Our pleas for attention to black poverty have caused renewed attention to the plight of poor whites."[54]

"I agree with that. But the civic republicans will say, 'We are ready to talk with you, ready to listen to your perspectives, absorb and reflect on your insights.'"

"I'm afraid that conventional dialog, at least without fundamental reevaluation of its terms and rules, will just reinforce the status quo. It's like trying to see the back of your head. If you take a look at the footnotes and citation patterns of the civic republicans, you will see that they are little better than other writers at incorporating the ideas of outsider scholars. So, I'm afraid that increasing dialog will not deter conventional thinkers from embracing measures like immigration controls and English-only initiatives, while the more liberal ones embrace limited forms of affirmative action, which do little good, as you and your friends have argued."[55]

"Aristotle was quite candid, if I recall. He thought dialog should take place only with one's equals—with the white-male aristocracy of Athens. Today's versions are much more egalitarian, but I gather you think they need to go much further."

"Dialog won't work for systemic social ills. Society doesn't see—can't see—faults in the paradigm, the very structures by which we communicate, make ourselves understood, explain, understand, and construct reality. We won't listen to blacks, because we have assigned them low status, low credibility in the stigma-pictures we've made of them and still disseminate. The master narrative includes conquest, disparagement, and subordination of the darker races, not loving inclusion, much less respectful attention to their ideas and world views.[56] Aristotle wrote that one should help one's friends,[57] a rule that would disadvantage blacks. But the contrary rule—treat everyone alike—will also disadvantage outsiders. Deliberation and moderation, indeed all the conventional virtues, are inadequate to deal with racism and other broad-scale social ills."

"So, Rodrigo, what do you advise? I know you realize it's a normative question, but one must do something."

"We need to confront the unfamiliar unmediated, take time to question our own presuppositions. We need to stand back and examine our own bubbles. For this, we need to seek out someone unlike us, someone who sees things with new eyes. If we do not do this, we will pay a price, namely the inability to see system-wide defects that cause our bubble, ever so imperceptibly, to drift downward."

"So, Rodrigo, your advice is . . ."

"For individuals, read books by unfamiliar writers. For civic republicans, stop talking with each other, seek out outsiders, the more strange and heretical the better, and get clear on the exogenous presuppositions that structure your own elegant dialogs and inquiries. For society, see what other societies have done by way of treating recurring problems more effectively than we have. For law professors, talk to your students—ask how they would like to be instructed, what they see wrong with the current system. Bring in outsiders, like the journalist-author of *Anarchy and Elegance,* and encourage your students to write about their impressions—and then listen and take them seriously."

"And if you are a law school faculty concerned with curricular change and the students' grumbling over pedagogy and the tenor of the law school classroom?"

"I know, Professor, I've got that report due," Rodrigo said with a slight grimace. "And you've got your encounter with the famous civil libertarian. I hope you've found this conversation as useful as I have."

"That and more," I replied.

Rodrigo picked up his papers. Almost as an afterthought, I asked him: "But won't we just be co-opted, you and I, I mean? We'll take our 'outsider perspective,' as you call it, in your case to the law faculty committee, in mine to the audience at my conference. Won't we just join the bubble, merge whatever meager insight we can offer into the general cultural mix, reinscribing ourselves in the current dysfunctional, hierarchical, and often racist culture of which we both complain? Won't we just become part of that bubble?"

Rodrigo paused at my door a moment, then looked up with a smile. "At least it'll be a larger bubble," he said as he disappeared from my view.

Conclusion

As his footsteps echoed down the hall, I reflected on what we had said. I wondered whether he and Ali would meet with success in revamping their school's curriculum. I wondered how my own audience next month would respond to the idea of normativity and *civitas* as denial. I wondered how

Rodrigo would fare when he entered the job market. I remembered that bubbles had surface tension—would he be able to get inside one? Through my window, I watched as Rodrigo greeted a slim, dark young woman on the sidewalk—Giannina, I assumed. As they strode away, hand in hand, I wondered if my own bubble was drifting downward. I wondered whether, once the Owl of Minerva has flown, it ever returns, and whether the new place can indeed be larger and more humane than the old one, as Rodrigo had so cheerfully intimated. I wondered when I would get to meet the elusive Giannina.

I picked up the heavy pile of bluebooks and started home.

6

RODRIGO'S SIXTH CHRONICLE:
Intersections, Essences, and the Dilemma of Social Reform

Introduction: In Which Rodrigo Tells Me about an Urgent Problem

I was returning to my office from the faculty library one flight below, when I spied a familiar figure hovering outside my door.

"Rodrigo!" I said. "It's good to see you. Please come in. You look a little agitated. Is everything OK?" Rodrigo had been pacing my office while I was putting my books down and activating my voice mail. I hoped it was intellectual excitement and his usual high-pitched energy that caused his restless demeanor.

"Professor, I'm afraid I'm in some trouble. Do you have a few minutes? There's something I need to talk over with someone older and wiser."

"I'm definitely older," I said. "The other part I'm not sure about. What's happening?"

"There's a big feud going on in the Law Women's Caucus at my school. The women of color and the white members are going at it hammer and tongs. And like a dummy, I got caught right in the middle."

"You? How?" I asked.

"I'm not a member. I don't think any man is. But Giannina is an honorary member, as I might have mentioned before. The Caucus has tried to keep its struggle quiet, but I learned about it from Giannina. And I'm afraid I really—how do you put it?—put my foot in the mouth."

"In *your* mouth," I corrected. Although Rodrigo had been born in the States and spent his early childhood here, he occasionally failed to use an idiom correctly, a difficulty I had observed with other foreigners. "Tell me more," I continued. "How did it happen? Is it serious?"

"It's extremely serious," said Rodrigo, leaping to his feet and resuming his pacing. "They were having a meeting down in the basement, where I went after class to pick up Giannina. We were going to ride home together, and I thought her meeting would be over by then. I stood by the door a minute, when a woman I knew motioned me in. That was my mistake."

"Are the meetings closed to men?"

"I don't think so. But I was the only man there at the time. They were talking about essentialism[1]—as I've learned to call it—and the organization's agenda. A woman of color was complaining that the group never paid enough attention to the concerns of women like her. Some of the white women were getting upset. I made the mistake of raising my hand."

"What did you say?"

"I only tried to help analyze some of the issues. I drew a couple of distinctions—or tried to, anyway. Both sides got mad at me. One called me an imperial scholar, an interloper, a typical male, and a pest.[2] I got out of there fast. And now, no one will talk to me. Even Giannina made me move out of the bedroom. I've been sleeping on the couch for the last three nights. I feel like a leper."

A lover's quarrel! I had not had to deal with one of those since my sons were young. "I'm sure you and she will patch it up," I offered. "You'd better—the two of you owe me dinner, remember?"

Rodrigo was not cheered by my joke nor my effort to console him. "I may never have Giannina's companionship again," he said, looking down.

"These things generally get better with time," I said, making a mental note to address the point later. "It's part of life. But if talking about some of the issues would help, I'm game. I've just been reading these things"—I gestured toward some of the books and law review articles I had just carried up from the library—"on essentialism and feminist legal theory. They're for an annotated bibliography I'm preparing."

Rodrigo peered over at the pile on the corner of my desk. "I read that one last night. And I'm reading the two articles now. If you have the time, I'd love to talk. Since no one else will talk to me, I've got lots of time on my hands."

"Me too," I said. "Would you like a cup of coffee before we start?"

"I'd love one. I've been too distraught to eat."

I busied myself grinding the beans and setting the dials on my office espresso maker. "So, tell me what you know about essentialism. Cream and sugar?"

Rodrigo nodded. After I left the machine to its own devices and returned to my chair, he began.

In Which Rodrigo and I Review the Essentialism Debate and Try to Understand What Happened at the Law Women's Caucus

"The debate about essentialism has both a political and theoretical component," Rodrigo began. "That book," Rodrigo nodded in the direction of *Yearning: Race, Gender and Cultural Politics,* by bell hooks, lying open on my desk, "and those articles pay more attention to the political dimension. But there's also a linguistic-theory component."

"You mean the early philosophical discussion about whether words have essences?" I asked, pausing a moment to offer Rodrigo a cup of steaming espresso. I pointed out the tray of ingredients and said, "Help yourself if it needs more cream and sugar."

"Exactly," Rodrigo replied, slurping his coffee. "The early antiessentialists attacked the belief that words have core, or central, meanings. If I'm not mistaken, Wittgenstein was the first in our time to point this out.[3] In a way, it's a particularly powerful and persuasive version of the antinominalist argument."[4]

As always, Rodrigo surprised me with his erudition. I wondered how a young Italian-trained scholar had managed to learn about Wittgenstein, whose popularity I thought lay mainly in the English-speaking world. "How did you learn about Wittgenstein?" I asked.

"He's popular in Italy," Rodrigo explained. "I belonged to a study group that read him. The part of his teaching that laid the basis for antiessentialism was his attack on the idea of core meanings. As you know, he wrote that the meaning of a term is its use."

"I haven't read him in a while," I added hastily. "But you mentioned that the controversy's political side seems to be moving into the fore right now, which seems true. And I gather it's this aspect of the debate that you wandered into at school."

"In its political guise," Rodrigo continued, "members of different out-groups argue about the appropriate unit of analysis—about whether the black community is one or many, whether gays and lesbians have anything in common with straight activists, and so on. At the Law Women's Caucus, they were debating one aspect of this—namely, whether there is one, essential sisterhood, as opposed to many. The women of color were arguing that to think of the women's movement as singular and unitary disempowers them. They said this view disenfranchises anyone—say lesbian mothers, disabled women, or working-class women—whose experience and status differ from the norm."[5]

"And the others, of course, were saying the opposite?"

"Not exactly," Rodrigo replied. "They were saying that vis-à-vis men, all women stood on a similar footing. All are oppressed by a common enemy, namely patriarchy, and ought to stand together to confront this evil."[6]

"I've read something similar in the literature," I said.

"We may have seen some of the same things. The debate in the Caucus recapitulates an exchange between Angela Harris,[7] a talented black writer, and Martha Fineman, a leading white feminist scholar."

"Those pieces are on my list of things to read. In fact—" I paused, ruffling through the papers on my littered desk, "they're right here. I skimmed this one and set this other one aside for more careful reading later. I have to annotate both for my editors."

"Then you have at least a general idea of how the political version goes," Rodrigo said. "It has to do with agendas and the sorts of compromises people have to make in any organization to keep the group working together. In the Caucus's version, the sisters were complaining that the organization did not pay enough attention to the needs of women of color. They were urging that the group write an amicus brief on behalf of Haitian women and take a stand for the largely all-black custodial workers at the university. While not unsympathetic, the Caucus leadership thought these projects should not have the highest priority."

"I see what you mean by recapitulation of the academic debate. Fineman and Harris argue over some of the same things. Harris writes about the troubled relationship between black women and other women in the broader feminist mainstream, although she notes that many of the issues this relationship raises reappear in exchanges between straight and gay women, working- and professional-class minorities, black women and black men, and so on.[8] She and others write of the way in which these relationships often end up increasing disempowerment for the less influential group. They point out that white feminist theorists, while powerful and brilliant in many ways, nevertheless base many of their insights on gender essentialism—the idea that women have a single, unitary nature. They point out that certain feminist scholars write as though women's experiences can be captured in general terms, without taking into account differences of race or class. This approach obscures the identities and submerges the perspectives of women who differ from the norm. Not only does legal theory built on essentialist foundations marginalize and render certain groups invisible, it falls prey to the trap of overabstraction, something the same writers deplore in other settings. It also promotes hierarchy and silencing, evils that feminists should, and do, seek to subvert."[9]

"She spoke at my school recently," Rodrigo said. "I heard her say as much."

"And something similar goes on within the black community," I continued. "This community is diverse, many communities in one. Black neoconservatives, for example, complain that folks like you and me leave little room for diversity by disparaging them as sellouts and belittling their views as unrepresentative. They accuse us of writing as though the community of color only has one voice—ours—and of arrogating to ourselves the power to make generalizations and declare ourselves the possessors of sociopolitical truth."[10]

"I know that critique," Rodrigo replied. "We talked about it once before. It seems to me that they might well have a point, although it does sound a little strange to hear the complaint of being overwhelmed, smothered, spoken for by others, coming from the mouth of someone at Yale or Harvard."

"Like you at the Law Caucus, I found myself on the end of some stinging criticism.[11] I have Randall Kennedy and Steve Carter, particularly, in mind. They write powerfully, and of course many in the mainstream loved their message—so much so that they neglected to read the replies.[12] But let's get back to the feminist version, and what happened to you at the Law Women's meeting."

"Oh, yes. The discussion in many ways mirrored the debate in the legal literature and in that book." Rodrigo again pointed in the direction of the bell hooks book. "As you know, Harris's principal opponent in the antiessentialism debate has been Martha Fineman, who takes black feminists to task for what she considers their overpreoccupation with difference. Their focus on their own unique experience contributes to a 'disunity' within the broader feminist movement that she finds troubling. It weakens the group's voice, the sum total of power it wields. Emphasizing minor differences between young and old, gay and straight, and black and white women is divisive, verging on self-indulgence. It contributes to the false idea that the individual is the unit of social change, not the group. It results in tokenism and plays into the hands of male power." [13]

"And the discussion in the room was proceeding along these lines?" I asked.

"Yes," Rodrigo replied. "Although I had the sense that things had been brewing for some time. As soon as some of the leaders expressed coolness toward the black women's proposal for a day-care center, the level of acrimony increased sharply. A number of women of color said, 'This is just like what you said last time.' Some of the white women accused them of narrow parochialism. And so it went."

"The white feminists accusing the sisters of disloyalty, the sisters telling the others that they seem uncaring, and dangerously empowered?"

Rodrigo nodded assent, so I continued, "And what got *you* into trouble?"

"Well, I started to draw an analogy between the controversy they were having and the one raging about Great Books and the canon. [14] I had hardly gotten the words out of my mouth when both sides were up in arms. They accused me of butting in, of being condescending and of trying to preach to them. I got out of there in a hurry. But ever since, I've felt a distinct chill. Before, we all had good relationships. Now, even Giannina won't speak to me."

Rodrigo's distracted look impressed on me the seriousness of his predicament, at least in his eyes. So, I resisted the temptation to joke, and instead went on as follows:

"Rodrigo, you might not know this because you've been out of the country for—what?—the last ten years?" Rodrigo nodded. "These issues are really heated right now. And they're not confined to feminist organizations. Many of the same arguments are being waged within communities of color. Latinos and blacks are feuding. [15] And, of course, everyone knows about Korean merchants and inner-city blacks. Black women are telling us men about our insufferable behavior. We're always finishing sentences for them, expecting them to make coffee at meetings. Some of them with long memories recall how we made them march in the second row during the civil rights movement. We make the same arguments right back at them: 'Don't criticize, you'll weaken the civil rights movement, the greater evil is racism, we need unity, there must be common cause,' and so on. They're starting to get tired of that form of essentializing, and to point out our own chauvinism, our own patriarchal mannerisms and faults."

"Those are some of the things I got called at the meeting. It looks like I have company."

"We all need to think these things through. You and I could talk about it some more, if you think it would help. Can I offer you another cup of coffee?"

"I'd love some. And, yes, Professor, I'd appreciate it a great deal if you could help me sort things out."

"I'm sure I'll benefit just as much as you. Remember that I have all those annotations to write. You always help me get my thoughts in order."

In Which Rodrigo and the Professor Discuss the Perils of Making Common Cause

I started my espresso maker on a fresh pot. As it settled into its humming cycle, I looked up at Rodrigo. He began:

"What got me in trouble, as I mentioned, Professor, was the suggestion that the whole controversy mirrored the one about Great Books and the scholarly canon."

"How did that get you in trouble? I mean, I'm not sure I even see the connection."

"The white feminists were the maddest. I already told you some of the things they said. But even some of the sisters hissed. I got the sense that I should leave, and did. But before my hasty exit, I explained that essentializing struck me as the usual response of a beleaguered group, one that needs solidarity in a struggle against a more powerful one. It has a close relation to perseveration—something you and I talked about before—in which a culture in decline insists on doing over and over again, with more and more energy, the very things that once brought it greatness but that now are bringing it doom.[16] So you see how the Great Books analogy got me in hot water with the Law Caucus."

"I think I am beginning to understand," I said. "You are saying that essentialist thinking of any sort, white or black, male or female, is an effort to tame variety, to impose an artificial sameness on a situation that has bewildering diversity built into it."

"I think it's an insistence on a single narrative. You've been writing about narratives in the law, Professor.[17] I think this is something similar—an effort to impose a single 'story line' in order to make life simpler than it really is."

"I see," I said. "There *is* a sort of progression. In linguistic theory, Wittgenstein and others showed that words don't have central, unitary meanings. Later, the focus shifted to culture, where outsider groups began to insist that their books, texts, experiences, language, and special-interest courses were as valid as those in the mainstream's canon. There is no one valid set of stories, in other words. Those battles have largely been won, as well. Now the controversy has moved into the arena of politics and power. Groups are attempting to coerce or persuade subgroups not to splinter off. And a main weapon in this battle is the narrative of a common enemy."

"After leaving the meeting, I thought of a good name for it," Rodrigo added: "Relational essentialism. It's the idea that black women, for example, must join white women, not because both groups have the very same experience, perspective, needs, and agendas. They don't. Rather, it's because they stand on the same footing with respect to patriarchy. In this respect, they are essentially the same, that is, oppressed and in need of relief."

"Black men like you and me are guilty of the same thing when we tell the sisters to be quiet, to stop complaining of mistreatment at our hands or at those of certain famous black men, lest they weaken the community in general."

"I don't exempt us," Rodrigo said quietly. "We're all guilty of the same thing on occasion. It's a universal trait. We want to simplify the world by getting deviant, feisty, noncompliant others to come along. We want them to see the world and our struggle in exactly the same way we do. In essentialism's political guise, we need others—sometimes urgently—to join in our fight against a force that is oppressive. What essentialism's various guises[18] share is the search for narrative coherence. My audience at the meeting hated this idea."

"It's easy to see why," I said after a short pause. "Everyone likes to essentialize others—or themselves—on occasion. Is it possible that when you shared with me your concerns about being banished to the living room a little earlier, you and I were engaging in at least a mild variety of the same kind of essentialism? I'm sure you know the critique of 'male bonding' as based to a large degree on the sexual objectification of women. Some would say that your concern over the intimate consequences of your quarrel with Giannina reduces her to her sexual capacity as a woman."

"I know," Rodrigo replied. "I try not to do it. It just slipped out, like my remark at the Caucus meeting."

"We must all struggle against it—the desire to simplify others, I mean. It makes the essentialized person or group angry, of course. Plus, we miss a chance to learn something. You're right to suggest that it's a universal tendency," I said. "But nevertheless it's a power move."

"Which in turn is a response to a sense of one's own predicament, one's own disempowerment," Rodrigo said.

"Vis-à-vis someone else, I think you said. And I agree, it's often relational. A essentializes B, who essentializes C out of fear over D, and so on down the line."

Rodrigo nodded in agreement, so I continued: "It's easiest to see in personal life. The trick is to connect it to political and legal theory."

"I ran across a brilliant example the other day of why essentialism has real, sometimes debilitating consequences for individuals. Would you like to hear it, Professor?"

"I'd love to," I said. "Can I offer you a bagel to go with that second cup of coffee?" I motioned toward my compact office refrigerator, which I had just restocked. When Rodrigo nodded enthusiastically, I unwrapped my bag of bagels and spread them out on my desk. "Which kind would you like?"

"What are those?"

"Those are onion. Those others are sesame seed."

"I'll take one of those," Rodrigo said, pointing. "Giannina's not having anything to do with me, anyway. Where were we?"

"You were explaining your theory that essentialist thinking is not harmless."

"Oh, yes. The other author, Kimberlè Crenshaw, is the one who offers the example. Let me know if you've heard it. She points out that black women often experience discrimination at work on account of their black womanhood.[19] Often the employer is not particularly racist—that is, treats black men fairly decently—nor sexist, i.e., treats white women fairly. But the employer thinks black women are lazy, stupid, and sexually licentious. So the employer treats them poorly with regard to promotions and job assignments."

"Such a woman could clearly sue for employment discrimination," I said, "and recover damages."

"But how? I mean, under what theory? Crenshaw points out that a black woman plaintiff, until very recently, had only two options. She could sue for racial discrimination, in which case she would be able to use statutes and case law developed with blacks generally in mind. Or, she could sue for sex-based discrimination, invoking laws framed with women in mind. There was no legal category for black women who experienced discrimination on account of their black womanhood. So, they could either place themselves in a class of women dominated, numerically and in other ways, by white women, and use remedies framed with them in mind. Or, they could sue for racial discrimination, in which case they ended up lumped in a category containing black men. In either case, they wound up in a group—white women or black men—with more power, prestige, influence, and standing than they."[20]

"I believe the author and others have a name for this."

"Intersectionality," Rodrigo replied quickly. "It's related to essentialism. As we have seen, the law of remedies assumes that there is one essential black and one essential woman. The black is male, the woman white. The black woman has to choose, and neither choice is comfortable. Neither category is hers. Neither group has her agenda and needs in mind. And the law follows suit."

"But isn't it a wash?" I asked, offering Rodrigo some nicely aged brie I had overlooked in my refrigerator. "I got this on sale, but it's pretty good. Try some."

Rodrigo slathered his bagel with the cheese, and then continued: "I gather you mean that the person situated at the intersection of two categories, like the black woman, gets to have two sets of allies."

"Exactly," I replied. "In some settings, and in some eras, racism will be the major problem for her. When this is the case, she can call on black men as allies. In other situations, sexism will be the major concern. Then, she can call on the white women, who face the same problem. Black women may end up getting protection that has a poor 'fit' to their circumstances. But at least they can call on double the number of friends."

"So I thought, too. But then a cool remark that Giannina made as we rode home that night got me thinking that maybe it isn't so."

"What do you mean?"

"At first, I thought as you did. In fact, the algebra of it is kind of neat. Anyone who lies at the intersection of two categories gets halfhearted protection from each of the two groups. And so, you might think they are at least as well off as the others. This would, of course, blunt the criticism that persons marginal to a particular group are injured when the group essentializes its own experience, excluding these others from its agendas and planning. It would blunt it because the reply would be, simply, that the intersectional person can call on double the number of allies, can find two (or more) groups, not just one whose narrative will overlap, at least in part, with their own."

"But now you are thinking this is not so? I think I agree with you, but I can't quite put my finger on why," I said. Secretly, I was hoping Rodrigo would let his famous imagination loose. I had to write several annotations on these issues over the next few days, and was hoping our discussion would enable me to produce a better product.

"I hope you'll bear with me, Professor. This part of my theory is still pretty—how do they call it?—provisional. Please don't be too hard on me."

"Of course I won't. Intersectionality and antiessentialism are emerging as important issues in the law. If you can do anything to advance the debate, we'll all benefit. And besides, I've got a very concrete reason for wanting to hear what you have to say. So, please, go ahead."

"There are three reasons why I think that an outsider cannot play along, as it were, with the relatively more empowered group that wants to essentialize it. They're all related. And they all converge on a single moral that Giannina said she has come to live by: namely, that if you are a relatively disempowered person, say a black man or woman or a lesbian single mother, it is always a big mistake to take the perspective of the larger, more empowered group, even for strategic reasons."

"I'd like to hear how you are going to document that, and I assume it has something to do with your three reasons."

"Right," the irrepressible Rodrigo responded with alacrity.

Rodrigo's First Reason for Being Careful about Coalitions—On Marching in the Right Direction

"The first reason, Professor, is strategic. This is the one that Giannina was referring to that night. It's that it's better to march in the right direction rather than the wrong one. Suppose you're a black woman and you decide to go along with the feminist agenda, even if all the leaders are white, and all the goals seem more calculated to serve their interest than yours. You reason, what the heck, at least some of the things they hold important I hold important, too—for example, protecting the right to an abortion. Moreover, the group has access to power, money, and channels of communication. So, even though the group is lukewarm about programs that you feel are important, like Head Start, you at least get to march with them on an important issue."

"It's always nice to have company," I said.

"Unfortunately, it turns out that it's generally better to march along more slowly in your own direction. It assures that at least you get closer to your destination.[21] If you march with the larger group in a direction that is a little off from where you want to go—say, ten degrees skewed—you will have high morale. There will be great solidarity. There will be protest songs. Hands will be linked and you will have an impressive-looking phalanx. Your picture will be in the papers."

"But in time you'll notice that you are diverging, getting further and further away from your goal, right?"

"Yes. But the price of strategic essentialism is not only that you get away from your agenda and your heart-of-hearts goals. You'll develop what Antonio Gramsci calls false consciousness.[22] You'll forget who you are and what your original goals and commitments were. Goals and personal identities and loyalties are socially constructed. If we work and struggle with people—no matter how well-intentioned—whose perspectives, culture, and agenda are different from ours, we will eventually change. Goals are not atomistic. I can't say, I'll go along with the Republicans because I agree with their ideas on tax reform, but I'll be a Democrat with respect to this other policy, and so on. Spending time with Republicans means you will inevitably take on the mindset of a Republican. A black man active in a white-dominated civil rights organization will eventually take on the traits and concerns he finds there. A black woman working in a male-dominated group will risk losing her identity as a black feminist. Some social scientists call this 'alienation.'"[23]

"I'm not sure I quite understand all this high-Crit talk, Rodrigo. I do think that your metaphor of marching determinedly off in the wrong direction, with lots of company and all the bands playing, is a vivid and useful one. But you mentioned there were other reasons for caution."

Rodrigo's Second Reason—On the Need to
Avoid Triumphalism

"The second reason has to do with something you and other writers in the Critical Race Theory school have expressed—namely, skepticism of gains that seem to have been won through appeals to social altruism."

"I assume you mean our writing on the phenomenon of interest convergence and its pitfalls." [24]

"Precisely. You and others have written of the way in which civil rights gains for blacks and others always seem to coincide with white self-interest. In eras in which white self-interest and black justice are opposed, nothing happens. When, as happened around the time of *Brown v. Board of Education*,[25] elite white groups need to allow a 'breakthrough' for minorities, one miraculously appears. Altruism, a sense of compassion, and racial justice count for little, if anything." [26]

"I know and agree with that hypothesis," I said. "But how does it connect with your thoughts about essentialism, and your claim that the weaker party has little to gain by affiliating with the stronger, even where both are struggling against a common oppressor?"

"Oh, I should have explained myself better," Rodrigo said. "I didn't mean to be elliptical. What I meant is that temporary alliances always have a way of falling back, just as civil rights gains stemming from momentary interest-convergences between blacks and whites always erode."

"When the interest-convergence ceases, you mean?"

"Yes. Take *Brown v. Board of Education*. As everyone knows, the ringing words of the Court's opinion were quickly robbed of much effect by administrative foot-dragging, obstruction, and delay. The case ended up changing very little. School districts are as segregated today as they were in the days of *Brown*.[27] And of course much the same has happened with women's issues. The right to abortion secured by *Roe v. Wade* was quickly cut back by narrow interpretation, refusal to provide funding, and the fervor of the religious right.[28] Despite a smaller rate of increase in the number of abortions since *Roe v. Wade*, women who obtain them often have to run a gauntlet of opposition and hassling. Gianinna described an experience a friend of hers had. It was harrowing."

"And so the conclusion you draw is . . . ?"

"Gains are ephemeral if one wins them by forming coalitions with individuals who really do not have your interest at heart. It's not just that the larger, more diverse group will forget you and your special needs. It's worse than that. You'll forget who you are. And if you don't, you may still end up demonized, blamed for sabotaging the revolution when it inevitably and ineluctably fails."

"Sounds dire," I said. "I hope you'll explain how this happens."

Rodrigo's Third Reason—On Normativity and the Inevitable Egocentrism of Rights-Talk

"As I mentioned, Professor, the three reasons converge. The third one has to do with the way normativity—prescriptive discourse—is deployed.[29] Imagine that a group, say women, is successful in winning a concession from society at large, namely recognition of the right to an abortion. Who will reap the gains of the new right, and who will leave disappointed? Rights are precious things; they realign how we think about each other. Getting a new right recognized is a lot of work. In accomplishing this, one has likely made a lot of enemies and called in a lot of favors. The victory has not been cost-free. Who now will pay those costs?[30] With abortion, we saw how quickly the right was narrowed. Courts ruled that states need not fund abortions, and that governments may prohibit them entirely in state-supported facilities. Poor women often cannot afford abortions and are, therefore, in effect, denied access. A few women in the majority group protested, but many went along since the restrictions did not affect them. But it's not merely that the right was cut back in predictable fashion, as *Brown v. Board of Education* was for blacks. Worse, as soon as the political climate changed, black women's sexuality came under fire. The new rights-and-responsibilities movement,[31] championed by some well-known feminists, now designates black women's sexuality as irresponsible, and the employment of abortion as a means of birth control as an abuse of a right."[32]

"Much the same happened in the wake of various civil rights 'breakthroughs,'" I pointed out.

"I think it's a general phenomenon," Rodrigo agreed. "Rights, once won, tend to be cut back. And even when part of them remains, the price of the newly won right is exacted from the most marginal of its beneficiaries.[33] For example, affirmative action benefited largely the middle-class, upward-striving black person, like me—ones who likely would have succeeded anyway. Desperately poor blacks benefited little. And the remedy, affirmative action, was so visible and controversial that it drew fire, assuring that all blacks paid the penalty of the benefits to the few—penalties in the form of stigma, hostility by the majority, and the overriding belief by whites that all blacks are so undeserving or so stupid that they require affirmative action to have a chance."

"So your third reason has to do with the way gains won through coalescing with a more powerful group backfire, causing one to end up disappointed and demonized?"

"Normative discourse is always self-centered," Rodrigo replied. "The critique of normativity shows that in a number of ways. For example, society may tolerate or even inaugurate new rights for women or minorities. But then it will invariably declare that your and my exercise of those rights is not what they had in mind at all. When a low-income black woman has an abortion, that will seem like lasciviousness and hypersexuality, an irresponsible exercise of the right.[34] When a right to nondiscriminatory treatment in employment is recognized, everyone celebrates. But when a black man with credentials short of Albert Einstein's gets a job, that will seem troublesome and unprincipled."[35]

"So, the conclusion you draw from all this is . . . ?"

"That one should never adopt the perspective of the more powerful group, even strategically. Adopting another's perspective is always a mistake. One starts out thinking one can go along with the more numerous, better organized, and more influential group—say, white women in the case of sisters of color—and reap some benefits. You think that you can jump nimbly aside before the inevitable setbacks, disappointments, and double crosses set in. But you can't. You will march strongly and determinedly in the wrong direction, alienating yourself in the process. You'll end up having the newly deployed rights cut back in your case, even being criticized as irresponsible when you try to exercise them. Moreover, any small suggestion for deviation in the agenda, any polite request that the larger group consider your own concerns, will bring quick denunciation. You are being divisive. You are weakening the movement."

"Rodrigo, you have me half convinced," I replied. "I've long thought that the interest-convergence hypothesis was right. You've just elegantly extended that hypothesis to the essentialism debate and embedded it in a linguistic and cultural context. But if you are ever going to restore your credibility in the eyes of the sisters of color at your law school—not to mention the rest—you can't stop at that. They will want to know where you go from there. If essentialism and making common cause with a too-large group, one that doesn't pay attention to your unique needs, is always a mistake, what do you do to replace it? You need more than a theory to explain what's wrong; you also need to explain what we ought to be doing. Otherwise, you run the risk of being seen as a troublemaker, one who goes around stirring up animosity among potential allies and friends."

Rodrigo winced a little. "I think that may have something to do with what happened to me. And I've given a little thought to what you say needs to be done. But this part of my theory I'm much less certain about than the critique part. Do you have the time to listen? You're a great critic, Professor. And I have a most immediate need to refine my thoughts. Giannina and I may be finished if I don't."

I smiled at Rodrigo's earnestness, remembering my own youth.

"Can I offer you some fruit?" I asked. "We've been going at it for quite a while. I find I need something every now and then to keep my energy up."

Rodrigo nodded gratefully. I took down a small tray of nuts and dried apricots I kept stowed in a cabinet next to my refrigerator and offered some to my friend. Rodrigo selected a handful, then continued as follows:

In Which Rodrigo Outlines a Theory of Antiessentialism and the Relation of Small Groups to Social Change

"Interest-convergence never lasts long, as I said, Professor. And it's a bad idea to try to stage-manage it by aligning yourself with the next-less-disempowered group, the one just up the scale from you, for all the reasons I mentioned."

"But if we drop out of larger groups, people will accuse us of being narrow nationalists, of being poor team players, of being obsessed with our own parochial interests. And won't they have a point—at least in their way of looking at it?" I asked.

"There are two challenges," Rodrigo replied. "The first is to remain oppositional, not to give in to the welcome embraces of the group that is not like you. This is fairly difficult. All the pressure is the other way. We are taught, even indoctrinated, to be cooperative team players.[36] One who pursues his or her own way is depicted as disloyal, disruptive, and derided as a 'single-issue' person. In our society, those are not nice words. But one can persevere. The second challenge is to understand why pursuing a nationalist, counter-essentialist course is a good idea, to explain how it brings benefits to everyone, not just to one's own kin-group."[37]

"This I'd love to hear," I said, peeling an orange I'd just retrieved from the back of the refrigerator. "Have some."

"These are delicious. Where did you get them?" asked Rodrigo.

"At a place just down the street from where I live," I replied. "It's a Korean-run grocery store. They have great produce, and I go there in part to make a point. Have as many as you like. I've got more."

"The big market where Giannina and I shop doesn't have nearly as good ones. We may switch. Where was I?"

"You were starting to explain why antiessentialism is good for all, even the larger group, and not a case of disloyalty or excessive self-preoccupation."

"Oh, yes. My theory has to do with double consciousness. You're familiar with the term of course, Professor."

"Of course. The black scholar, W. E. B. Du Bois, wrote of it.[38] It holds that persons of color see the world in two ways at the same time. The black person, for example, sees himself as normal and abnormal at the same time—as others see him, and also as he sees himself. It's a familiar feeling we all know."

"And in recent times, black and other feminists of color have expanded that notion to include the idea of multiple consciousness.[39] A black female lesbian, for example, sees the world from at least those three different perspectives. Her experience is not the same as that of the average black woman, nor that of a black gay male. It's a complex interaction among those three points of view, and perhaps others as well."

"And you were saying, Rodrigo, that this somehow confers an advantage? To the person bearing multiple consciousness, or to others?"

"To both. The possessor of multiple consciousness learns to see everything through two or more lenses at once. This actually gives you a better grasp of reality. It's kind of like looking through a pair of binoculars. Binocular vision is always better than the kind you get by looking at something through just one lens. So, it gives the possessor an advantage."

"I've heard it said that slaves observed their masters better than their masters observed them. Is your theory related to that idea?"

"In a way it is. The slave perceived the master more accurately than the latter perceived him; he had to to survive.[40] Reading the master's folkways and moods was an essential skill the slave developed to avoid harsh treatment. But he also observed the master more clearly because he had double consciousness—he saw the master both as a master and as a human being. The master, on the other hand, regarded the slave one-dimensionally as a slave or worker only, not as a human being. There were a few exceptions, of course."

"It's coming back to me. The first time we met, you argued that multiple consciousness enables the outsider to see defects in the prevailing order before one immersed in that system could. You said that, in scholarship, this conferred an advantage, particularly with respect to grasping and deploying postmodern theory. But, if I hear you correctly, you are urging that outsiders ought to hang onto their peculiar form of social insight, maintain it pristine and separate, in order to benefit the larger group as well. But isn't it just this larger group that they plan to leave if they followed your advice?"

"I know it sounds paradoxical, Professor. But bear with me for a minute. Merging with the larger group causes you to forfeit a kind of sightedness. So it's bad for you. But it's also bad for the larger group because dissenters who agree to remain in the larger movements eventually become coopted and alienated from their own position, with the result that the larger group loses an important source of criticism, a kind of early warning signal by which they could learn something. Systemic evils, like racism and sexism, are never visible within the culture, because those evils are woven into the paradigm— into the system of meanings by which we construct and understand reality. [41] Speech is paradigm-dependent. And, if racism—or any other evil—is embedded in that paradigm, one can't speak out against it without being heard as incoherent. That's why racism and sexism are harder to correct than scientific error."

"I'm not sure I see that. How about an example?"

Rodrigo was silent a long moment. Then, he looked up thoughtfully:

"Professor, does your school have an affirmative action program?"

"Of course. I think virtually every one does. Yours must, as well."

"It does. But I learned something interesting when I was working on a report for the curriculum committee. As you recall, we've been working with some of the faculty in revising the first-and second-year curriculum. This came up sort of tangentially, but now I think it's important. At one point, my friend Ali, who is also on the committee, and I asked the law school for figures about employment, salary, job offers, and a few other things, etc. We were exploring quite a different hypothesis."

"What they call serendipity," I interrupted.

"Exactly. And what we learned turned out, as you will see, to have a great bearing on the matter we are currently discussing: namely, the invisibility of the status quo. We learned that the minority students, most of whom were admitted to the school under an affirmative action program, tended to graduate at a rate almost identical to that of law students in general. Not only that, they tended to get jobs at roughly the same rate. Last year, in fact, they did better than the whites. They also earned a slightly higher average starting salary. More of them got judicial clerkships—I mean on a percentage basis, of course."

"That's fascinating. I remember hearing one or two figures like those at my school. What do you make of that?" I asked.

"Ali and I were intrigued, as you can imagine. So, we looked around further. It turned out that years after graduating, the same holds true. The minorities end up appointed to judgeships and commissions at a rate greater than their proportion in the alumni body. All the students, of course, are smart, and many of them go on to quite distinguished careers. But the minorities tend to do a little better. We checked at some other law schools and found the same thing: The minorities did a little better than the whites, or at least not worse. Not in every case, of course, and not on every single measure, but in general."

"And the conclusion you draw from this is . . . ?"

"I thought that there has to be some form of cultural preference encoded and deeply buried in the way we admit and grade students, something, perhaps in the way we use letters of recommendation, evaluate extracurricular activities, or perhaps the LSATs, that gives an edge to the whites and disadvantages the minorities. The output figures imply strongly that the minorities are just as able, or more so. But they get admitted in quite small numbers. My law school has only a handful of students of color."

"Mine, too."

"Yet the ones who do get in, excel."

"From which you conclude that some form of favoritism is going on?"

"Some encoded cultural preference for the slightly less qualified whites. I don't want to overstate this, Professor. As I mentioned, all the graduates do well. But judging from output statistics, the minorities are superior to or undifferentiable from the rest."

"Perhaps they have an unfair advantage," I quipped, "namely, a sense of mission." I immediately regretted my tongue-in-cheek remark when Rodrigo shot me a rueful look.

"I'm joking. You've pointed out a serious problem. I don't mean to make light of it. I've often reflected on how brilliantly many of my minority students acquit themselves in class and later. But I think you were mentioning this en route to a point about perception, right?"

"Exactly. I found when I ran some of these figures past people of the majority race that they did not draw the inference I did. Rather, they looked puzzled or disbelieving. They wanted to know where I got my statistics, and when I said the placement office, they were flabbergasted. Several said that the minority-success figures I had must themselves be the product of affirmative action in wider society."

"In other words," I said, "they begin with the premise that minorities are inferior, indeed must be—otherwise why would there be affirmative action? Then, when it turns out that the minorities, despite everything, nevertheless do well, it must be because judges, employers, appointments committees, and so on are giving them favored treatment. You draw one conclusion, they another."

"And that's the whole point of a canonical mindset. It means that if you have two possible inferences from a set of data, one in which minorities are the equal of whites, or even have a slight edge, and one in which they don't, you immediately think of the second."[42]

"I agree that preconception—what you call canonical thinking—functions that way. Paradigms always preserve themselves. But I'm unclear what connection all this has to your argument in favor of an antiessentialist cultural nationalism that would renounce coalition politics."

"Let's see if I can bring myself back on track." Rodrigo was silent for a moment, his fingers lightly touching his forehead. I was glad to see that my quick-witted young friend, who often seemed able to dance miles ahead of me, occasionally needed to regroup. At length he continued:

"The connection is this. The larger group always has a canon—a set of principles, articles of faith, ways of seeing the world. These may not include you—at least as fully as you might like. If you go along with them, there will inevitably arise occasions like the one I just mentioned between blacks and whites, except that you will be on the receiving end of poor or uncomprehending treatment from a group with whom you thought you had a lot in common."

"Since their narrative is designed for a different purpose—namely, theirs—your requests will seem like distractions, evidence of disloyalty or overpreoccupation with self. They may seem like reverse essentialism—a perverse insistence on the importance of such a petty and divisive thing as race."[43]

"And so you are generally—maybe always—better off with your own," Rodrigo concluded.

"Yet you said, I think, that accepting this would benefit not just the insurrectionist group but the larger one from which it secedes, as it were. I'm curious how you see that. How can it benefit white women in the feminist movement, for example, if the black women go their own way? Is it the binocular vision idea you mentioned before?"

"The main benefits inure to the secessionist group. But the larger group benefits, as well. They get careful outside criticism. They get a certain degree of protection from complacency by reason of the need to vie for the support of potential allies in outsider groups. They get constant reminders that their perspective is not the only one. I got one just the other day," Rodrigo concluded, a little ruefully.

"But Rodrigo, aren't you overlooking that the next-larger group, the one that suffers the defection, needs the smaller group? It needs it to consolidate cultural change, to install new conventions, to institute ordinary, concrete reforms, like new civil rights laws. What might look to you like loyalty to self looks to others like a case of weakening a revolution that desperately needs you—needs your numbers, needs your genius, needs the credibility you bring by virtue of your very diversity. Revolutionary groups of all sorts need solidarity. When a reform movement starts to fragment, isn't it in trouble? Rodrigo, I think for once you are guilty of excessive optimism. You ignore the costs of fragmentation. I don't see how antiessentialism can possibly benefit the group whose solidarity is weakened. I think one revolution dies to give birth to another. Isn't that the best you can say?"

Rodrigo smiled as he listened to my earnest objection.

"Professor, I was about to say that I had a response and that it had to do with the role of hunger. Then I noticed that it is past dinnertime."

"We could get a bite to eat at the little Persian deli next door," I offered. "They just opened up last month. I've been there twice. They're pretty good, although I think they close at seven."

"It's a few minutes of. What do you say we get some take-out? I'll treat this time."

"Please let me," I said. "Your life is disrupted enough right now, and I assume you have interviews coming up?"

"Starting next week."

"You'll have extra expenses. Let me pay. If you make up with Giannina, perhaps the two of you can have me over when you're back from the circuit."

"Okay, if you'll promise to come. Giannina has been wanting to meet you."

"It will be my pleasure."

Wherein Rodrigo Posits a Theory of Social Change and the Role of Oppositional Groups in Bringing It About

Ten minutes later, we were riding up the elevator to my office, balancing cups of hot tea and plates of dolmas and pita bread. "I'm glad to hear you plan to elaborate on your theory of social change, Rodrigo. In one of our earlier discussions, you kind of left that hanging.[44] As you know, I am a skeptic on that score. A number of friends and I have been developing a theory of what we call the 'empathic fallacy' to explain why reform is so halting and slow.[45] The last time we talked—or maybe it was the time before last—you said something to the effect that social reform through law was unlikely. But you left open the possibility that it might come another way."

We arrived at my door. As I struggled to get out the key without spilling my food, Rodrigo said, "My theory—it's only vague and sketchy at this point—consists of two parts. I think I know a further reason, I mean in addition to the ones you and your friends are developing, why we never get lasting reform through litigation, legislation, etc. That's the first part. The second part consists in showing how reform does come about, when it comes."

"Which is rare enough."

"Agreed," Rodrigo said. "Need some help with that key?"

"No, I've got it." Moments later we were seated comfortably back in my office.

"This is like having a picnic," Rodrigo said as he dived into his meal. "I'm glad we got there before they closed."

"You should go there sometime while they're open," I said. "The service is good, and they let you stay as long as you want. I sometimes go there with my students to continue a discussion we had in class."

"Are you ready for the first part of my theory?" Rodrigo asked impatiently.

I took a last bite of my dolmas, washed it down with a swig of tea, and said, "I'm all ears."

Rodrigo Lays Out a Natural History of Social Ideas

"I think that virtually all revolutionary ideas start with an outsider of some sort," Rodrigo began. "We mentioned the reasons before. Few who operate within the system see its defects. They speak, read, and hear within a discourse system that is self-satisfying. The primary function of our system of free speech is to effect stasis, not change. New ideas are ridiculed as absurd and extreme, and discounted as political, at first. It's not until much later, when consciousness changes, that we look back and wonder why we resisted so strongly."[46]

"Revolutionaries always lead rocky lives. You'll see that too, Rodrigo, although I don't know if you classify yourself as one or not. All the pressure is in the direction of conforming, of doing what others do, in teaching, in scholarship, in fact in all areas of life."

Rodrigo shrugged off my counsel. "So, new ideas and movements come along relatively rarely. And when they do, they are beleaguered. For a long time, they garner little support. Then, for some reason, they acquire something like a critical mass. Society begins to pay attention. Now, the situation is in flux. The group at this point needs all the allies they can muster. They begin to make inroads and need to make more. They see that they are beginning to approach the point where they might be able to change societal discourse in a direction they favor."

"Including the power to define who is 'divisive,'" I added.

"That, too—especially that," Rodrigo said animatedly, seeing how my observation fit into the theory he was developing. He looked up with gratitude, then continued:

"At this point, they need all the help they can get. If they are you, they need Gary Peller and Alan Freeman.[47] If they are feminists, they need Cass Sunstein.[48] Earlier, they needed the religious right in their campaign against pornography. And so on. With a little growth in numbers, they may perhaps reach the point at which power begins to translate into knowledge.[49] And knowledge, of course, is the beginning of social reform. When everyone knows you are right, knows you have a point, you are well on your way to victory."

"And for this, the group needs numbers."

"Right. With them, they can change the interpretive community.[50] They can remake the model of the essential woman, say, along lines that are genuinely more humane."

Rodrigo and I Discuss the Role of Reformers and Malcontent Groups

"So, Rodrigo," I continued, "you are saying that new knowledge of any important, radical sort begins with a small group. This group is dissatisfied, but believes it has a point. It agitates, acquires new members, begins to get society to take it seriously. And it's at this point that the essentialism-antiessentialism debate usually sets in?"

"Before it wouldn't arise. And later, when the large group is nearing its goals, it doesn't need the disaffected faction. So it's right at this midpoint in a social revolution—for example, the feminist movement—that we have debates like the one I got caught in the middle of."

"But you were saying before that the disaffected cell ought to sit out the revolution, as it were, and not just for its own good but for that of the wider society as well?"

"It should. And often such groups do, consciously or unconsciously. I'm just saying that when they do, it's usually not a bad thing."

"And this is because of your theory of knowledge, I gather, in which canonical thinking always gets to a point where it no longer works and needs a fundamental challenge?"

"And this, in turn, can only come from a disaffected group. Every new idea, if it has merit—has staying power—eventually turns into a canon. And every canonical idea at some point needs to be dislodged, challenged, and supplanted by a new one."

"So maverick, malcontent groups are the growing edge of social thought."

"Not every one. Some are regressive—want to roll back reform."

"I can think of several that fit that bill," I said shuddering. "But you said earlier that the outsider has a kind of binocular vision that enables him or her to see defects in the bubbles in which we all live—to see the curvature, the limitations, the downward drift that eventually spells trouble. But just now you used another metaphor. What was it?"

Rodrigo thought for a moment. "Oh, I remember. It was just before we went out for food. The metaphor was the role of hunger."

"I'd love for you to explain."

"It's like this." Rodrigo pushed aside his plate. "Change comes from a small, dissatisfied group for whom canonical knowledge and the standard social arrangements don't work. Such a group needs allies. Thus, white women in the feminist movement reach out to women of color; black men in the civil rights movement try to include black women, and so on. Eventually, the larger group makes inroads, changes the paradigm, begins to be accepted, gets laws passed, and so on."

"Can I take that plate?" I asked. Rodrigo passed it over and I put it in the nonrecyclable bin outside my office, along with the other remnants of our snack. "This is what you argued before, so I assume you're getting to your theory about hunger."

"Correct. But you see, as soon as all this happens, the once-radical group begins to lose its edge. It enters a phase of consolidation, in which it is more concerned with defending and instituting reforms made possible by the new consensus, the new paradigm of Foucault's Knowledge/Power,[51] than with pushing the envelope towards more radical change. The group is beginning to lose binocular vision, the special form of insight most outgroups have, about social inequities and imbalances."

"And so the reform movement founders?" I asked. "We've seen many examples of that. As you know, legal scholarship is now extremely interested in that question. Many in the left are trying to discover why all our best intentions fail, why the urge to transform society for the better always comes to naught."

"I'm not sure I'd say the movement founders," Rodrigo interjected. "Rather, it enters into a different phase. I don't want to be too critical."

"But at any rate, it peters out," I said. "It loses vigor."

"But then, eventually, another group rises up to take its place. Often this is a disaffected subset of the larger group, the one that won reforms, that finally got the Supreme Court or Congress to recognize the legitimacy of its claims. It turns out that the reforms did not do much for the subgroup. The revolution came and went, but things stayed pretty much the same for it. So, it renews its effort."

"And that's what you meant by hunger?"

"In a way. Those who are hungry are most desperate for change. Human intelligence and progress spring from adversity, from a sense that the world is not supplying what the organism needs and requires. A famous American philosopher developed a theory of education based on this idea."

"I assume you mean John Dewey?"[52]

"Him and others. He was a sometime member of the school of American pragmatists. But his approach differed in significant respects from that of the other pragmatists like William James and Charles Peirce. One was this. And so I'm thinking we can borrow from his theory to explain the natural history of revolutionary movements, applying what he saw to be true for individuals to larger groups."

"Where you think it holds as well?" I asked. "It's always dangerous extrapolating from the individual to the group."

"I think the observation does hold for groups, as well," Rodrigo replied. "But I'd be glad to be corrected if you think I am wrong. The basic idea is that groups that are victors become complacent. They lose their critical edge, because there is no need to have it. The social structure works for them. If by intelligence, one means critical intelligence, we become dumber all the time. It's a kind of reverse evolution. Eventually, society gets out of kilter enough that a dissident group rises up, its critical skills honed, its perception equal to that of the slave. It challenges the master by condemning the status quo as unjust, just as Giannina challenged me. Sometimes the injustices it points out are ones that genuinely need mending, and not just for the discontent group. Rather, they signal a broader social need to reform things that will benefit everybody." [53]

I leaned forward; the full force of what Rodrigo was saying had hit me. "So, Rodrigo, you are saying that the history of revolution is, by its nature, iterative. The unit of social intelligence is small; reform and retrenchment come in waves. This fits in with what you were saying earlier about the decline of the West and the need for infusion of outsider thought. And, it dovetails with other currents under way in environmental thought, [54] economic thought [55]—and, as you mentioned, in American political philosophy. Maybe you'll start a resurgence of attention to John Dewey, who I always thought was a neglected, but very brilliant, philosopher."

"Do you see any defects in my theory, anything I should consider?"

After a pause, I said, "Well, there's the World Trade Center issue." [56]

"I'm not sure what you mean."

"Isn't the intelligence of radically disenfranchised groups and subgroups just as likely to turn criminal and take destructive forms, like blowing up the World Trade Center, as it is to take the constructive critical turn you posit."

"This may happen occasionally," Rodrigo conceded.

"But it's no small objection, Rodrigo," I pressed. "Many believe that the need today is not for further fragmentation, further nationalism, further multiplication of small groups along lines of ethnicity, politics, or religion. Rather, the need is for the opposite—for peace, for cooperation, for everyone to acquire a large, ecumenical understanding of the world and our place in it. [57] We can't solve problems piecemeal. Everything is connected. What's needed is a holistic vision, not the parochial concern, say, of certain third-world nationalists. We need to see problems in national, if not global, perspective."

"But we won't get that unless the world is fair." Rodrigo was speaking slowly and emphatically now. He leaned forward in his seat. "You see, Professor, the ecumenical view requires that everyone see the regime as just. If not, they will unite with others disaffected like themselves, and struggle their hardest to bring their grievances to the next-larger group. The next-larger group inevitably will preach to them about the errors of division, partisanship, and disloyalty, and will tell them their cooperation is necessary to forward the larger group's agenda, whatever that is. But if the Palestinians thought their situation was fair, they would not be disturbing the peace in the Middle East. If black women thought they were being dealt with fairly in the women's movement—or at the hands of the black brothers, for that matter—they would not be agitating for increased attention to their needs."

"So justice comes before peace?"

"Logically, yes, and also in the natural history of ideas," Rodrigo replied. "Of course, if one is a member of a more-empowered group, as you and I are vis-à-vis black women, one's need will be for peace, for unity, for consolidation, for other virtues of a stable and just age. But the smaller group will think just the opposite—that the age is not just and has no business being stable."

I was silent for a moment. "Now, Rodrigo, isn't there a lesson in this for you and your quarrel with Giannina?"

"I think now I understand better the conflict between me and the women. Women themselves are outsiders from the mainstream. Maybe they're better able to see the patriarchy in the system than I am. The problem is that I didn't realize that my point about essentialism being a power struggle between groups is generalizable to men and women, even to me and Giannina. As far as what happened at the meeting, I realize that much of my thinking follows from Giannina's own analysis of what was taking place between the white women and the women of color."

Just then I heard the phone ringing in my secretary's office down the hall and realized we were about to be interrupted by call-forwarding if the caller persevered beyond four rings. While waiting for the call to flip over, I mused to Rodrigo:

"Rodrigo, I think I agree with you about your general analysis. Moreover, I want to write your epitaph. It will say . . ."

Just then my office phone started to ring, so I quickly finished my thought: "Justice first, then peace—a motto that others have employed in different versions to highlight the incompatibility between an oppressive regime that contains structures of unfairness, and social stability. Such a regime is inherently unstable because of the ever-present possibility of revolt."

Rodrigo smiled in appreciation. I picked up the phone. What I told him made him smile even more:

"It's Giannina," I said. "She wants to know if we would like to go to a movie."

Conclusion

Seconds later, Rodrigo was scrambling out of my office, cramming notes and papers in his book bag. As I watched his lanky frame disappearing rapidly down the hallway, I reflected on our conversation. I thought that his analysis of essentialism had considerable merit, especially as a descriptive theory accounting for the divergent views of commentators like my friend Martha Fineman, who writes about the need for solidarity, and those of writers of color like Angela Harris and Kim Crenshaw, who see the need for separate treatment of subgroups. His further step of connecting the antiessentialism debate to theories of Critical thought and social change gave me greater pause. The literature was replete with scholars trying to make sense of the failures of twentieth-century reform movements, including ones I hold dear. My colleagues and I had been exploring the role of normativity, of misplaced faith in the law, and of the "empathic fallacy," in hopes of making sense out of the train of setbacks. His idea that things are cyclical seemed appealing, and corresponded to my own sense of how things worked. And, of course, I was rather flattered at the prominent role it afforded mavericks and discontent scholars, like me, whom Rodrigo considered useful mutants! Yet I hoped for further support for his thesis. Would I receive anything comparable to Rodrigo's printout, which he had so quickly and generously provided me following our first conversation?

As I walked down the darkened corridor on my way home to change clothes before the movie, I looked through the glass window on the door to the faculty mailboxes. I was startled to see a small gray envelope there in my box. I had checked my mail only shortly before. I fished out my key and walked in. Alas, no printout of articles and books. Instead, I saw, written in a small, neat hand, the following poem:

Docket Entry in the Birmingham City Jail

in a hallway of the library
behind a glassed-in wall
the warden's docket lies
open to the page
where twenty-seven years ago
minus two weeks exactly
at 5:50 in the afternoon
on the twelfth day of April 1963
The Reverend Martin Luther King
thirty-four years old
was booked as number 607
for violating section 1159
of the City Code of Birmingham
creating a disorderly disturbance
by walking down the middle of the street.

the Reverend Ralph Abernathy
and five other black persons
some male, some female
preceded him into the Avenue "F" jail.

at 6:06 after
all the commotion subsided
one Robert Groves
number 608
white and male
joined them
drunk

Giannina (1990)

As I continued down the hallway, I reread the poem and wondered: Why did she write it? And what did it mean? I knew, of course, that a text had no single, determinate meaning, least of all a poem. On some level, Giannina's poem may have been an effort to reach out—a peace offering. Perhaps she was reminding us that the feud was just a small thing, that noble ventures, like King's, must struggle not to lose themselves in banality: On one level, we are all brothers and sisters. But if one fails to notice differences, then Martin Luther King becomes just another prisoner, like the drunks—important features erased. I left the building and walked in the direction of my apartment to prepare for the evening and for my first chance to meet the elusive Giannina.

7

RODRIGO'S SEVENTH CHRONICLE: Race, Democracy, and the State

Introduction

The familiar voice in my receiver gave me quite a start: "Professor, it's me, Rodrigo Crenshaw. I'm at the corner grocery store just down the block from your building."

I had been getting a number of calls from former students wanting to know if I would serve as a reference for the bar examiners or an employer.

"Sorry it took me a minute to recognize your voice," I said. "Come on up if you have time. It's been awhile."

In a few minutes, the tall, lanky Rodrigo was standing in my doorway. "How has your summer been going, Professor?" Rodrigo cast his eyes over my desk. "Looks like you've got your bluebooks done."

"I had to grade fast this year, because—did I tell you?—I received a grant to spend a month at a study center in northern Italy. I just got back, in fact."

"I didn't know. The last time we talked, I was so wrapped up in my own problems I neglected to find out about your plans. So, what did you think of my old country?"

"I loved it. The countryside and food were great. I'm sure I've put on a couple of pounds. And I used the time at the center to finish that book we talked about before."

"Were the working conditions good?"

"Ideal. It's right by a lake. I thought of writing you, but they said the mail takes weeks. I would have called you up in a day or two, if you hadn't called me first."

"The government's been in turmoil. Did that affect your trip?"

"No—all was calm so far as I could tell. You have relatives there, though, right?"

Rodrigo nodded. "Distant ones. In Bologna, mainly."

"Are they okay?"

"Fine. I talked to them last week. They say it's no worse than usual. You probably know that in Italy, as in many parliamentary democracies, the government changes easily and often."

"And not just the national government," I offered. "Regional and even city governments vary. You can travel three miles and be in a completely different regime. In one town, the government can be centrist or socialist. The next town over can be communist, and so on."

"I know. It makes life there interesting. When I came to the States, I went through the reverse adjustment. Here, there are only two basic approaches to politics, each linked with a competing conception of the state. Things seemed to me static, almost boring. Of course, there's nothing a European intellectual loves better than to sit in a café and discuss politics. I did some of that myself."

"Do you miss the ferment there?"

"A little. I couldn't help being struck by the contrast. Here, there are twenty different theories or approaches to law, ranging from right-wing law and economics to left-wing Critical Race theories, like those you and your friends are developing.[1] Yet, thinking about the state seems frozen at a fairly simple level."

"Compared to other countries, you mean?"

"Yes, it's remarkably dichotomous. For example, I've noticed that exactly one-half of my professors think government should be large and powerful, an agent for change."[2]

"We both know what political party they are apt to belong to."

"Of course. And the others believe in the minimalist state. For them the larger the government, the more harm it is likely to do.[3] Of course, there are the communitarians and civic republicans, who want a greater identification between the citizen and the state.[4] But aside from those, the possibilities seem quite limited. My friend and fellow LL.M. student Ali says he almost never runs into a Marxist."

"A growing number of the students are libertarians," I observed.

"I've noticed that," Rodrigo agreed. "They strike me as a variant of Republicans, even if they don't identify with that party. Their fascination with deregulation, personal privacy, and laissez-faire economics reminds me of the strain of political thinking that prevailed during your period of rapid expansion a century ago."

"But you were saying that all those categories were played out."

"I think so, Professor. For example, consider the age-old problem of race—something both of us care deeply about. Proponents of both the activist and quietist state say they have our interests at heart. Yet people of color seem to do little better in the one regime than the other. In some respects, we folks of color have the worst possible situation here."

I made a mental note to ask Rodrigo something about that later if the opportunity arose, but resisted the temptation for now. Instead, I said, as noncommittally as possible: "Some of us have written about that."[5]

"I know."

"And I suppose you think the solution to our social ills is bound up with the concept of the state in some fashion, so that a different—or at any rate, better—form of government is a necessary step toward resolving those problems?"

"We talked about some of those things before. As always, it's easier to see what's wrong with the current system than to figure out what to put in its place. But if you have the time, Professor, I'd love to run some ideas past you. I'm thinking of using them for the last part of my dissertation, a draft of which is due by the end of the summer."

"I'd be happy to listen. As always, I'm sure I'll learn as much as you. Would you like some dinner?"

"Actually, Giannina and I just ate. But I'd be glad to join you for a snack."

"The two of you made up, I assume?"

"Yes, we're doing fine."

"I'm glad to hear it. I enjoyed meeting her that time." As I gathered up my keys and sweater, I asked, "And what are your plans?"

"Well, I've got a teaching job. My friend Ali got one, too. Mine's in the Midwest. I'm not sure what Giannina and I are going to do. We're getting along really well now. But she's reluctant to leave the city, where she has all her writing contacts."

"Sounds like a difficult decision," I commiserated. "I know couples who have tried commuting. Some find it grueling; for others, it's not so bad. There's a little dessert shop just down the street," I said. "Can I interest you?"

"Great. I can always eat dessert," my young friend said with enthusiasm.

In Which Rodrigo Explains the Connection between Racism and Democracy

A few minutes later, we were comfortably seated in the pastry shop down the block from the law school. After selecting our desserts from a tray the waiter brought, I said:

"You were saying something about the relationship between government and racism. Something about our form being the worst of all for minorities. I'm sure you mean in theory, Rodrigo, because, in practice, other cultures are just as bad, if not worse."

"Both in theory and in practice, Professor. It may sound paradoxical."

"It certainly does," I burst in. "What about Cambodia? What about ethnic cleansing? What about the religious tyranny of Iran? And what about the honorable moments of our own history, like *Brown v. Board of Education?*"

"Let me explain, Professor," Rodrigo replied mildly. "There is plenty of blame to go around. Other cultures have been vicious, too. But they have tended to victimize outsiders, generally nonmembers or historic enemies. We—I mean Western democracies—are practically alone in our systematic mistreatment of our own minorities.[6] I mean, of course, African-Americans, Native Americans, Asian Americans, and Latinos. And this is a major problem for any theory of government—understanding and regulating the relation between the majority and the minority, I mean."[7]

"You have a theory, I assume?" Rodrigo brightened, whether at my question or the arrival of the waiter with our desserts, I couldn't tell. "What are you having?"

I looked at his plate. "Flan," he replied.

"Looks good," I said, taking a spoonful of my own lemon sherbet. "Now tell me about your theory of government and race."

"I didn't mean to be too harsh earlier, Professor. Your—I mean our— system has some of the best formal values in the world. We have language declaring that all men and women are equal, about the brotherhood of man, and so on. On the Fourth of July, when all the flags are flying, and on a few other occasions of an official nature Americans can be counted on to be genuinely fair-minded, genuinely antiracist."[8]

"A few of them can be counted on other times, too," I interjected.

"To be sure. Yet in moments of informality, those same Americans feel free to tell an ethnic joke, to complain about blacks, or talk to a woman condescendingly."[9]

"We've all seen that. We know that there are certain places, bars and the like, where we are not safe. And we know that even those white folks whom we can ordinarily trust, who would not think of saying anything hurtful, change. At certain times, in a certain atmosphere, at a certain party, in the company of certain others—you have to watch out."

"I think the axis has something to do with fairness and formality," Rodrigo said. "On formal occasions, such as in court, when serving on a jury perhaps, the average American can sometimes get beyond race. You have all those reminders—the flag, the robes, the judge, the solemn words—that cue you that this is an occasion where the formal values, the higher, official ones, are to preponderate. Other, more intimate occasions do not evoke those same values. The same person can be racist one minute, then nonracist the next, depending on the setting."[10]

"Interesting," I replied. "I think I agree with you. But what about a country like South Africa?"

"There the situation is exactly reversed. The public values, until recently, were officially racist. But on occasion South African whites could be counted on to show real compassion in their private lives. If you were a black and in trouble of some sort, a private citizen, not the government, would be your best source of hope."

"Maybe that's why American blacks like big government and historically have looked to the Democratic party and the federal government as our salvation."

"I think it may have something to do with that," Rodrigo replied. "But more and more, it's beginning to appear a vain hope. Neither political party does much for us. Our fortunes are little better under the more big-spending Democrats than under the less-is-more Republicans."[11]

"I agree. In fact, I've written so myself. And so, I gather you think we need some wholly new approach?"

"I do," Rodrigo replied. "We can't rely on formality forever. Otherwise, our young people will get jobs in exactly two areas—sports and the Army.

Superimposed on the entire system is a layer of antiblack sentiment. To get beyond that, we must do more than look for the chinks in the system, the few islands of relative safety. We must first understand, then do something about, the system that demeans and submerges our people at every turn."

"A large undertaking, Rodrigo. Would you like to discuss it over coffee?" We had both finished our dessert. Rodrigo looked as though he could handle another one.

"Or, would you like something more to eat? My sherbet was very good."

"No thanks, Professor. Just coffee. Understanding what's wrong is not too hard. I can lay it out for you in a few minutes. Where to go from there is another matter. Waiter!"

Rodrigo had caught the attention of the waiter circulating behind me. Soon we were sipping cappuccino, decaffeinated on my part, the real thing on his. After a moment, he began: "Professor, have you read Catharine MacKinnon's work?"

"Of course. I admire it greatly. Her analyses of the operation of patriarchy are at once illuminating and hard-hitting. She wrote several pieces on sexual harassment of women in the workplace,[12] and on pornography.[13] Her book *Feminism Unmodified*[14] is a classic in its time, but she has written much more."

"Then you know how she regards sexuality as the essence of women's subordination."

"I do. It's one of her most controversial theses. She says that the sexualization of women, the construction of her in that role, is the very instrument of her oppression, and not in any contingent or means-ends sense. It is not possible to be a female sexual being in our society and not be relegated to second-class status. Sexuality is women's subordination, pure and simple. It doesn't just happen that women are both sexualized and oppressed. They are two sides of the same coin."[15]

"And had you thought whether something similar is true for us, Professor—whether there is not some parallel mechanism that accounts for our subordination?"

I was silent for a moment. I reflected on such theories as socioeconomic competition, the colonized mind, interest-convergence, and various psychological theories that authorities had put forward to explain the persistence of racism.

"I'm not sure I can think of anything precisely similar, if you mean a simple psychological or political mechanism, like sexuality, that accounts for black subordination and the maintenance of a racist regime. I suppose you have one to propose?"

"I think it's democracy," he replied.

"Democracy?" I was thunderstruck. "The crowning achievement of the West, the legacy of Athens and Rome, the jewel in political theory. You think it's this that explains white-over-black power relations and the oppression of our people?"

"Yes," Rodrigo replied with the remarkable insouciance that was his trademark, "at least one variant of it. Western-style democracies, even with their formal, for-public-consumption rhetoric of equality, brotherhood, and all the rest, basically don't mean it. Whether they ever could change to be fair toward minorities, nonconformists, and other outsiders, I seriously doubt. I think minorities always have done better—relatively speaking—and will continue to do better—in other types of regimes. And this is systemic and intrinsic, not accidental."

"Rodrigo, of all the things we have discussed, this idea of yours strikes me as the most counterintuitive. I can think of innumerable counterexamples. But let me put them on hold for a moment. I want to learn more about your—how shall I put it?—jaded attitude toward the West. What on earth do you see in democracy that renders it the root of our mistreatment of minorities?"

"It's the idea of enlightenment," Rodrigo answered. "It functions for minorities as sex and sexualization do for women. You recall MacKinnon's thesis. She holds that sexuality, or, rather society's construction of it, is the very medium of women's subordination. I think enlightenment-style Western democracy is its parallel, the source of black people's subordination. Not just in a causal sense. Rather, racism and enlightenment are the same thing. They go together; they are opposite sides of a coin."

I recalled a powerful scene in the movie *Malcolm X*, in which the young Malcolm was first introduced to the systematic nature of color-imagery in the words of Webster's dictionary by his prison mentor.[16] I asked Rodrigo, "Do you mean the way in which color-imagery and symbols operate to devalue dark skin and place a premium on white?"

"That and much more," Rodrigo replied. "I think the system of imagery, the metaphors, the myths and stories of Snow White, white man's burden, dark villains and continents, and the rest are but surface manifestations of something deeper, something that lies at the heart of Western-style government and politics."

"And this something distributes power, privileges, social roles, disapproval and approval, niceness and its opposite—and has to do with Enlightenment philosophy?"

"Yes. The word itself is no accident. Locke wrote essays justifying slavery.[17] Hobbes, Mill, and even Rousseau either did the same or wrote of a hierarchy of cultures and the natural subservience of the darker-skinned ones to the lighter.[18] The framers of the United States Constitution used color imagery.[19] Many were slaveowners.[20] The few who decried slavery publicly nevertheless thought people like you and me were inferior and devised schemes to send our unfortunate dark-skinned forefathers, as they called them, back to Africa; others blithely justified the institution as the lesser of two evils."[21]

"Perhaps that was a historical anachronism which Western society has outlived. No one would advocate those things today except the lunatic fringe. Indeed, less than two centuries after the period you are describing, Quakers and others were turning Enlightenment ideas around to challenge slavery."

"I don't think it was simply a stage, something we have outgrown. The Framers put in place a structure of government that is inherently biased against the minority. They thought they were establishing a perfect machine, one predicated on the separation of powers and similar doctrines that would assure that it remained forever in perfect balance, like the heavens, whose celestial laws of dynamics and motion Galileo, Descartes, and Newton described.[22] Such a perfect machine could scarcely need serious systemic correction—that would be contrary to its nature. Intrinsic to Enlightenment thought are the ideas of order, balance, symmetry, and control.[23] So, the idea of perfection, of perfect arrangement, made it hard for the minority to get its pleas heard or taken seriously. It remains so today. Have you ever tried to get a white person to take complaints of racism seriously?"

"It's not easy. They either deny them, or say racism lies in the past. If you point out an example they can't deny—the black Nobel Prize winner denied a job in favor of a no-good high-school dropout white—they say, 'Well things are better now than they used to be, don't we have to admit that?'"[24]

Rodrigo smiled, then said: "It's part of the idea of perfectionism, which in turn is an integral part of Enlightenment philosophy."

"And that makes us seem like ingrates for complaining. But you mentioned that there was more."

"There is. Another component of Enlightenment thought is the idea of hierarchy—of one culture or mode of thought being always and forever better than another. Light over dark. Enlightened over savage. We over they. Think of all the light-type words with favorable connotations—'enlightened,' 'brilliant,' 'insightful.' Enlightenment implies a progression, with ourselves— which originally meant Western white male aristocrats in lace shirts—at the top. Our class, you see, knows mathematics, physics, the laws of motion and philosophy, while *they* are benighted, ignorant, superstitious, mired in darkness. Naturally, it should fall our lot to develop theories of government, and to run things. We have sanitation and they don't. Q.E.D."

"Quite a combination," I replied, ironically. "A balanced, perfect machine. And my own class in charge, pulling the levers. The one confers authority, legitimacy. The other assures stasis, resists challenge. But perhaps we're dealing with benevolent despots, ones who are wise and compassionate. That wouldn't be too bad. Consider the Western missionaries, for example. Surely they did some good."[25] I was determined to play the Devil's advocate as long as possible.

"You're right," Rodrigo conceded, "except for one thing. Enlightenment thought and politics imply exclusion, imply disdain for those falling outside the charmed circle. It is not a warm, embracing philosophy, like some you might have run into in the villages and small towns of my country, Professor. In its images, metaphors, and foundations it has exclusion and cruelty built in."

"I'm not sure what you mean. Are you referring to something more than the near-universal human tendency to prefer, to be most comfortable with, to trust, one's own kind?"

"I am. Enlightenment thought is exclusionary by its very nature. Consider what a beam of light does. It illuminates a narrow circle or band, leaving the rest unlit. It attracts the eye there, discourages it from going to the rest. That is the guiding metaphor of Enlightenment thought, and it has exclusion built in. And I don't mean in any accidental, contingent sense, but inherently and necessarily. Any political system, such as democracy, built on such a foundation will be bad for the minority. It is not just happenstance that Western democracies pioneered the slave trade, plantation system, coolie labor, Native American relocation, and Bracero programs.[26] The United States was one of the last Western countries to abandon slavery.[27] It maintains and tightens strict immigration controls at the very time when other countries are loosening them.[28] The West used color imagery to justify empire—recall the white man's burden—as well as the Discovery Doctrine by which we forced the Native Americans off their ancestral lands.[29] Domination and exclusion are implicit in the idea of democracy. All can't govern, literally—that would be impossible. And in the West, the basis of that exclusion is color, followed by sex and property, in that order."

"I thought you said sex was the basis of female subjugation."

"I said sexuality, or rather, MacKinnon did. The way society constructs sexualized woman is the very means of her subordination. You can't have sex, as currently understood, and female equality at the same time. But that's her thesis. Mine is that democracy is the counterpart mechanism for us. If you are black or Mexican, you should flee Enlightenment-based democracies like mad, assuming you have any choice. Enlightenment philosophy is the very means by which you are rendered a nonperson, always one-down. A thousand myths and tales, a thousand scripts, plots, narratives, and stories will paint you as hapless, primitive, savage, lascivious, and not-so-smart, suitable only for menial work.[30] It's as rigid a system as the Middle Ages, yet harder to change because it's all informal and implicit. There is nothing to rebel against. Indeed, the formal guarantees are impeccably egalitarian. A black person can be president, even though none ever has, and only three of us have ever been in the Senate."

"Then why are you here?" I asked. "You just said black persons should flee this place, yet you took a teaching job in the Midwest!"

"I have a mission," Rodrigo replied levelly, "as I mentioned before. Besides, I was born here. We have work to do."

"And the thing we have to work on is that which all have been taught to treasure—democracy, which you see as the means of our oppression?"

"The very instrument," Rodrigo replied cheerfully. "Liberal democracy and racial subordination go hand in hand, like the sun, moon, and stars. Enlightenment is to racism as sexuality is to women's oppression—the very means by which we are kept down."

"And to think I once studied mathematics and Descartes," I shuddered in mock disbelief. "Rodrigo, do you have any idea how strange your equation is? Democracy as the very source not just of majoritarian oppression—many have warned of that—but of racism, of steady, enduring, systemic subjugation on the basis of color!"

"All truth is paradoxical," Rodrigo replied. "It starts out with a question, goes underneath what is accepted."

"There are paradoxes and then there are paradoxes. As I have done more than once, I must encourage you to keep these ideas to yourself, at least until you are finished with your degree and have tenure. I see nothing but trouble ahead if you air them too freely. Our white friends have a healthy self-image. For them, Enlightenment philosophy is the crown jewel of civilization, the pride of Western culture. To portray it as the source of bigotry and oppression—along that way lies trouble. If I were you, Rodrigo, I would keep these ideas of yours quiet for a while."

Rodrigo looked at me mildly. "I know you're on my side, Professor. I appreciate your counsel."

"Besides," I added, "there's an economic side to all this. It's very complex, having to do with laissez-faire capitalism, a companion system to what you call Enlightenment political thought.[31] Its practitioners maintain that everything should be efficient. How does your indictment of Western liberalism deal with this? It's not particularly liberal or romantic, but pretends to be hardheaded science."

"I've actually given it some thought. Will you scold me if I tell you about it?"

"No, please, I'd love to hear."

In Which Rodrigo Explains the Connection between Racism and Free Market Economics

"The scientific trappings of economics are no guarantee against racism," Rodrigo began. "You recall what anthropologists were saying about us as late as 1925.[32] Note the parallels—both free market economics and Enlightenment political philosophy are erected on mechanistic premises. The one visualizes government as a grand, noble machine, perfectly in balance, as we mentioned. The other regards economic activity in much the same way, as a broad summation of private choices, endlessly and forever perfecting itself as stronger actors and businesses drive out weaker ones. Processes, products, inventions, and services get better over time. People trade things—services and labor—and the whole system improves ineluctably and endlessly. The less regulation, the better, for if people act according to their own self-interest—pursue their own gain—society will be better off. We'll have more jobs, products, services, and wealth."

"And I'm sure you see some flaw in this design?" I asked.

"A kind of flaw. One the seriousness of which depends on your position in society. Some might regard it as minor. For others, it would be more serious."

"And I gather those others are us—people like you and me?"

"Yes. I was discussing this with Ali the other day. Are you familiar with Garret Hardin's refutation of socialist economics?"

I searched my memory. "Do you mean his work on lifeboat ethics, or the tragedy of the commons?" [33]

"The latter mostly, although the former comes into play as well. In his famous article he points out that socialism—any form of collective organization, really—has a built-in difficulty, namely the free rider problem." [34]

"You mean the individual who agrees to the collectivist arrangement but with an unspoken reservation. This person is happy to have the village or group set aside land—or any other resource—for common use. He uses it, but when it comes his turn to pay or care for it, mowing it for example, he shirks his duty. One of the other 99 members of the cooperative has to step in. After a while, people start to notice that certain members of the collective are drawing a share of the crops but not doing the work. Eventually, they follow suit and the whole thing falls apart. Socialism contains the seeds of its own self-destruction, since everyone learns, sooner or later, that they can do better by withdrawing, by investing as little as possible."

"But doesn't this hold true just for lazy people, a small fraction of any group?"

"No. It holds true for the industrious just as well. By inconspicuously withdrawing from the collective enterprise, remaining members in name only, they can devote the extra time to private activity—making shoes, for example. That way, they get both shoes and crops. The others get just crops."

"So, in Hardin's view, socialism is flawed, and tends in time to flip-flop over into capitalism," I said in summary. "But I gather you had something different to point out."

"Oh, yes," Rodrigo replied, taking a quick gulp of his cappuccino and draining his cup. "Without controls, collectivism tends to decay. But something similar happens with free market capitalism. There is a mirror image flaw on the other side, one with special implications for minorities."

"Do you mean the way that color preferences exclude us from market transactions, deny us access to trades? [35] People just won't deal with us, at least if a white person is equally available."

"We talked about that before. And I think what we said then holds true: The market does not cure racism, but accentuates it. But on thinking about it further, I believe I've found an even more basic mechanism, one that generates a climate in which vulnerable groups, particularly those of color, cannot flourish."

"I'm anxious to hear what you have to say. But, first, how about a refill? Or would you like more dessert?"

"Fine. All this talking makes me hungry."

I caught the waiter's eye and gestured Rodrigo to continue.

"Individualistic market economics teaches everyone to seek his or her own profit, to rely on his or her own resources and effort to support him- or herself through life. Yet there must be rules and laws, against stealing or setting fire to your competitor's shop, for example, requiring the payment of taxes, and so on."

"Our friends in the law-and-economics movement would set that level as low as possible."[36]

"But even they believe there must be some laws to assure security, public safety, and some degree of social cooperation.[37] Yet even that minimal level tends to erode under market pressures, with the result that Western societies get rougher and rougher over time."

"More or less the opposite of Hardin's thesis, but for capitalism," I commented.

"And, as I mentioned, with sobering consequences for minorities and other outsider groups. In a free market society, every actor is rewarded for coming as close to the line as possible. A merchant who cuts corners, who takes liberties with labor, fair-weights-and-measures, tax and reporting rules, will have an edge on competitors who are more law-abiding, more generous toward their staffs, and so on. When everyone learns this and begins to do the same, by a sort of tacit agreement the line moves back. Eventually the legislature formalizes the new line. Driving speeds on the freeway are a good example. Even people who would like to drive slowly and safely can't."[38]

"And you think the same holds true for matters of race?"

"Yes. Even those whites who would otherwise care about us, who left to their own devices would work for a nonracist society, don't. They lose interest, devote themselves to their own concerns, drop out of the civil rights movement."

"As I think I mentioned, it happens all the time. Even those students who begin law school as idealists, wanting to help the poor and downtrodden, change. By the time they graduate, they are ready to go into corporate practice, or become house counsel for the rest of their lives—anything-other than the public interest work that attracted them to law in the first place."[39]

"I've noticed that, too. Competitive pressures drive out altruistic, other-regarding impulses. Pretty soon, the formal rules change, and we don't even notice how this happens. If a free market society does contain an impoverished or minority group, all things being equal, that group's situation will worsen over time because the majority will come to care less and less about it, will be willing to devote fewer and fewer resources to redressing its needs. Eventually, things get so bad, competition so cutthroat, the agony of the inner city so intense, that society intervenes. We pass a few laws, establish a few programs, and we all feel much better."

"It *is* like Hardin's thesis," I mused. "And it certainly accords with historical experience. The last twenty years for us have been some of the worst I've seen. And certain earlier periods of rapid economic development—or times of economic distress and competition—saw the introduction of harsh measures against Asians, Mexicans, and other immigrant groups."

"And I think these resurgences of nativism and other unlovely sentiments are not simply aberrations, Professor, but markers in what is generally a steady decline in civility and generosity and tolerance. All of this, of course, has very real consequences for our people."

"In a way, Rodrigo, your thesis is similar to the counter-majoritarian difficulty which many have pointed out in connection with theories of judicial review,[40] but includes it as a special case. Enlightenment-based Western-style democracy poses not just the possibility, but the near-certainty of domination and rough treatment of minorities—a treatment that comes in time to seem more and more natural and deserved, and less and less in need of correction. Legal self-seeking comes to be defined as what white people do."

Just then, the waiter arrived with a tray of tempting-looking desserts. "Those look good. Have one. This is on me," I said.

Wherein Rodrigo Explains the Persistence of Western Racism

As we started on our desserts, I recapitulated what I had heard. "So, Rodrigo, you believe that the source of our troubles lies with Enlightenment philosophy. You've deployed cognitive psychology to show how that outlook generates a willingness to disdain others, and works together with color imagery to assure that our people are always despised and overlooked. You have said that Enlightenment notions are for blacks what sexuality is for women, the very means by which society constructs and justifies our subordination. In democracy not all can have a voice. Enlightenment democracy assures that ours is the one that is excluded. And even if we could be heard, the perfectionist strain that Enlightenment breeds makes criticism seem like fly-specking, making the listener prone to ask questions like, 'But aren't you better off than you were in Africa?'

"Further, you have argued that free market capitalism works together with Enlightenment political thought to keep blacks and other people of color down. In a kind of reversal of Garret Hardin's thesis, you argued that capitalism eventually destroys fellow-feeling and identification with the group. Those who start out caring for us, wanting to join our struggle, fall away, go off to tend their own gardens lest they get too far behind the competition. I agree with you on most of these points. But is there not still hope? Is not democracy an open social arrangement, one in which talented outsiders like yourself may work for change? If not, what's the point of struggle?"

Rodrigo took a mouthful of his raspberry torte and looked up. "It's not particularly open, at least compared with other social systems. And whether there's any point in struggling, I think everyone must decide for himself. The system does resist change, both practically and on a level of theory. Have you noticed how uninterested most Americans are in hearing about their own racial injustices?"

"I have. And I assume you attribute this to the same factors of perfectionism and the sense of one's own culture's infallibility that make change difficult," I ventured.

"Yes, those plus the other things we talked about earlier. Color imagery and the cognitive psychology of visual imagery and light make it difficult for persons in the society to focus for long on the troubles of outsiders. Plus there is law's contribution to freezing things."

"Locke-ing things in, so to speak," I quipped.

"I kind of like that," Rodrigo replied appreciatively. "Mind if I steal it?"

"Not at all. You've been doing most of the talking today. I've gotten much more out of this discussion than you."

"You're the one that got me started, encouraged me to pursue this vein of thought in the first place. I can never thank you enough. You're a good mentor and friend."

I marveled, once again, at how even grizzled old veterans like me learn at least as much from our students as they from us. Even their half-formed ideas often trigger responsive ones in our minds, enabling us to go on in what is often an arid and desolate landscape.

But I said, "Tell me more about how the system resists change."

In Which Rodrigo Explains Further How Racism Gets Locked In: Law's Contribution

"Law—I mean the legal system—is one of the ways," Rodrigo said. "Can I interest you in a gelato? I notice they have it here, and it's one of the things I miss from Italy."

"Of course," I quickly replied. "It's one of the many fine foods from your country that I got hooked on during my visit. It's better than what we call ice cream, with all that butterfat. My doctor told me to cut down."

I gestured to the waiter and waited while Rodrigo tried to make himself understood concerning what I gather was his favorite flavor. He settled for something second best, after which I ordered *mandarino*, a tart variety of near-orange that I had first bought from a street vendor in Bologna.

When I mentioned this to Rodrigo, he looked up with interest. "No kidding—you were in my old city?"

"Three days. I loved it. I thought the arcaded walkways were gorgeous. I loved the old churches. And I stopped in at the law school completely unannounced, but managed to talk with one professor and three students."

"Did they speak English?"

"They did, for which I was grateful. It struck me as both a sophisticated and highly political place. As you mentioned, the students did know of Critical Legal Studies. So did the professor, and one of the students had even read Bell and Matsuda, I assume in translation."

"It's possible, professor. But I think it's equally possible they struggled through in English, just as they did in talking with you. Left and progressive movements in Italy read more work from the States than you might think."

"I recall that when we first met, you had already read an impressive amount."

"No more than many of my friends. Ali may have read even more than I, but he was a philosophy major while I studied comparative cultures, as you remember."

"I do. But tell me more about the persistence of racial inequality."

"Well, one additional mechanism—beyond the ones we've already discussed—is simply law's conservatism. There is no particular reason why a legal system needs to be on the wrong side, needs to perpetuate racial or other injustice."

"At a few periods, the American judiciary was actually pro-reform," I interjected.[41]

"In the sixties and early seventies, and sporadically before then. But on the whole judges have turned a deaf ear to minorities seeking change more than they have welcomed them and forwarded their causes."

"And the reasons they have done so are—?"

"The usual ones—judges' class and economic backgrounds. But a further one is simply that the legal system, in the U.S. at any rate, is past-oriented. *Stare decisis* and the rule of law mean that judges are bound to continue the previous regime even if it is unfair."

"That's certainly true. But every now and then, a great jurist like Thurgood Marshall, William Brennan, or William Douglas has seemed able to rise above that culture and stake out a position that is genuinely forward-looking and humane."

"But the new rule or decision has a way of slipping back. You have written about that yourself, along with your friends."[42]

"I know," I said. "Some of us explain that cycle of lurching forward and falling back in terms of interest-convergence.[43] Others write that whatever its cause, it's an ever-present reality that argues against putting too much reliance on the courts for social change."

"Girardeau Spann comes to mind."

"I read his brilliant book.[44] And agree with it to a large extent."

"Me, too, though I have a slightly different explanation for the dismal picture of dashed hopes and betrayals he depicts so remorselessly."

"I'm sure you do, Rodrigo. For one so young, and with such a cheerful disposition, you certainly have some downbeat ideas."

"Not much more than some of yours, Professor. Although one or two of your recent things have had almost a—how shall I put it—spiritual quality?"

"Well, optimistic, anyway. I'll concede that in my younger days no one matched me for skepticism about our people's future. A few people described me as the originator of 'bleak chic.'"

"Now *that* I hadn't heard," Rodrigo exclaimed. "I kind of like it. It fits."

"But what about the occasional judge who champions our cause, what about the breakthrough *Brown v. Board of Education* decision that comes along every decade or two?"

"Decisions like *Brown* produce a lot of hurrah-ing and singing and dancing in the streets, as you have pointed out. Then, they are quietly stolen back by narrow construction, foot-dragging, and administrative delay. We end up little better off than we were before—or even worse. Everyone hears about the great decision and assumes our problems are solved. Our friends go off to save the whales, or to other causes. And our enemies paint us as whiners and complainers. For, after all these beneficial laws and landmark decisions, if we aren't making it, well—what can be done? Perhaps there is something intrinsically wrong with us. So they get to blame us even more than before."

"But you said there was a new element. These things I think both of us know and have talked about before—right?"

"Right. It's that the legal system can't bring about any sort of significant change because it operates piecemeal. It can only solve the case before it. Doctrines of standing, mootness, ripeness, and political question assure that.[45] And since racism is systemic, rather than episodic, intrinsic to the culture rather than an aberration, the normal rather than the abnormal, law cannot see or redress it.[46] The gravitational tug of the familiar is too great. And the familiar—the ordinary state of things—is racism, rather than the opposite."[47]

"I could use an example."

Rodrigo was silent for a moment, while I scooped up the last drop of gelato in the bottom of my cup, wishing I could have more. I was struggling with my conscience when Rodrigo broke in with an insight that made the wait worthwhile:

"Imagine that the Supreme Court one day decides that a voting regime in which black electoral power is canceled out is, by virtue of that simple result, unconstitutional. It decides in favor of something like the 'proportional representation' that your friend Lani Guinier has been writing about.[48] So that any structure that produces only a handful of black representatives from a heavily black district, and allows those few to have their effect canceled out by the need to make trades and compromises, is a violation of the Constitution or voting rights laws designed to implement it."

"I gather you are going to say that such a decision would end up making little difference."

"Very little. Such a decision would be interpreted as the extraordinary thing it is. Local authorities, voting registrars, congressional leaders, and so on, would say, 'Well, of course the Supreme Court didn't mean *that*.' Because of the interlocking web of cultural understandings, meanings, and presuppositions about the sort of country this is supposed to be, local officials will gut the landmark decision. In every close case requiring an interpretation, they will say to themselves, 'Surely the Court meant X,' when it actually meant Y. And of course X will be the status-maintaining interpretation."

"And that's what you meant when you said that everything would have to change at once, and not piece by piece, precedent by precedent."

"Yes—otherwise, the rest of the system will simply drag the new rule down, and we'll be back where we were before."

"And this is just the sort of wide-ranging change that law cannot usher in, by its very nature, for the reasons you mentioned."

Rodrigo's Second Reason—John Calvin and the Culture of Individualism

"I think there is a grain of truth to what you say, Rodrigo. It captures a growing sense that legal culture is structurally biased against racial reform. It's not so much that judges hate us. Rather, it's something about the milieu in which they work."[49]

"In your country, are most judges Protestants?" Rodrigo asked.

"Interesting question. I really don't know. Probably so, although I can think of many exceptions. And of course, in the legal academy, many are Jewish, and not a few Catholic. Why do you ask?"

"Because I have the sense that Calvinism plays a part in rendering race reform even less likely than it would be in its absence."

"What do you mean?"

"Capitalism arose around the same time as Calvinism did, shortly after the Reformation. Both turned society's attention toward the individual. Calvinism and its variants eliminated intermediaries, such as priests, and focused on the role of the individual believer. Capitalism did much the same in the economic sphere. Both doctrines remain alive and vital today."

"And have something to do with majoritarian oppression of African-Americans and other people of color, such as Native Americans, Puerto Ricans, and Mexicans?"

"It's related to the individualism we just talked about. Anyone not succeeding by his or her own efforts must not be trying very hard. Failure is a sign of moral sin or sloth. And any focus on group redress, which African-Americans need to correct the systemic injustices we have suffered over four centuries of domination, is alien to individualistic thought. Before the Reformation, the Church was at least allied with the king and the aristocracy. Over time, it could have come to expand its allegiance to include workers and the poor, as a few liberation theology groups have done.[50] But in the main, religion in the West has been more concerned with individual sinners—and patrons—than groups in need of help."

"Direct democracy, as they have it in the Western states, in which the people get to enact laws and constitutional amendments by referendum and initiative, has been responsible for some notably antiminority and antigay measures.[51] Do you see any connection between this mechanism and the individualism you attribute to our religious tradition?"

"I hadn't thought much about that," Rodrigo conceded. "But it stands to reason that representative government supplies at least a slight momentum in favor of consideration of groups. Representatives are always making trade-offs, weighing the interests of one set of constituents against those of others. Of course, they sometimes blithely trade away *our* interests, as we discussed earlier. But when the people vote in the privacy of the ballot booth, they are even freer to vote their preferences—which are sometimes quite unlovely, as you and I know."[52]

"All too well," I acknowledged.

"And then there's the judiciary's well-known deference to the authority of other branches, or of the people acting through direct democracy. Although the judiciary is supposed to act in a counter-majoritarian fashion, to protect weak and insular minorities from tyranny,[53] they do this less and less these days. And when they are asked to do so, they naturally interpret the request against a background of what seems natural to them. And what seems natural is tyranny. The current system of white over black seems natural. The reigning narratives, myths, and meanings operate to invalidate black claims, so that judicial deference to quite pernicious practices passes, at the time, as the right thing to do.[54] American courts and other branches of government are more apt to write off a poor man's or group's pain than are more collectivist governments. I imagine you saw examples of this on your European sojourn, Professor?"

"I was surprised to see how few homeless people there are, or beggars, particularly in your country. And the elderly seem less destitute than many are here. I assume that's because there is always someone to help them."[55]

"Yes—either a family member or social service agency. The system isn't perfect, and there are of course exceptions, as we discussed before. But on the whole the caregiving function is carried out more effectively there."

"I wouldn't be surprised if this is related to the way our version of democracy emphasizes Enlightenment ideals. Calvinism lets us blame the poor and the lame. Judges and others come steeped in perfectionism, so that the system changes slowly. And, as you pointed out, incremental reform won't work for racism or other systemic social ills. Everything has to change at once, but can't, because of *stare decisis* and law's commitment to piecemeal treatment."

"Much more than other disciplines, law is caught up in old-style formalistic, mechanical approaches to reason and analysis, which it is just beginning to abandon. Postmodern and Critical currents have caught on almost everywhere else, providing powerful new insights into our condition and the nature of knowledge itself. With some exceptions—like you and your friends, Professor—law remains committed to outmoded approaches."[56]

"You give me too much credit, Rodrigo," I quickly interjected. "I'm just an ordinary foot soldier, toiling in the trenches. I don't talk this high Crit stuff very well. I'm afraid it's for young people like you, who have the time and flexible minds to master it. I find much of it interesting and provocative, although I often wish the writers who deploy it would learn to write more simply. Sometimes, I almost feel I have to read with a dictionary of 'Criticalese' in hand."

"I know," Rodrigo conceded. "Some of us do get caught up in impenetrable jargon. I've taken a vow to try to write more clearly, myself. My thesis adviser has been your strongest ally. I'm not sure if you know him, but he's a stickler for the straightforward phrase."

"Don't let my lament sidetrack you," I interposed. "I think postmodern analysis holds enormous promise for a new program of racial reform. It's just that I think you're the one to develop it, not me."

"You've already been doing it," Rodrigo added quietly. "You don't know what an inspiration you and your generation have been. You've shown how formalistic, precedent-based civil rights law built along the liberal model fails over and over again. You've pointed the way, developed the evidence, the prima facie case, so to speak. We're just filling in the gaps, developing theories to explain what you've shown."

"You're too kind," I said. "But all this flattery will get you nowhere if you cannot do two things. Your readers, especially those of majoritarian hue, will want to know, first, how you deal with certain counterexamples, like Cambodia, Iran, or India under the caste system. Other societies seem to have had no trouble perpetrating and justifying cruelty toward minority or despised populations. How can it be connected with Western thought and government if it happens everywhere? And, second, they will want to know what you plan to do about it, about the local version, I mean. Law types are pragmatic. They will want to know not just your diagnosis of our racial ills, but your prescription."

"On the first point, I guess I'd have to concede that there's enough cruelty and racism to go around. My purpose was to explain its persistence in the West. My basic point is that in the West, the disadvantage that blacks and other people of color suffered initially, that is, in connection with the way they were brought here, never ends."

"What about Thomas Sowell? He's shown that blacks from the West Indies rise rapidly. He attributes the failure of older African-American groups to thrive to their lack of industry, reliance on failed liberal programs, and to a culture of poverty."[57]

"It is true that Sowell found those differences. But you should note that West Indians rise rapidly up the economic ladder when we generally do not, but only for one generation. U.S.-born blacks have lived in a racist society longer than the newcomers and thus have had longer to become demoralized. In time, we may well find that West Indians sink to the same levels. Or, possibly society will construct a new category, like Bill Cosby—nice blacks, the other kind.[58] White folks never see their own racial and class advantages—the family friend who got them a summer job when they were a teenager, the carefully constructed recommendation letter for a college, the receptive teacher who discussed extra credit, which led to an A-minus in an Honors English course—things that happen to our kind almost never. But they do see as radically, shockingly, bitterly unfair the advantage a rare black gets when he or she gets into a good college under an affirmative action program. They promptly declare—'*That's* what I mean by unfair,' overlooking the inheritance, the loan from father, the childhood help they received of various kinds."

"Rodrigo, the hour is late, and you set a fast pace. An old man like me needs his rest. As stimulating as I find all this—and I think your thesis advisor will too—I'm going to have to head home soon. Maybe we can share a cab. But I'd love to have you outline your solution to our racial predicament—the one you hinted at earlier."

"This part of my paper is still—how do you say it?—sketchy. I can do it in ten minutes. How about another coffee?"

As luck would have it, the waiter hovering nearby in the now nearly deserted restaurant overheard Rodrigo's remark, and asked, "Can I bring you gentlemen more coffee?" I noticed he was a man of color and remarked, once again, how much better treatment people like Rodrigo and me get from service folks of color, even in today's world.[59]

"Decaf for me. Doctor's orders."

Rodrigo shot me a sympathetic look and said, "The same. I kind of overdosed during finals, so I'm cutting back. Besides, Giannina's been after me to reduce my intake. She says it makes me hyper."

"Funniest thing," I remarked, smiling to let Rodrigo know I appreciated his high-energy manner. "You were saying you have the outlines of some sort of solution."

In Which Rodrigo Explains How to Begin to Address Our Racial Predicament

The waiter quickly returned and poured our coffee. Rodrigo added cream and his trademark four teaspoons of sugar; I added NutraSweet. Then he began:

"The trick lies in dealing with the source of our problem, namely Enlightenment thought. I'm skeptical of any other way out. The structures of domination are so deeply engrained that the current regime seems just and natural to most folks within it, in need of little correction."

"But you said you had some thoughts."

"The beginnings. Some notions of where one might start if one thought the will were there, which I don't. For example, we've both noticed how color imagery, and metaphors of light, of eyesight play a part in our domination. We're the great Unseen, invisible, dark, the Other. We are equated with bad things, with a thousand connotations and narratives that make it difficult for white folks, even ones of good will, to think we might be their equals, might be as nice, as talented, as worth getting to know as one of them."

"And what would replace that system?"

"Well," Rodrigo replied with that nonchalance I had come to enjoy and appreciate, "we might try to get them to abandon the sight-based metaphors that lie at the heart of Enlightenment philosophy and adopt instead another sense organ, for example, touch."

I put down my cup of coffee. "You mean that you want to get white people to learn to hug the world, including the dark people in it, gays and lesbians, and other outsiders?" I was incredulous. "Rodrigo, I've got to hand it to you. This is a truly novel idea. But it will never go over."

"I'm not sure why not," Rodrigo replied. "Families love and hug each other. The human embrace is the means by which our most basic collectivities form and replicate each other. Handshakes, embraces, pats on the back—these are all primordial human experiences. We could build on this model of human relations, with its much more inclusionary impetus, rather than the more hierarchy-producing and -maintaining metaphors of our Enlightenment heritage."

"With environmentalism, you hear the remark, 'Go hug a tree,'" I said, immediately feeling a little lame. The idea of a society whose political structures were built on love and hugging struck me as a little, well, New Age, not quite befitting scholars of my station and in Rodrigo's case, station-to-be.

"There's also the bumper sticker, 'Have you hugged your kid today,'" Rodrigo added. "White folks might be persuaded to hug us, too. That's all I'm suggesting."

"That one's promising, if a little, well, frontal. Maybe it's worth proposing for its shock value, as a way of getting people to focus on sight metaphors and the pernicious quality of much Enlightenment theory. But you mentioned you had other avenues in mind."

"A second approach would tap a theory you and your friends have espoused, Professor, namely interest-convergence.[60] Everyone likes and can easily be gotten to act in their own self-interest once it's explained to them."

"So, you want to get the majority group to see that improving their treatment of groups of color benefits them."

"Yes, and to do that we can bring out themes that you and I discussed earlier in connection with the decline of the West, particularly the United States, whose slipping quality of life, economic status, and so on, have now become apparent to practically all.[61] We could gently let them know that the solution to their various predicaments—the environmental crisis, old-age care, and so on—lies with approaches now in the possession and experience of outsider groups. This would, of course, provide a new and compelling basis for affirmative action—namely, the majority group's self-interest. In a sense, some of this is already going on. White folks are turning to Native American thought for approaches to environmental protection,[62] to Southwestern culture for satisfaction and renewal.[63] It reminds me of how society discovered and exalted all things black during the Harlem Renaissance,[64] but with less condescension. The U.S. is beginning to realize it needs answers. Otherwise, it will soon be overtaken decisively by Asia and the Common Market."

"Do you think that the flirtation of some law professors with deconstruction and other postmodern approaches shares some of that emphasis?"

"You could look at it that way," Rodrigo replied. "There's the sense that the old kind of case-crunching analysis, full of mechanical, formalistic reasoning, has played itself out. Doctrinal analysis holds very few, if any, new insights any more. New scholars are moving beyond it into perspectivism, interdisciplinary 'law-and' scholarship, and cultural studies. There's a general sense that we've reached the end of a road."

"Rodrigo, now that I come to think of it, I much prefer this approach. Though an expert at poststructuralism, Criticalese, semiotics, contextualism, and all the other fancy new approaches I am not, I think Americans are much more apt to go for them than for the hugging solution. At first I thought you were being facetious, and I'm your friend and advocate."

"I wasn't being facetious. Any change of paradigm strikes one as peculiar when it's first suggested. Other cultures often complain that Anglo culture is cold, find Americans arrogant and superior. These other cultures are more on the hugging model—by which I mean collectivist. They don't have such a perfectionist hang-up, so they are less judgmental. In that respect, they share something with perspectivism, positionality, and some of the new approaches being written about by Pierre Schlag, Steve Winter, and others.[65] It is much easier to be inclusive if one isn't committed to the idea of one right answer, as classical thought inclines one to be."

"I did notice the difference you mentioned while traveling in the Mediterranean. And of course I find much the same warmth and support when I'm with my own people. But I had thought the difference had to do with my own reaction: I'm much more guarded when I'm operating in white circles.

But maybe it's not me, but them. And you actually think that the new legal-theoretical approaches, besides having more of an emancipatory potential, could lead the way to a more loving, inclusive society?"

"I do. They certainly are less hierarchical. But what postmodern poverty or labor law would look like is anybody's guess. We do have the beginnings of postliberal analysis of race in CRT.[66] And postmodern approaches underlie much of radical feminism, and some of the newer schools of interpretation and constitutional theory."[67]

"But surely, Rodrigo," I said, "you are not saying that an academic movement, subscribed to by a handful of ivory-tower academics and leftists, can lead the way to a revolution in the material and social conditions under which twenty million people live. Doesn't that ascribe far too much efficacy to what we intellectuals do?"

"Of course it does," Rodrigo replied gloomily. "Although in a hundred years, things may look different. Postmodernism is a powerful critique. If it succeeds in mounting a serious challenge to Enlightenment thought, that may lead to new ways of relating to one another and ultimately a new form of society. But I doubt change is anywhere over the horizon."

"You're a complete pessimist, then? You think insight and hard work are not enough?"

"There is little the academy can do. Oh, I suppose one could go around turning off all the TV sets in the ghetto. Or, better yet, blow up all the transmitters.[68] Television is one of the most pervasive purveyors of color imagery there is. That might help a little. But basically I think our troubles are unlikely to yield to a quick or simple fix. The Constitution was color-conscious in its inception, selling out the interests of blacks in no fewer than ten places.[69] Women and the unpropertied were excluded, as well.[70] It was a document shaped by Enlightenment images and structures, one that had white supremacy practically written all over it. The leading Framers had slaves,[71] thought those slaves were intellectually inferior to whites, and equated science and higher thought with European values and civilization. Law, perfectionism, free market economics, and other mechanisms now lock in the system of white-over-black supremacy the Constitution instituted two hundred years ago. There is no need for chains and laws enforcing separate-but-equal. It's all nice and neat, and I'm afraid the system is likely to go on forever."

"We could contest Eurocentric, honorific notions that equate linear thought, mechanics, etc., with whiteness, with superiority, methodically show the narrow, self-serving nature of all the prevailing myths and narratives."

"If that task is done well, I think it can do some good," Rodrigo replied soberly. "The trouble is that white folks will think it's all sour grapes. Or they may quickly embrace 'folkways,' much as they did the Harlem Renaissance, jazz, and other black arts, deeming them interesting and vital—but not really on a par with the Western greats."

"It's the credibility problem again," I said.

"Which, in turn, is part of our construction."

"Which itself is dictated and determined by Enlightenment philosophy. We are not just one-down. We are the kind of people who are created and constructed so as to be unable to change our positions, so as always to be one-down."

"The reductio ad absurdum of the counter-majoritarian principle, which is supposed to be soluble merely by having the right kind of friend in court."

"Well, professor, even if you don't have a friend in court, you have one in me. You're looking a little tired, and the hour is late. You mentioned earlier that you wanted to get a good night's rest after your trip, and here I am keeping you up late. They're starting to stack the chairs. What do you say we try to get a cab?"

"I'm going strong," I protested.

"But I'm out of ideas. I mentioned that my solution was still at the formative stage, that it's much easier to see what's wrong with the world than how to set it right."

As I fished out my credit card and motioned to the waiter that we would like to pay our bill, Rodrigo paused. Then, after the waiter walked away to record our charges, he continued:

"I wonder if you saw that conservative's column the other day. The one that spoofed the spate of women's books that have been coming out?"[72]

"You mean the one that complained that there were so many of them?"

"Yes, that one. The writer complained that all the recent books seem to be about women. He was referring, of course, to perhaps ten or twenty books, mostly by women, on women's problems, like child abuse, the 'three-job syndrome,' menopause, and the like."

"I remember the review. It had a plaintive, almost whiny tone. The author was feeling neglected because none of the books was about him."

The waiter returned with our check and wished us good evening. As I signed the credit slip and started to get up, Rodrigo completed his thought:

"That review drove home to me how perspective works. Tens of thousands of books are published every year, many of them on fishing, hunting, sports, mechanics, war, and so on. Yet to the columnist these did not seem like 'men's books,' but just books. And the small number, amounting to no more than a few dozen or hundred a year that in very recent times have been addressing issues of interest to women, seemed to him to skew the distribution all out of proportion, when in reality a huge majority of books deal with things men want to read about."

"And the moral you draw from this is . . . ?"

"Two things," Rodrigo said, opening the door and helping me get in the cab he had inconspicuously flagged outside the restaurant. "One is that night owls like me should never keep our friends up too late. The second is that racial reform will often seem outlandish, one-sided, and unjust to those who are unused to sharing power. They will oppose and hector us at every turn. Which means, among other things, that we had better take care of each other. And so, Professor, I think we had better continue this another time. We had talked about dinner."

I gave my apartment address to the driver, who had been waiting none too patiently.

"How about next Saturday at our place. Giannina has been dying to have you over."

"I'd love to."

"You're on. I'll call with the address and time."

Conclusion

As I rode rather sleepily homeward through the dark streets, I reflected on what we had said. Rodrigo's ideas on Enlightenment as the source of racial oppression seemed to me plausible, even powerful. I wondered how his new colleagues would see them, and how they would receive this new wunderkind with his audacious ideas. I wondered whether the racial problems of our people were really rooted in some basic flaw of our form of government, so that only a radical reconception of the state could enable us to go beyond cosmetic changes and periodic peaks of progress. Like many, I had grown up thinking that democracy was a good thing, and it pained me somewhat to hear Rodrigo's remorseless indictment, on fairness and formality grounds, perfectionism, color imagery, the association with Calvinism and individualistic mindset, law's contribution to stasis, and free market economics.

I thought how kind and courteous, almost tender, Rodrigo had been of my aging frailties in calling an early halt to the evening and hailing a cab for me. Was that not a root example of democracy, namely, considering the other person's feelings? Or was it socialism?

My reverie didn't last long. "We're here, Professor," the cabby said in a voice just this side of sharpness. I paid, trudged up the steps to my building, and prepared to deal with jet lag and the new week.

8

RODRIGO'S EIGHTH CHRONICLE:
Black Crime, White Fears—On the Social Construction of Threat

Introduction: In Which I Learn about an Event at Rodrigo's Institution

I was staring disconsolately at the flashing light on the vending machine in the student lounge, where I had gone in search of a much-needed late afternoon pick-me-up, when I heard a familiar voice from behind me:

"Professor, do you need some help?"

"Rodrigo!" I said. "It's good to see you." To tell the truth, I felt slightly uncomfortable at being surprised while trying to satisfy my physical needs on someone else's turf, but glad to see a person who might help me out of my predicament.

"What's the problem, Professor? Out of change?"

I stumblingly tried to explain the dilemma that just minutes ago had caused me to curse my fate. "As luck would have it, I have exactly fifty cents in change." I held out my palm with the quarter, two dimes and a nickel. "But the Diet Pepsi I desperately need to keep going costs fifty-five cents. I also have this dollar bill. As you can see, the machine takes dollars, but it won't take mine. It keeps rolling right out. 'Use exact change,' it says. So I'm stuck. Would you have a nickel, by any chance?"

"I wish I did, Professor, but the subway took my last dime. But let me try something. Could I have all that money?"

"Sure," I said, handing it over. "What are you going to do?"

Rodrigo first inserted all my change. Nothing happened. Then, muttering something to himself, he inserted my dollar bill and pressed the button.

Jackpot! The machine disgorged both the Diet Pepsi I had been waiting for and a great clatter of change. Scooping it up, Rodrigo counted it out. "Ninety-five cents, just as I thought."

"How did you know to do that?" I asked appreciatively.

"It's simple, Professor. The machine doesn't have the right change. That's why it can't take your dollar. But if you put everything in, the machine then has enough money to make change for you. And since it's honest—has a simple computer that remembers how much you've put in—you get your change back. And your Diet Pepsi."

"Thanks!" I said. "At my age, I've learned I really need to take an occasional break, especially in the afternoon."

Rodrigo smiled. "Maybe it's a metaphor for all of life, Professor. Sometimes if you put in more than anyone expects, you get more in return."

"My, you are getting upbeat in your old age," I retorted, "especially for someone trained in Bologna and steeped in neo-Marxism and economic-determinist analyses of race. But what brings you around? It's good to see you—it's been a while."

"I was hoping you could give me a few minutes. I tried calling, but your line was busy. I need to run some ideas past you. They're about black crime."

"I'd be happy to talk with you about that. As you know, there's already a burgeoning Critical literature, including the piece by Regina Austin we talked about before.[1] And, of course, there are the three Chronicles by Derrick Bell."[2]

"I'm familiar with those. What I'm really interested in pursuing is the cultural phenomenon itself. I'm intrigued by the way the whole issue tends to be framed."

"What got you started thinking about this?" I asked. "I hope the INS is not on your trail again."

"No, nothing so personal. I'm thinking of adding a section to my dissertation on society's treatment of black crime. Did you hear about the professor at my school who got mugged and sent to the hospital?"

"My God!" I said. "I did. It was just in the paper. There was a lot of talk about it here. Do you know him? How is he doing?"

"No, I don't know him, and he is much better. He had a lot of bruises and a cracked rib or two. But he's back from the hospital now and it looks like he'll recover completely."

"I'm relieved. We were all shocked. Some of us talked about getting more safety features and lighting in the parking lot. I think the administration is going to do something."

"I'm glad, Professor. Not that I don't think you couldn't outrun most thieves. You look pretty fit for a man your age. I imagine you run every day."

"Most days," I replied modestly. "But I don't have the speed I once had. I went running with Professor Bollicker the other day, and immediately regretted it. He's much faster."

"You and I should go jogging one day, Professor. I've started up again. Giannina says it makes me less hyper, and it does help me sleep."

"Maybe sometime. Now, what are your thoughts on black crime? I gather the professor's mugger was black?"

"Well, as it happened he was. And the professor, as you probably know, is white. He's also a much-loved figure around the law school, a veritable institution. Everybody admires him and was furious when he got robbed and sent to the hospital."

"A natural reaction," I replied. "And so where does all this lead you? Are you surprised by the amount of crime you find in this country? I imagine it's greater than when you left. You were a teenager then. It was a safer era."

"I guess it's not the amount of crime that surprises me. I had read about that in Italy. Every major industrialized society has crime. Italy has some, too, although a little less than here—of the violent, interpersonal variety at any rate. What surprises me more is the way it's perceived. The reaction at my law school was a prime example."

I drew myself up in mock horror. "I can't think of a worse crime than mugging a professor," I said. "It's like desecrating a cathedral. Besides, I have so few brain cells left functioning, I fear it would take just one good knock and I'd be finished."

"I agree," Rodrigo said, then blushed. "Not about you, but about what happened to the other professor. It *was* a despicable act. Yet, what surprised me was the way some people generalized the event. I heard snatches of conversation—things like 'those people'; 'something has to be done'; 'they're out of control.' Even white folks I had come to think of as liberals were talking about the 'breakdown of the black family,' and so on. Some of us African-American students felt distinctly uncomfortable, as though people were looking at us, wondering why we didn't do something, wondering if we were going to mug *them*. There was even a graffito in the bathroom: 'Bernhard Goetz was right.'"

"Ugly," I commiserated. "But not exactly new. Every widely publicized black crime seems to bring out the same reaction. I'm sure all this strikes you as shocking, coming from a more peaceful, sunny clime. The U.S. has changed in the last ten or twenty years. You're seeing it with new eyes."

"Maybe so," Rodrigo replied. "And maybe you'll think my vision is a little skewed. That Diet Pepsi is getting warm, Professor." Rodrigo looked in the direction of the unopened can in my hand. "Can I take you somewhere for a drink, or were you in the middle of something? There's a health food bar Giannina and I discovered the other day. It's only a short walk from here. They have fresh fruit juices, salads, and organic soft drinks."

"Organic soft drinks?" I said. "I'll try anything once. Maybe my doctor will approve. She's been trying to get me to cut down on caffeine."

"They also have snacks. I could use one if you have the time."

I recalled my young friend's famous appetite. "Okay," I said. "This will be on me. You paid for the movie the other day."

On the Social Construction of Black Crime

A few minutes later, we were comfortably seated in the health food bar Rodrigo had recommended.

"I've never been to a place like this," I said. "Although I should." I patted my stomach. "I gained a couple of pounds when I visited your homeland earlier this summer. What are you having?"

The waiter arrived and stood by expectantly. "I'm having their Avocado Supreme. It reminds me of something I used to have back at Bologna."

"I'll have the same," I said. After the waiter disappeared with our orders, Rodrigo continued:

"Have you noticed, Professor, how your society—I mean, our society— virtually equates crime and the black underclass, as though they were practically one and the same thing?"

"I have," I answered. "The conservatives want to crack down on it, build walls around their communities,[3] more prisons, and get tougher on what they call 'career criminals.'[4] The liberals, for their part, lament it and want to do something about what they see as the causes of black crime—poverty, lack of jobs, and so on."

"We talked a little about these things before," Rodrigo replied. "But my thinking has taken a slightly different turn since then. The reaction to the professor's mugging got me to thinking. What's common to both the liberals, who want to attack the problem at its root, and the conservatives, who want to solve it with harsher punishment, is that both construct black criminality as *a problem*."

"But it *is* a problem," I insisted. "Rodrigo, I hope you're not going to put me through another one of your postmodern tours-de-force and try to make something disappear which everyone knows exists. Black crime, especially among young black men—your age, I might add—is a serious problem. About one-quarter of young African-American males are caught up in the criminal justice system.[5] The jails are about 45 percent black. Homicide is the leading cause of death for young black men.[6] Drugs and gangs run rampant in the inner city. I hope you're not going to deny the very real pain our community suffers as a result of the criminal activity of its own youth. Nothing could bring you quicker disrepute."

"Not at all," Rodrigo replied mildly. "I know the problem exists. In fact, it touched me just the other day. I was shopping in a men's clothing store, looking for a tie, when the house detective asked me to empty my pockets and book bag. He seemed disappointed when all he found was lecture notes and a leftover apple from my lunch."

"I'm relieved you concede that our young—some of them, at any rate—commit crimes. But you said that you found something about society's perception of those crimes interesting?"

"Yes." Rodrigo stopped for a moment while the waiter put down our plates and asked us if we'd like anything to drink.

"Just a refill," I said, pointing at my water glass.

"Do you have espresso?" Rodrigo asked. He ordered a double and then continued:

"I've been looking at some of the statistics, Professor. And I don't think black criminality is a more serious problem than many other forms of it. But it's interesting to see how we came to think that it is. I believe that, in conjunction with other sociocultural developments, four or five books and a couple of well-known reports played a major role in creating our modern conception of black criminality. Before then, there was simply crime. Some of it was committed by white people, and some by blacks. Then, beginning in the mid-1960s with three national reports,[7] the Moynihan study,[8] the

Blumstein article,[9] and three or four books that I'm sure you're familiar with,[10] the whole thing changed. Now, crime became identified with us—people like you and me, I mean. Before this time, crime was no more identified with us than, say, playing the trombone, having a cold, or any other human activity that crosses racial lines. Everyone knew that many of us were poor and sometimes took things. But so did people of other colorations—it was not seen as a peculiarly black problem."

"I'm not sure that's literally true, Rodrigo," I cautioned. "I have seen some studies of ethnic stereotyping and imagery that seem to indicate the opposite.[11] In certain periods, blacks, Mexicans, and other minority groups of color were depicted as lascivious, immoral, bent on raping white women, and so on. It's a control device. The authors say the images change from period to period, according to whether society needs to justify control, repression, or yet some third position vis-à-vis the group.[12] But the image has been negative in virtually every period, and criminality is often part of it."

"It's the violent, interpersonal type of crime that intrigues me," Rodrigo explained. "Because *that* part of our image has not always been there. In the thirties and forties, for example, everyone knew that young black kids sometimes stole hubcaps. But white kids did, as well. The extraordinarily negative depiction of our people as violent muggers and burglars who might break into your house at night and surprise you with a knife at your throat—that's relatively new."

"Hmmm," I said. "You're not saying it doesn't happen, are you?"

"Not at all. But some people wake up at night, and the burglar is white. Other crimes are committed predominantly by whites, and they're just as devastating as those our people, our kids, perpetrate. At one time in history everyone knew the Irish did one sort of thing, and blacks another. Then the hubcaps became more serious stuff. It became a problem. Then their problem. Then, our problem. Which is where we are today. Everyone wants to crack down on their—I mean our—problem, Professor."

"Rodrigo, as you know I'm not a great fan of your poststructuralist theories. I'm just an earnest plodder trying to work in my own way for racial justice. It seems to me that society could not, as you put it, construct an image of our people as criminal if there were not a grain of truth to it. Some of our young people do commit crimes—violent, interpersonal ones, like the one that laid your professor low. I'm not sure what utility there is in focusing on the social construction angle. If the media were lying, that would be one thing. But there *is* a problem. And isn't it up to us to do something about it? I hope you're not trying to whitewash a serious social problem."

"Not at all, Professor." Rodrigo was silent for a minute. "Can I give you an illustration from another area?"

"Of course."

"Consider a different example, namely that of the teenager. In some ways teenagers are the opposite of blacks. They are a relatively favored segment of our society. Everyone tolerates their foibles. They have a lot of free time. Marketers are always trying to sell them things. They have allowances, and so on."

"Well, that's the social image," I replied. "Although the reality is often quite different. Some teenagers are troubled, work twenty hours a week, take care of their younger brothers and sisters, and so on."

"I'm not denying any of that. I'm just asking you to question where the concept came from. Today, it's part of the culture. But it was not always there."

"It wasn't?"

"The flesh-and-blood humans were always there, of course. People between the ages of 12 and 20 or so, who stand about three-fourths to four-fifths of their final height and have been or are going through puberty—those have always been there. But that's not to say there have always been teenagers."

"You mean no special term for them?"

"Exactly. They were just human beings who happened to be between those two ages. They had no more special status than people between the ages of five and twenty-two, or thirty-seven and forty-eight."

"No special name for them," I said. "No category of their own."

"Nor any special clothes, magazines, marketing strategies, or musical groups. Before the category was created, teenagers were just medium-high people who went through the daily tasks of life. Some mowed lawns. Most went to school. And so on."

"I see what you're saying," I said. "A self-conscious interest group, whose main purpose is to consume things—such a category would be wonderful for the economy."

"I'm not so sure I'd be quite that deterministic, Professor. But the category does serve certain purposes. In that sense, it didn't just happen. By the same token, there were periods in history when blacks were not seen as particularly criminal. Hapless, perhaps. Carefree, musically talented, lazy, happy-go-lucky—you name it, the many sides our image takes on from time to time, none of them particularly flattering."[13]

"But you think the criminal image whites imposed upon blacks came about as a response to some social need, perhaps for repression?"

"It would certainly serve that purpose," Rodrigo replied. "A group that is criminal, vicious, animal-like, with designs on white people's lives and pocketbooks—such a group would need to be controlled. At other periods such an image would not serve society's purposes, for example when blacks (or members of other racial groups) were needed for their labor or for service during wartime."

The waiter arrived to take our dessert orders. "Would you like something?" I asked. "Please go ahead. I'm thinking of trying their *gelato*."

"It *is* good here," Rodrigo replied. "Giannina and I had some last time. It's not quite like what we have back in Italy. But it's the next best thing."

In a moment, the waiter had taken our orders and disappeared. I looked at Rodrigo expectantly.

"The social construction of us as criminal did not come about by accident," he continued. "There were black breakthroughs and successes in the 1960s and early 1970s.[14] The need for repression set in shortly afterward as a way of limiting our gains."[15]

The waiter set down our desserts. "That looks good," I said. "What kind are you having?"

"Mandarino," he replied. "What's yours?"

"Lime. I'm counting calories. But back to your point. Other ethnic groups had crime, too: Irish rum-running, Italian numbers rackets. Mayor Daley's machine in Chicago. Tammany Hall. And others that come to mind, as well. What's the difference between the social construction of these other groups and ours?"

"There are two or three differences," Rodrigo said. "First, the kind of crime we associated with these other groups was often relatively harmless. At any rate, we winked at it, tolerated it, smiled at it, almost. Second, to the extent to which members of these white ethnic groups actually engaged in it, the group benefited. Crime, for many, was a way of upward mobility, a means by which fortunes were amassed and family empires created. The next generation left crime when their parents sent them to college. They became senators and members of Congress, had country homes, opened or managed legitimate businesses."

"So crime was a path of upward mobility for other immigrant groups, but one that was denied for us?"

"Correct," Rodrigo replied. "For African-Americans alone this avenue was closed. Society decided to repress, not tolerate, crime from our group."

I made a mental note to ask Rodrigo about something later, but instead asked, "Why do you think that was so? I assume you have a theory?"

"Nothing especially original," Rodrigo replied. "We're a large group numerically, so a good deal was at stake. Moreover, society has more to live down with respect to us. And, of course, there's the color question. For all these reasons, society decided fairly recently that it did not want us to get ahead in this way. The notion of the sinister, out-of-control black served this purpose admirably."[16]

"Rodrigo, I hope you're not saying there was something like a conscious conspiracy. That strikes me as a little paranoid."

"No," Rodrigo replied. "Not any more than the creation of the teenager was a conscious conspiracy. No group of executives sat down and said, 'Let's see. What group can we create that will have a lot of money to spend and that we can persuade to buy clothes and magazines and make-up and music?' Yet, the category did get created, did operate to produce benefits to the merchandising sector. I think that good and bad categories just sort of come about naturally, with little effort or conscious design, when society needs them to appear."

"I wish I could be convinced," I said. "It sounds almost too pat."

"Let's walk back to your office, Professor. Do you still have your computer?"

"Yes," I nodded.

"And it's still hooked up to your databases?"

I nodded yes, and Rodrigo gestured for the waiter. "I've been doing some research on just this question."

I wasn't sure what he meant by "just this question," but wanted to hear what he was looking into, so I said, "Sure, come on over. I have some new art work up in my office. I think I told you that I was lucky enough to get a permanent job here, following that one-semester visit. So we're neighbors. At least until you go off somewhere else."

"I'd like very much to see your stuff, Professor. I loved that poster you had of the State Fair."[17]

As we walked out of the little restaurant, Rodrigo looked at me and said,

"I hope you'll be careful, Professor. Even the streets around here aren't one hundred percent safe. We need to have you around for a while."

I mumbled something about being neither that old nor hard to replace, and a few minutes later we were walking up the steps of the law building to my office.

Rodrigo's Third Printout: The Statistics and Politics of Crime

"Say, you've rearranged things. The computer used to be over there."

The alert Rodrigo pointed out my recent redecorating efforts, of which I was proud. "Yes, I moved all the plaques over to that wall, the couch over there, and switched my desk and computer to face the window. What do you think?"

Rodrigo ignored my question. His eyes were on my computer. "Do you mind if I sit here, Professor? I should have brought my notes. But this should just take a minute."

"Go ahead," I said, moving to where I could see the screen. As he had done once before, Rodrigo's fingers flew over the keyboard. Accessing databases I did not even know existed, he brought up a wealth of information from articles, book abstracts, the U.S. Census, and FBI annual crime reports. I envied his technological wizardry, and lamented that I had come to computers so late in life.

"See, Professor," Rodrigo said, pointing at the screen. "Here are the figures we talked about before. It was in your footnote, as I recall. They show that the total for white-collar crime exceeds the dollar losses from all the crimes associated with African-Americans put together. If you just take . . ." Rodrigo punched a few more keys. "See—if you add all the losses from street robbery, including mugging and purse snatching, and add to them this other figure for . . ." Rodrigo interrupted himself briefly while my screen flashed, dissolved, then flashed again—"for all household burglaries, you get . . ."

I squinted, then said: "A lot of money. It looks like almost $8.3 billion per year."[18]

"Now, we *could* throw in malicious mischief," Rodrigo muttered, punching some other keys. "Oh, yes, I remember where I got that. It's here. See, the total for graffiti is about $600 million."[19]

"That's a lot of losses," I replied. My young friend went on:

"And, oh—here it is. Just as I thought. The figure for white-collar crime is not just higher than the one for street crime. It's . . . let's see . . . *much* higher. I was working on this before but didn't quite finish. I hope you've got a minute, Professor. I have a feeling this will surprise you." Click, click, click. I wondered, once again, how Rodrigo had become so proficient at electronic searching while studying world cultures, then law, in Italy. "What are you trying to do?" I asked.

"I'm trying for a total. Does your computer have a split screen? No, too bad. I was trying to make a running tally. Here, let me borrow some paper— can I use that pad? There. Just as I thought. If you divide out by the proportion of the country that is white and the proportion that is black, it looks like . . . the figures for the sort of crime white people do are greater than the figures for the sorts of crime they associate with us."[20]

"You mean," I said, "that our people commit less crime than people of the majority race?"

"The per person losses are actually a lot lower. I'm assuming, of course, that most white-collar crime is perpetrated by white people—I mean the classic categories of that kind of crime, such as embezzlement, bribery, price-fixing, and insider trading.[21] Actually, I'd better check." Click, click, click. "Here we are. The crime reports. Just as I thought, mostly white. And when you add in *corporate* misconduct—marketing unsafe autos and dangerous pharmaceuticals, Love Canal, the Dalkon Shield, the savings and loan scandal, the General Electric price-fixing conspiracy . . ." click, click, click, "the Lockheed fiasco, Three Mile Island, asbestosis, and Agent Orange—you find that almost all the top executives were white."[22]

"That's really interesting," I said.

"This is more or less where I stopped last time. But, there's more. This is what I was going to do."

I watched quietly as Rodrigo once again performed feats on my computer, stopping only to scribble a new entry on the rapidly growing list of figures on the yellow pad next to him.

"See, Professor. If you add these other figures to the total of white-collar crime that we got earlier . . ." Rodrigo looked down at his list. "For *corporate* crime, including defense procurement fraud and bribery,[23] consumer fraud,[24] and, let's see, oh yes, the savings and loan scandals.[25] You have a net figure of . . . hmmm. It looks like many times the per capita figure for black crime.[26] So, in one way of looking at it, the crime that elite white people do, especially white males, is much more serious than that committed by blacks of all ages and types."

"Amazing," I said. "I wonder why this never comes out?"

"It's inherent in the social construction, Professor. No one focuses on white crime or sees it as a problem. In fact, the very category, 'White Crime,' sounds funny, like some sort of debater's trick."

"But there it is, right in the crime reports," I said.

"Yes, where it's hidden in a mass of statistics where no one focuses on or makes a big production of it. The other kinds, the ones laid out with precise charts in the FBI's annual compilations, attract all the attention and seem like 'the problem.'" Rodrigo gestured toward the electronic bookmark he had stuck in my computer, a feature I did not even know I had.

"Oops!" we both said in unison, as the phone rang loudly. I looked at my watch and remembered the journalist I had promised to speak with around this time, half wishing I had not agreed to talk with her.

"Do you need privacy, Professor?"

It was the journalist. I covered the receiver. "No problem. This shouldn't take long."

Rodrigo pressed a few buttons, my printer started whirring, then he wandered out into the hallway. I was depressed to learn that the journalist, with whom I had spoken before and was friendly, wanted a comment on hate-speech directed at *lawyers*. I had done some writing on hate-speech against blacks, and the journalist wanted to know what I thought of a state bar association president's suggestion that vilifying an attorney be considered a hate crime.[27] I said a few guarded things, tried to explain Harry Kalven's thesis[28]—which the reporter refused to take down as too technical—and after a few minutes hung up. A moment later, Rodrigo walked back in.

"What do you think of my printout?" he asked, gathering up the long, flowing computer sheet my printer had obligingly produced in his absence. "Oh—and what did your journalist friend want to know?"

"I haven't looked at your printout yet, but I will—I'm fascinated by your evidence that white people commit as much crime as our youth do. And, as for the journalist, never mind. Talking to the press is both one of the best and worst aspects of this job, as you'll find out soon enough. Some of them are really smart, understand everything, and take their time to get the story straight. Other times, they just want a quick quote—usually something specific they have in mind and try their best to coax you to say."

"Do you generally oblige them?"

"I do. I think it's important to be helpful and forthcoming to the press, despite the occasional disappointments. Maybe when you start teaching, I'll refer calls to you. I'll tell them, if you don't know the answer you can find out anything in less than thirty seconds. You're pretty good with a computer."

Rodrigo beamed. "I've been working on it. Part of my dissertation is going to be statistical, so I've been boning up. You looked like you were going to ask me something."

"I can't remember what it was."

"Did it have something to do with street crime?" Rodrigo asked. "I was pulling up the figures on muggings when you looked like you wanted to interject."

"Oh. That's right. If you are going to make the case that black crime is a social construction, an illusion, or at any rate no worse than white crime . . ."

"Less bad, actually," Rodrigo interjected quietly.

"Then you're going to need to deal with the objection that black crime is scarier. It's violent. When a savings and loan officer carries out a scam or causes an institution to fail, it costs the investors and depositors money. But losing five hundred or a thousand dollars is not the same as being mugged and sent to the hospital, even if the medical bill turns out to be the same. Embezzling and tax fraud are bad, to be sure. But they're just plain not as terrifying as waking up in the middle of the night and seeing a shadowy figure standing behind a curtain."

"I agree," Rodrigo said.

"And not only that," I continued. "You are going to have to supply at least the outlines of a solution. It's not enough to say that the United States has two kinds of crime, nor that there's a lot of it, maybe even more than in Canada, Sweden, or your own homeland. People here think America is great, the most wonderful country on earth. Your criticism will seem like fly-specking. They'll be mad at you for pointing out that there's more crime than they like to think, and especially mad that you're saying their own group—privileged middle-aged white males—are just as bad as young African-American inner-city toughs, walking the streets in packs of four and looking mean."

"So you want to know my thoughts about violent crime, and also my solution. No small challenge, Professor! These parts of my thesis are not fully fleshed out. But I do have some ideas on how to begin to address them. Can I interest you in a bite of real supper? I noticed on the bulletin board just a minute ago that the Latino Law Students are having a feed in the student lounge. And judging from the smells in the hallway, it's already started. You still like Mexican food, right?"

"I love it," I replied a little ruefully. "But I should eat more of the kind we had before. My doctor's been after me. It is late, though, and she *did* tell me to have lots of small meals as I go through the day . . ."

"Maybe a corn burrito, Professor?" Rodrigo asked solicitously. "They're not too high in calories or cholesterol."

"Tell you what. If you agree to help me hold the line at just one, I'll help you critique the remaining parts of your paper in return."

"It's a deal," Rodrigo said.

In Which Rodrigo Explains His Theory about Violent Crime

Twenty minutes later, as we rode up the elevator, balancing paper plates and munching on the remains of our burritos, Rodrigo continued: "I'm learning to love Mexican food. Italian is my favorite, of course. But for some reason, Mexican is more plentiful in the neighborhood where Giannina and I live. And the prices are a little lower."

"Easier on a student budget," I commiserated, placing my plate on the wooden chair next to my office door while I fished out the key. "Have a napkin," I said once we were inside, indicating a stash on the end of a bookshelf. "I have cold drinks in the mini-fridge. I showed it to you before, right?"

"Yes, you did. I'm not thirsty, but maybe I'll have one of your famous coffees, if you're up to making some."

"I was just thinking that myself. I got in a new supply of beans. You were going to address my objection about violence. Much black crime is violent and, while the net losses from white-collar and black-collar crime may be similar, there's no comparison in terms of their *in terrorem* effect."

Rodrigo looked pensive. "You're right, and I would be the last person to try to excuse muggings or Central Park beatings. Did I tell you I've taken up jogging? Anyway, I think the answer lies in recognizing two things. The one has to do with the construction of reality idea we talked about earlier, the other with the way these figures look in the light this analysis reveals."

"I'd love to hear," I said, flicking the switch to *On* and adding the beans. "I assume you want the real kind, with caffeine?"

I knew the answer already. "I love coffee," Rodrigo said. "And it's not too late. Giannina wants me to cut down. She says coffee makes me too hyper. But if I have my last cup before about six p.m., I find I sleep well."

I poured him a cup, then measured out the decaffeinated beans from the other jar.

"Mmmm. This is good. You make some of the best coffee I've had since leaving Italy, Professor."

"So, a new construction of crime and a sharper look at the statistics will yield an answer to our problem?" I prodded.

"Have you ever wondered about all the white people's derelictions that are not crimes at all, but torts or administrative offenses, punishable if at all by fines, but rarely imprisonment?[29] At the same time, the things that black and poor people do—shoplifting, stealing hubcaps, joy riding, selling or buying marijuana, can net you quite a few months or years behind bars."

"I have noticed. It seems to me that society has neatly arranged to have the types of things high-level executives do—even ones that are clearly unethical or antisocial—be handled nonpenally, the same way they handle the youthful indiscretions of clean-cut suburban youth. You rarely hear of a corporate executive going to jail—for long, at any rate—even if the malfeasance is fairly serious, like marketing DES or Ford Pintos once these products are known to be lethally dangerous.

"No one thinks of these as violent crimes, but of course they are. We treat them as a case of boys-will-be-boys, as ordinary, red-blooded business zeal that got a little out of hand. The perpetrators rarely serve prison sentences. If they do, it makes the news—and then they're out again in a few months."[30]

"I read of one that was quietly released just the other day. He had been sentenced to several years for bilking the public of millions of dollars. A few months later, he was walking the streets again."[31]

"Much such misconduct isn't even treated as a crime. For example, I'm sure you've heard of doctors who perform Cesarean sections on women during childbirth, not out of medical necessity but for the doctor's convenience.[32] Giannina was reading an article the other day on excessive medical procedures—including mammograms and hysterectomies for women and prostate operations for men.[33] These cost millions of dollars a year, and result in a great deal of pain and in some cases, deaths, yet are almost never included in the yearly totals for white-collar crime."

"I've read, too," I added, "of physicians who refer patients for laboratory tests to facilities in which the doctors have an interest. These result in more unnecessary tests, with all the inconvenience, expense, and in some cases pain that these entail."[34]

"There are also many deaths each year caused by the marketing of infant formula in Third World countries."

"Yes. The mother frequently cannot read the preparation instructions, because they are printed in English. Sometimes, the mother simply cannot read. Safe water for mixing the formula is almost never available. The result is an expensive but unsafe formula to replace the mother's perfectly safe and completely free breast milk. Even if the mother eventually realizes that the formula is causing her baby's illness, she has stopped lactating. Her baby will die."[35]

"None of this is regarded as a crime," Rodrigo went on. "And then there is toxic dumping. We've already mentioned the sale and marketing of dangerous products. Toxic dumping adds another several thousand deaths a decade."[36] Rodrigo gestured toward my computer. "Mind if I turn that on again?" I waved no, so he continued. "Let me see, where did I find that figure for dumping. Let's try fulltext and Love Canal. Oh, look, here's the atomic fallout test case, *Allen v. United States*.[37] Add a few thousand more thyroid cancers. . . ." Rodrigo stopped to jot a few more figures down on the yellow pad, rapidly filling up with numbers. "And here's one on children's car seats.[38] For some reason I didn't bring that one up before. And if you add . . ."

Rodrigo was silent for a moment while he added up a column of figures. "How many white people did we say there are in the country? Okay, divide out and we get . . . oh, look. Once again, just about the same. Hmm. Actually a little higher for the whites. And if you add undeclared wars . . ."

"Undeclared wars?" I asked.

"They're illegal, and they kill you just as dead. Every last one violates the War Powers Act,[39] not to mention the Constitution, which provides that only Congress can declare a war.[40] All the others are technically illegal. Virtually all also violate international law, including treaties to which the United States is a signatory, like the United Nations Charter.[41] Tens of thousands of lives lost, millions if you go back to the two world wars. These are things that elite whites do. They kill and cripple. They are violent crimes, just like rape, homicide, and assault and battery, and but for our social construction of black crime, these white-collar crimes would have the same *in terrorem* effect as street crime currently does."

"And if you add them in?" I asked.

"I had the figure before, when Giannina and I were doing this back at our place. But I'd better not rely on memory. Let's see. Wars. Where did I get that. Oh, I know—let's try this. There we are. Over 40 million deaths, if you go back just through the Second World War.[42] If you include noncombatants and deaths on the other side . . . Oh, here we are. All wars—over 87 million since the beginning of the century."[43]

Rodrigo scribbled again while I watched transfixed.

"If you add wars and military excursions, elite whites cause about three times the number, I mean ratio, of deaths and dismemberments, as blacks.[44] Without wars, they're only slightly ahead." Rodrigo turned off my computer.

"Well, Professor?"

"You can't be sure that no African-American sat on the board of the corporation that marketed DES or dumped toxic wastes into Love Canal. And a recent Chief of Staff, as you know, was black—Colin Powell." I quickly realized how lame my challenge sounded, so retracted it.[45] "On the whole, though, I have to admit, in the United States, at any rate, white folks have caused more death by violence than anyone else. And that's not even including slavery."

"That's at least another 7 to 14 million deaths[46]—more if you add the Indians," Rodrigo replied soberly. "And of course Amnesty International and other organizations have been after us for years to reduce our number of executions, which in their opinion is far too high.[47] Higher than in any other nation except the old Soviet Union."

"Not to mention that we alone execute the mentally retarded and the under-age,"[48] I said.

"Death row is disproportionately black, as the Georgia study showed.[49] Juries convict black men who commit crimes against white victims at a rate several times greater than when the victim is black.[50] The jails are nearly half black,[51] and over 60 percent minority.[52] All these are crimes in the eyes of many international authorities."

"And of course it's not black people who are declaring these wars, operating these criminal justice systems that treat black offenders so harshly."

"In general, no. And, studies of race-by-race sentencing show that black offenders are punished more harshly than whites for the same offense, right across the board."[53]

"I hadn't realized that," I said. "But it stands to reason."

We were both silent for a minute. "I think neither of us gets much pleasure from these dreary statistics," Rodrigo said. "But I think it's important to get them out, because without them, our people become more and more demonized. Society deems us the source of its miseries, the insecurity of life in the cities, the reason why life today is not as safe, not as sweet as it used to be. These are unfortunate facts, and no one can blink them."

"But laying them at our doorstep is not fair," I summarized. "The empirical analysis you just conducted showed we should be *more* fearful of the depredation caused by white-collar crime than by street crime. It's more serious, more common, *and* more hurtful."

"Crime and suffering in the ghetto are serious problems. No reasonable person should dismiss them. Conservatives and progressives alike ought to be working to ameliorate the pain, the poverty, the blighted lives that occur there. The dropout, infant mortality, and incarceration figures for the poor black community are tragic. But the challenge is to find an approach that recognizes that crime and delinquency are society-wide problems, not ours exclusively."

"I gather you've been thinking about that challenge," I said.

"I have some ideas—an outline, little more. If you'd like to hear I'd love the feedback. My draft's not due 'til the end of the summer. It doesn't need to be a long chapter, but I think I need to talk about solutions."

"Let's hear what direction your thinking is going in."

In Which Rodrigo Proposes His Solution to the Crime Problem

Rodrigo reached for the pad of yellow paper. "I hope you don't mind if I take notes. I find that talking with you stimulates me, Professor."

"No more than it does me," I said. "As I think I mentioned before, I'm participating in a Federalist Society debate next month, and someone is sure to bring up the crime-and-punishment question. This talk is helping me at least as much as you."

"You're a good friend, Professor. I like the way you push me. This part of my thesis I've told to no one except Giannina. So I really value your opinion."

"Please go on," I said.

"I think the key lies in getting a handle on white-collar crime, including the corporate variety. It would help, too, if we could cut down on military crimes—mainly all those undeclared wars. Defense procurement fraud is a big item, but it's all those young bodies, brains, and bones that bother me. If we could reduce white-collar, corporate, and military crime and adventurism, I think we could make the desert bloom."

"We'd all be safer, surely, but how would that help our people, particularly our youth who are caught up in gangs, crack, drugs, drop out of school, and get pregnant at depressingly early ages?"

"It wouldn't address these issues directly," Rodrigo conceded. "Although reducing military adventurism would save many young black lives. Most of the gain would be indirect. If my calculations are right," Rodrigo looked down at his scratch sheet, "the average American loses between five hundred and a thousand dollars a year to white-collar crimes. If you define the category broadly, to include corporate fraud and misconduct, the figure is even higher."[54]

"That's a lot of money," I replied. "Are you sure of your figures?"

"They're about what I got before," Rodrigo said. "I can leave you this printout, and you can check for yourself."

"Thanks. I appreciated it when you did that before. It made my job easier. So, what do you think we could do to stem the tide of white-collar crime? And even if we did, why do you think society would want to spend any of the savings to relieve the pain and poverty of ghetto youth, rather than apply it for lower taxes, trips to Disneyland, a second car, or that long delayed family vacation overseas?"

"Let me try to deal with each of those separately," Rodrigo said.

I sat back expectantly.

Wherein Rodrigo Explains How He Would Go about Reducing White (-Collar) Crime

"To reduce the excess amount of crime white people commit, especially those in the executive suite, I think we have to go to the source of it."

"And that source is . . . .?" I asked.

"The white family," Rodrigo replied.[55] "That and the crime/tort loophole we discussed a minute ago. The two work together. White people's peculiar family structure inclines them to commit certain kinds of crimes, engage in certain kinds of antisocial behavior. And the soft treatment they afford each other when they're caught encourages them to act irresponsibly, never to develop a full sense of responsibility for their acts."

"I'd love to hear more about the kinds of family pathology you have in mind. I think I have a pretty good grasp on what you mean by soft treatment of offenders, by coddling of white-collar and corporate criminals. But it's the family dynamics that interest me right now." (I had both a professional and personal interest in the relation of families to crime. As Rodrigo had been speaking, I remembered with a slight pang an incident in our own past when my wife and I had received a call from the neighborhood police station. Our eldest son had been arrested on suspicion of shoplifting. He was only ten at the time, and was later cleared, but the experience had left a deep impression on all three of us.)

"Would you like a cup of coffee first?" I asked.

Rodrigo nodded vigorously, so I got up, motioning him to continue while I prepared the espresso machine for another batch.

Getting to the Root of the Problem: The White Family Structure

As I busied myself measuring out the ingredients, Rodrigo began:

"As we were saying, Professor, white-collar and related crimes are a serious social problem. They are committed mostly by white folks, and their net social costs exceed those of street crime by a large margin. Indeed, if my figures are correct, they exceed those committed by the black population on a per capita, not just a net basis. Many of them go unpunished, even though they cause injury, disfigurement, and death. Moreover, the amount of personal violence associated with this type of misdeed is greater, on both bases, than that associated with black crime."

"Here's your coffee."

Rodrigo stirred in some creamer and his trademark four teaspoons of sugar and began slurping his drink. After a short interval, he continued:

"We need a major study of the white family. Social scientists could examine what features are contributing to the large amount of white-collar crime associated with it. Psychologists would study the contribution of child-rearing patterns, punishment, inculcation of attitudes toward authority, TV-watching, and so on. Sociologists would try to figure out whether mobility, changes in jobs and job security, and divorce have anything to do with it.

Statisticians would look for correlations—all converging on the central problem of high levels of white-collar crime, particularly ones of stealth and theft."

"And I suppose you have a hypothesis regarding what they will find if they do?"

"I do," Rodrigo replied. "Crimes of stealth and theft tend to be associated with small family size. In Italian culture, for example, families tend to be larger. There are more generations under one roof, with grandparents and aunts living with the nuclear couple and their children. The children get plenty of adult attention.[56] Plus, there's always someone there to watch them. There are very few latchkey children. For all those reasons, there is much less theft, even when you take into account that it is a much poorer country."

"Some American corporate criminals I have read about come from large families."

"I know. Small size is not the only factor. Many American families—upper-class, white ones, I mean—are also intensely private. Every child has his or her own bedroom. Children are urged to cover up. There is little nudity, even when the child is very small, and so on. I have a suspicion that this encourages a spirit in which crimes of silence, of secrecy can flourish. A third element is acquisitiveness. In the U.S., most children quickly learn that material things—toys, the latest clothes, musical equipment, and so on—are a measure of their worth. For some, later in school, this takes the form of competition for the highest grades. Little wonder that children raised in such a warped atmosphere grow up committing one of the highest rates of white-collar crime in the world."

"Competitiveness isn't so bad. It enabled us to develop the wilderness, set up a commercial empire, invent new machines and medical cures."

"But not when it spills over into the realm of crime," Rodrigo retorted, "as it too often does. For example, in my law school, one of the librarians told me that books disappear all the time. Imagine—stealing a book! In some societies this would be unthinkable. And, one of my fellow students, who is in the J.D. program, told me that during exam and moot court times, people scissor pages and whole articles out of bound volumes. The library has to Xerox or buy a replacement sheet or article, and glue it back into place. This looks funny—I've seen them—and must cost a fortune."

"I'm sure it does."

"And then this attitude spreads into the world of work," Rodrigo continued. "Corporations have learned that they can make more money by taking over each other, by issuing fraudulent or near-fraudulent junk bonds, and so on, much more easily than they can by working hard to sell better products or services.[57] I ran into an old friend who is now working for the mergers and acquisitions department of a major law firm on the other side of the river. He says they have a saying: 'We make money the old fashioned way—we take it.'"

"Even when legal, there's obviously a limit to how long American business can go on simply buying and selling and taking over each other," I said.

"But hardly anyone thinks to ask that question. The prevailing ethic and family structure tell all who grow up in the culture that if you can get away with taking something—if no one sees you or the law doesn't flatly pronounce it criminal—it's okay to do it. There is no ethics, no social network of caring or responsibility. It all goes back to the family structure."

"Of course, that's the same accusation they make against us—that our families are pathological, too many single mothers, gangs, irresponsibility, and so on."

"There is some of that," Rodrigo acknowledged. "But the black family is the strangest possible scapegoat for America's social ills today. The real causes of our economic downturn, of our festering cities, and soaring unemployment rate, are white-collar crime and corruption."

"You think it's that pervasive?"

"I do. But leaving that aside, the train of abuses I just documented for you on your computer is largely the source of our business downturn. Today the U.S. has only the world's fifth strongest economy.[58] It used to be first by a large margin. And to return to your question, yes, I think the solution to blacks' problems is interconnected with the solution to whites' problems."

"You mean in the sense that any general benefit redounds to the improvement of all?"

"In more than that 'trickle-down' sense, Professor. I believe the connecting link is the great middle class and its sense of what we can and cannot do as a nation."

I probably looked puzzled, for Rodrigo stopped for a moment, drained his coffee cup and continued:

"The white middle class has most of the votes. And currently, they will not vote for, or tolerate, costly programs that benefit the black poor. And the reason is not hard to understand: The members of the middle class are themselves hurting. Both parents in many families are already working, yet the families are barely able to make ends meet. Their own children are exhibiting social pathology because of the inattention they receive at home. And the economic indicators show that things are unlikely to get better soon."[59]

"In an atmosphere like that, no one is likely to feel generous toward outgroups, toward people even poorer, more desperate than oneself."

"No, but if we could get a grip on white-collar crime, there would be an immediate improvement in everyone's situation. Look at the figures we jotted down earlier—five hundred dollars per year per American citizen, not even counting the costs of wars and other military aggressions.[60] If every family had that much more in their pocket, they might be more generous toward those who have even less. We could help young black men in trouble. We could have Head Start programs and pediatric care for every black youngster. We could turn things around, reduce the amount of pain and desolation in our inner cities—not overnight, but in relatively short order."

"We could even give some of the white people's land back to the Indians," I said.

Rodrigo shot me a piercing look. "I'm serious," I said. "It's not a minor issue."

"I'm glad," Rodrigo replied. "Because it's a serious issue with me, too. Our indigenous tribes have poverty, dropout, and suicide rates that are some of the worst in the world. It's time society took making amends seriously."[61]

"And you think that by encouraging white folks to get a grip on their own criminality, rein in the malefactors and malefactors-to-be in their midst, all this would become possible?"

"Five hundred dollars per person is a lot of money. Right now, neither the money nor the spirit is there. The money has flowed into the pockets of the corporate elite, which is richer and more confident than ever before, while the middle class of all colors is hurting.[62] If we clamped down on the tax cheats, procurement fraud artists, and so on, the average American taxpayer would have a lower bill, would see more returns on his or her money, and would be less reluctant to vote for programs that benefit the poor and the black underclass."

"But what makes you think that the extra money will change people's political views? The average conservative middle-class voter will attribute the windfall to his own hard work and ingenuity. He will continue to believe that he is comfortable because he deserves it and that the poor are in their position because they have gotten what they deserve. And the wealthier may not even notice the extra money; they may simply notice with disapproval that the law is really cracking down on them, but that the kid who stole their hubcaps has yet to be apprehended."

"I'm sure some will react that way," Rodrigo conceded.

"And even if the extra money is there and if the taxpayers are willing to use that money for the benefit of all society, rather than for their trip to Disneyland or Susie's tuition, I am not sure that they would agree to have that money spent on the underclasses. Many middle-class people believe that too much is being spent already on 'those people.' And with the recent emphasis on the deficit and national debt, I'm not sure the middle class want to raise taxes only to increase spending. They want deficit reduction."

Rodrigo shot me a quizzical look, then replied:

"Yes, and we thought that third party candidates couldn't have much of an impact on national elections. But I don't guess I'm saying that the spirit to deal with the oppressive conditions of the inner city will necessarily come with the financial means of doing so. What I am saying is that, in these recessionary times, if we don't come up with the money by cutting waste or crime then the desire to help the plight of the poor will definitely not be there. With the extra money, the will may come."

"That is still a very optimistic view of things for a neo-Marxist."

"I realize that, Professor, but there is more. Even if the middle class does not see the savings or attribute them to the crackdown on white-collar crime, some of the savings will automatically accrue to the poorer classes. Particularly the savings from consumer fraud. Because the poor spend a higher percentage of their income on consumption than do the middle class or the wealthy, they will receive a higher proportion of their income in savings than will the wealthy."

"And with that higher income will come improvements in quality of life, and with that will come less of a need to steal and commit the various other street crimes that we talked about."

"Cracking down on white-collar crime can help two ways. There will be benefits from the savings automatically accruing to the poor as well as to the middle class. And there is a chance that the extra money will help the middle class get out of its own financial bind and enable it to think about others."

"But you would still have what you call the social construction problem, would you not?"

"I think this would ease as society began to see that our folks do not include the biggest and worst criminals by a long shot. They would see us for what we are—a population that contains many poor, some desperate, people living lives of danger because of the legacy of slavery, racism, and separate-but-equal treatment. Americans can be generous toward groups they do not see as demonized—flood victims, for example."[63]

"Or children lost in the bottom of a well," I added.[64]

"You have put your finger on an important point, though, Professor, one I'll have to ponder. I've argued that the social need generated the stigma-picture, the stereotype of the black criminal. The question is, if we could destroy that stereotype would things reverse—would the repression and cold treatment wither away, or would it return in yet another form and supported by yet another rationalizing structure?"

"That's a tough question," I replied. "It has to do with one's basic attitude to human nature, the fundamental goodness or badness of mankind. Some days, I think our people will not overcome, that we will never be saved, that we will be doomed to enjoy at most periodic peaks of progress, followed by a sickening thud as we fall right back where we started from—that white self-interest calls the tune. When it serves the purpose of elite whites to permit us an occasional 'breakthrough,' then we get a *Brown v. Board of Education* or Civil Rights Act of 1964. Right now it seems to be in the self-interest of powerful and articulate whites to depict us as criminals. I doubt we'll escape that stereotype until conditions change."

"Some white folks will listen," Rodrigo replied, a little hesitatingly. "My thesis advisor is white, and he seems genuinely open."

"But it's the opinion makers who really count," I replied. "And for all his brilliance, your professor really is not an opinion maker in the way the humblest reporter, news broadcaster, or assistant city mayor is."

Conclusion

We both sat back in my rapidly darkening office. The night was falling. I knew Rodrigo and I would soon have to make our ways back to our respective shelters, me to my nearby apartment, he to his and Giannina's place across town. The coffeepot's red switch glowed faintly in the gathering gloom. I reflected on the powerful case Rodrigo had made, both with statistics and interest-convergence, social-construction-of-reality theory, for why our people are invested these days with such a devastatingly negative image. I wondered if there was any hope for its abatement. Only strong friends with access to and a command of the media, the mechanisms of public information and opinion, could help us, I thought. I reflected on the huge costs of that other kind of crime and wondered what chance, if any, our nation had of bringing it under control. Further, if we did, what assurance was there that the gains would be transferred, put to the benefit of poor families in the ghetto?

The phone rang again. I picked it up, and as I feared, Rodrigo stood up and indicated he had to go. "By the way, Professor," he mouthed, "your office looks very nice."

I nodded, listened to the phone for a moment, then smiled broadly. Covering the receiver I told Rodrigo, who was about to disappear out my door:

"It's the reporter. She wants to know how to spell 'Harry Kalven'!"[65]

9

RODRIGO'S FINAL CHRONICLE:
Cultural Power, Law Reviews,
and the Attack on
Narrative Jurisprudence

Introduction: Rodrigo and I Meet at the AALS

I was sipping a cup of nondescript institutional tea in hopes of soothing my
jangled nerves in the low-budget take-out restaurant in the basement of the
huge, 1200-room hotel where the AALS was holding its annual meeting.[1] It
was only the third day of the conference, and I felt wearier than usual. I
wondered whether this was because of my advancing age, or because I was
simply suffering from overload. Too many colleagues, too many hyperkinetic
five-minute conversations with persons I hadn't seen in years, too many
panels, too many speeches.

I had escaped to the dimly lit dive in hopes of dodging the flocks of highly
wired law professors, all dressed in neat suits and carrying green vinyl AALS
briefcases, who frequented the more high-toned eating establishments upstairs. This year's meeting was being held in a resort city and many of the
conferees had brought their families. Along the restaurant wall a group of
young teenagers were playing at the video arcade. After the steady diet of

high-paced talk I had been bombarded with the last three days, their aimless chatter oddly reassured me.

I was halfway through my tea and had just noticed that my hands were no longer shaking when I heard a familiar voice from behind me.

"Professor!"

I looked up. "Rodrigo! What are you doing here?"

"I'd been hoping to run into you," my young friend and protégé replied. "But this place is crawling with law professors. No offense intended, but after awhile they start to look all the same. I'd practically given up, when I came down here. And here you are."

"I like your beard," I said. "How long have you been in Orlando?"

"Four days. I came for the new professors' workshop, then stayed on. Giannina joined me yesterday. We're both on a panel tomorrow."

"I came down here to get away, but to tell the truth I'm delighted to see you. Sit down. I was going to leave a note on the message board if I didn't run into you soon. How are things going with your new position in the Midwest? And did you and Giannina ever figure out how to arrange things with your far-flung jobs and the commute?"

"It's not working out too badly. She's keeping her place in the Village and I got a flat in town not far from the airport. We take turns commuting. She says her total travel time to come see me is no greater than that of some of her friends who take the train to work every day."

"How's the teaching going?"

Rodrigo looked up to catch the waiter's attention. "Not bad. Do you mind if I join you? I could use a cup of coffee or a snack."

"Not at all. I have nothing on my calendar tonight except getting caught up on what has been happening with you."

"The classes are a lot of work. Fall semester I had two new preps, but this spring I have just my seminar. I finished grading my bluebooks last night in the hotel, and I'm looking forward to getting some writing done, starting next week, in fact."

"You don't waste any time," I said admiringly. "What are you going to write about?"

"Either trusts and estates . . ."

I must have made a face, because Rodrigo quickly said, "I know. It's one of the courses they assigned me. But I have a topic that I find kind of interesting. The other one is civil rights. Actually, I was hoping to ask your advice on something. Whichever one I write first, I'm thinking of writing in the narrative, or storytelling, mode."[2]

"Storytelling?" Secretly, of course, I was delighted, since I had been writing in that mode myself, indeed am considered to have made a modest contribution to the genre. Yet no one was more aware of its risks than I.

"Rodrigo, as you must know, the whole movement is under attack.[3] Some consider it mushy, unrigorous, even nonlegal. You should think carefully before writing in that vein, unless you have exceptional colleagues. It might be best to hold off until you have tenure."

"I've heard of the attack on narrativity, in fact, I've been reading about it right now. I'd love to talk things over with you, if you have the time, because I'm genuinely undecided."

The waiter appeared. "Are you gentlemen ready to order?"

In Which Rodrigo and I Discuss the Critique of Narrativity and What a Young Professor Should Do

A few minutes later, we were finishing our sandwiches—pastrami on Rodrigo's part, a vegetarian special on mine—when Rodrigo looked up and began:

"As I see it, the attack on narrative scholarship takes two or three forms. Farber and Sherry say that narrative writing, especially within Critical Race Theory, rests on essentialist premises,[4] which of course isn't true. None of us is under the illusion that *all* minority scholars write in the voice of color, much less that we always employ narratives or stories."[5]

"Of course not," I said. "Derrick Bell's famous 'Serving Two Masters' article[6] is a classic of the cases-and-policies mode. And every now and then one of us tosses off the standard 300-footnote blockbuster full of case-crunching citations and cites to Fuller and Dworkin."

"The kind that are passing into history."

"Agreed. Yet other Critical Race scholars do write chronicles, parables, and narratives. We use them to explore ideology and mindset. Stories are a great device for probing the dominant narrative. We use them to examine presupposition, the body of received wisdoms that pass as truth but actually are contingent, power-serving, and drastically disadvantage our people."[7]

"But these are exactly the types of writing that are under siege right now. In addition to the essentialist accusation, Farber and Sherry charge that stories—our kind, at any rate—are inauthentic, atypical, and untrue. Moreover, they are apt not to be tied adequately to legal analysis and doctrine. They wonder why articles of this sort appear in the law reviews, and ask why law schools should give their authors tenure. There is no way to evaluate them, because they are *sui generis* and fall outside the scholarly paradigm."[8]

"That's not all," I added. "Scholars like Mark Tushnet say we don't merely fall outside the scholarly paradigm. We are positively damaging it.[9] The degradation of constitutional discourse, of which he not so delicately accuses us, includes flat-out lying and distortion, carried out by some of the genre's best exponents.[10] He also accuses us of playing politics with our stories, of choosing just one interpretation—say racism—in explaining an incident at a clothing store, for example, when other explanations are just as valid."[11]

"Pretty harsh," Rodrigo replied. "But we do have our defenders. Tom Ross,[12] Gary Peller,[13] Jane Baron,[14] and Kathy Abrams[15] write of the legitimacy and power of narratives, and the way they help readers understand the social world."

"Don't forget a third group," I added. "There's a vast iceberg out there of skeptics who are basically friendly to narrative scholarship, but want us to play by conventional rules. I'm thinking of people like Ed Rubin[16] and Mary Coombs.[17] They think it's fine if we write in stories and narratives, so long as we can be evaluated and graded in some way. They're worried that when young firebrands like you come up for tenure, their colleagues won't have the slightest idea how to vote. They won't understand what you've written, or if they do, won't know how to evaluate it. With case analysis the norms are well understood. But who's to say if Derrick Bell's *Chronicle of the Space Traders*[18] is better or worse than Patricia Williams's Benetton's story,[19] or Marie Ashe's *ZigZag Stitching* piece?"[20]

"That's not so hard," Rodrigo said. "Pungency, irony, insight, vividness. Illumination of a new perspective or angle of analysis. Narrative coherence. I don't see why it's so difficult to come up with criteria. The ones I just mentioned would be a start."

"I agree that eventually those ideas may take hold. But in the meantime, narrative writing is highly controversial. You know, of course, about Lani Guinier.[21] And how Derrick Bell had to leave Harvard."[22]

"But she didn't write narratives. And Derrick left on principle, because his school refused to hire a black woman."

"But his narrative scholarship may have played a part. And she was a Critical Race Theorist who challenged current notions of political and electoral fairness."

Two of the boys from the video parlor interrupted us politely to ask if we had any change. Rodrigo and I exchanged amused looks, dug deep into our pockets, produced what we had, and the youths nodded wordlessly and ran off.

"Nice kids. Where were we? Oh—maybe we need to distinguish different kinds of storytelling," Rodrigo continued. "I've noticed that there are at least two types, with one being much more controversial than the other."

"And the two are . . . ?" I coaxed.

"Actually there are three. On our side, there is the so-called 'agony' tale, or first-person account, usually of some outrage the author suffered.[23] And then there is the 'counterstory,' the one that mocks, jars, displaces, or attacks some majoritarian tale or narrative, such as without intent, no discrimination; or, the free market will drive out discriminators, or some other such tenet of the majoritarian faith."[24]

"And you mentioned that one of these is more controversial than the other?"

"Yes, by far."

"Which one?"

"Everyone loves the agony tale. They find them so poignant, so moving, so authentic, so true. They accept them immediately, call them poetic and soulful."[25]

"I agree," I said. "The reaction often reminds me of the Harlem Renaissance, when white folks discovered black culture. Suddenly, black writers, jazz musicians, and painters found themselves in vogue, their work a counterbalance for the predictability and blandness of the broader culture.[26] But you think counterstories are another story, so to speak."

"Yes, they don't go over nearly as well. Consider, for example, the strong reaction Derrick Bell's *Chronicle of the Space Traders* elicited. The point of the Chronicle is that white self-interest drives the civil rights movement, accounting for the many zigs and zags of our racial history. It ends by showing that white America would sell out the cause of black rights today, just as it did two hundred years ago, if the price were right."

"When one of us takes on one or more of these comforting myths of racial progress, of course there is trouble. But you mentioned that there is a third kind of story."

Rodrigo was silent for a moment. "Oh, yes. There is the majoritarian story or tale. White folks tell stories, too. But they don't seem like stories at all, but the truth. So when one of them tells a story such as, the pool is so small, or affirmative action ends up stigmatizing and disadvantaging able blacks, few consider that a story, or ask whether it is authentic, typical, or true.[27] No one asks whether it is adequately tied to legal doctrine, because it and others like it are the very bases by which we evaluate legal doctrine. White tales like these seem unimpeachable—when one of us tells a counterstory, the counterstory comes under attack, not the original story itself."

"Something like that once happened to me," I said. "Early in my career I wrote an article that in some respects was a classic 'agony tale,' except I didn't tell stories, just quoted cases and social scientists. It was an early piece on hate speech. I pointed out that the tort system provided little remedy for racial insults and name-calling."

"I know that article. Even though it's not on the computerized databases, I ran across a citation to it and looked it up. I liked it."

"So did all of my friends, including, interestingly, a lot of white people. I would go to conferences like this one and people I never even knew would come up to me and say how much they loved the article, how moved they were, and how terrible it was that the law didn't redress the harm of racist insults."

"And you say you find this surprising?" Rodrigo looked up with interest.

"Don't misunderstand me—I still think you should be very careful if you plan to write in the narrative mode. You can do it, just be cautious, and maybe wait till you have tenure. You see, I finally figured out *why* everyone loved that first article. It's because they could empathize with the black subjected to the vicious racial slur. They could say how terrible it is that our legal system doesn't provide redress. They sincerely felt that way. Indeed, I think it allowed them to say to themselves how much they loved the First Amendment. They loved it so much that they had to sacrifice these unfortunate Negroes and Mexicans, for which they were genuinely sorry and apologetic."

"So that was your agony story. But you said there were two others," Rodrigo prompted.

"Oh, yes. A few years later I wrote one on the campus hate-speech controversy. In this one, I didn't so much make a case for curbing hate speech as I did for the indeterminacy of the usual First Amendment analysis. I showed that the problem of campus hate speech can be approached in one of two ways. You can either see it, basically, as a liberty or an equality problem, with mirror-image consequences flowing from the two approaches, except of course going off in opposite directions. This one my liberal friends welcomed much less, although in a way it was a more sophisticated analysis. Then, recently, I published a piece showing that the marketplace of ideas is unable to redress systemic injustice—although it can correct minor social ills and errors—because the more deeply inscribed, systemic ones are simply invisible—we don't see them as such at the time. My ACLU buddies absolutely hated this one. They ignored my argument, and all my historical evidence for what I called the 'empathic fallacy,' and kept saying, 'I know a case . . .' where speech in their opinion worked."

"Which of course wasn't your point at all," Rodrigo added.

"No, it was that the First Amendment doesn't work, not speech itself."

Rodrigo was silent for a minute while we sipped our drinks. "So, professor, you think I should hold off on writing this sort of stuff until I get tenure?"

"I know it's ironic. I myself was counseled to do something similar in my early days.[28] And here I am telling you to do the same thing."

"I could write about something safe, like civil procedure. But what if I do write narratives, and the piece gets accepted at a top review?"

"You might think that ought to satisfy any tenure committee. But there's the risk that your colleagues will dismiss it as the product of yet another level of affirmative action, namely that of the law review editors who lean over backward to accept an article written by a minority professor. It's a case of the reverse reasoning you and I discussed before.[29] They insist that we meet the merit criteria, but when we do, they dismiss our accomplishment. Since professors of color virtually by definition lack merit, when we do demonstrate it in any of the classic ways, this is disconcerting. There must be a reason for such a strange event. And they find the reason in the very factor, affirmative action, that raises a question about our competence in the first place. When faced with deciding between two propositions—Rodrigo Crenshaw, the affirmative action candidate, had merit after all (indeed more than most of them, who have never once published in Harvard in their entire careers)— and a second proposition—affirmative action accounted for Rodrigo's article getting accepted at the top law review, guess which one they will choose to believe?"

"We can't win. Our successes are laid to affirmative action of one sort, and our failures to another."

"A double bind," I said.

"I could write a 600-footnote case-cruncher," Rodrigo said, a little doubtfully.

"I'm sure you could," I said. "And some of your colleagues would love it. That's the kind of article they wrote to get tenure twenty-five years ago. They'd see themselves in you. They'd be all smiles."

"The trouble is that I'd never get an article of that kind in Harvard. They're passé. The good reviews realize that that vein of formalistic scholarship has run dry, is producing fewer and fewer breakthroughs."[30]

"If it ever produced any," I added.

"All the good writing these days is either Critical or interdisciplinary. Yet the old-timers on our faculties roll their eyes when they meet this kind. Especially when it's written by one of us."

"Well, let's put format aside. What are you thinking of writing *about?* You mentioned something about Trusts and Estates. Sounds a little dull— but I'm sure you'll find a way of making it interesting," I added.

"I'd like to show that the famous public-trust doctrine that Joseph Sax pioneered in environmental protection law a quarter of a century ago put a halt to the search for more far-reaching reform in that area. I would argue that the theory was both conservative and progressive at the same time; conservative, because it imported ideas from trust law that ultimately froze environmental law into an unproductive model, and progressive because it offered a way to control some of mankind's worst impulses. The other paper I'm thinking about writing is a civil rights piece."

"It seems to me you could write the first one in the standard cases-and-policies mode."

"I could. But I could also write it employing narratives, analyzing the rhetoric and logic of reform. I could show, for example, that the language and mental pictures of Sax's trust approach are male, revealing an unconscious fear of what might happen if we did not place the valued property beyond our reach, in the hands of someone else. It's a little like what wealthy men do for their children—fearing that they otherwise might be tempted to spend the child's college funds on a sports car."

"Like Ulysses lashing himself to the mast. I like this other approach much better. It lets you do more, go to the core of the problem, namely the way we think about natural goods like parks, beaches, and animal species."

"I thought so, too," Rodrigo replied a little wryly. "But then I talked to a few of my colleagues. They all preferred the standard version. A couple of them showed thinly disguised scorn when I spoke of using a storytelling and narrative-analysis approach."

"There was a session at this very conference yesterday on problems of law review publishing. The program note says the session was to be a gathering of legal scholars concerned about the battle for what they call authorial authority. Evidently many law professors think that law review editors are pushing them around, exercising too much control, too much judgment over articles." [31]

"I heard about that," Rodrigo replied. "I couldn't go. But I heard that some of those present voiced unhappiness over the way in which law reviews are publishing storytelling articles, feminism, and Critical Theory pieces all to the exclusion, as they see it, of 'real law.' Many of those in attendance argued that the only solution is a faculty takeover of the law reviews." [32]

I shuddered. "I hate to think what that would mean for innovative scholarship. Students are not perfect, and the law reviews every now and then do make mistakes. A bad article creeps in; a good one gets turned down. But on the whole, students are much more open to new forms and authors than our colleagues are. Some of the latter are open-minded, to be sure, but too many would use their position on the board of advisors to perpetuate sameness—to assure that law review writing today looks exactly like what they remember from their youth—boring, circular 100-page treatises full of case analysis, shuffling and reshuffling doctrine and going nowhere. [33] Nothing could bring greater disrepute to legal academia. In the eyes of sister disciplines, we are seen as always being a little behind. A faculty takeover of the law reviews would make us the laughing stock of the scholarly world."

"I agree," Rodrigo said. "And that's why this session on control of the law reviews worries me."

"But that's not solving your own problem. Are you going to write that trusts-and-estates article in the narrative mode or not? And what was that other topic you were talking about?"

"It's all tied up with figuring out why there is such resistance to narrative scholarship and storytelling. I'd love to explore this with you, if you have the time."

"Of course I do," I said. "It sounds like you have been giving this some thought—not surprising since your career may ride on it," I added.

"I'm torn," Rodrigo replied. "I want to write the best possible article, yet I want to survive to fight again another day. Maybe we can discuss it over dessert. Could you use another bite?"

"I could."

In Which Rodrigo Puts Forward His Theory on Why Appeals for Reform Spark Such Strong Resistance

We returned from the counter with our desserts, a fluffy apple concoction for my rail-thin friend, an abstemious-looking sherbet for me, and Rodrigo began as follows:

"Professor, have you ever wondered about the connection between law, especially academic law, and social change?"

"Every day of my life. Sometimes I wonder if I'm not just greasing the wheels of industry, turning out young lawyers who will advance the aims of the capitalist state. I wonder whether all my teaching and writing about racial justice do any good. The job structure out there is fixed; my students have to fit in. Possibly I'm making them even more discontent by preaching to them about a better world when the realities of law practice, billable hours, corporate clients, and so on, mean that they are locked into a certain type of life and practice."[34]

"Some of your students go into public interest practice. You may be more of an inspiration to them than you know."

"But even those who do, find that law is not the trusty instrument of reform that we like to think."

"And the reasons for that have begun to be explored in recent scholarship, including your own, Professor.[35] Law can do little to bring about fundamental social change because it operates piecemeal.[36] Courts can only adjudicate the case before them. Doctrines of *stare decisis*, standing, mootness, and ripeness assure that.[37] Yet, fundamental reform requires that 'everything change at once.' If you only change one thing, leaving everything else in place, the remaining elements simply swallow up the new decree. Even such a mighty case as *Brown v. Board of Education* ended up changing relatively little in the fortunes of black schoolchildren, whose plight today is little better than it was forty years ago.[38] Pupil assignment rules changed only slightly, especially in the South, and white families compensated by simply moving away, with the result that more African-American children attend dominantly black schools today than did in *Brown's* day.[39] Shortly after *Brown*, the number of black teachers and school administrators actually dropped, and today the graduation and dropout rates of black, Hispanic, and Native American children are an embarrassment to any industrialized country."[40]

Rodrigo was speaking intently now, and leaning forward slightly. I nodded and encouraged him to continue: "And you believe all this is not due simply to a lack of will or changes in the political climate, but to a basic limitation in law reform?"

Rodrigo nodded emphatically. "Consider what I'm thinking of calling 'cultural weight.' Every legal decree operates against a background of assumptions, presuppositions, and agreed-upon meanings.[41] In addition, it has to contend with a network of existing social practices and narratives.[42] All of these exercise a kind of gravitational field back in the direction of the familiar, the known. Thus, when *Brown* was decided, a thousand local officials and lower courts were faced with figuring out what it meant in particular situations. Separate is no longer equal—but what did that mean for teacher assignments, public swimming pools, school bus routes, college counseling in the schools, disciplinary due process, and a myriad other practices?"

"I suppose you're going to say it meant very little. Is this because local officials were determined to resist *Brown?* Sounds like a conspiracy theory to me."

"No, I don't think that was the main way it happened, although *Brown* did indeed spark some ugly resistance, especially in the South. I think the mechanism was both more and less sinister than that."

"What do you mean?"

"It's the general weight of culture that stands in the way. No one person does, usually at any rate. Rather, it's a host of background forces, against which legal decrees are played out, that confines reform. There's actually been some recent writing about this."

"You mean the narratives, presuppositions, and existing practices that landmark cases like *Brown* have to contend with?"

"Yes. These sabotage a decree without any conscious effort on anyone's part. When the *Brown* decision came down, Southern officials interpreted the decree in terms of their own experience, training, and common sense. To them, it meant the only thing it could mean—desegregation that came not too quickly, went not too far, and that changed existing personnel, curricula, and general culture as little as possible. Indeed, Southern officials at first interpreted the case as applying only to primary schools, and not to public swimming pools, meeting halls, and other facilities.[43] A few even took the view that *Brown* only applied to the school districts immediately before the Court. It took years for the message to get out that *Brown* meant what it said. Even today, 40 years later, more black children attend segregated schools than did in *Brown*'s day."[44]

"And you think this is because of culture and not because of outright resistance?" I pressed.

"There was outright resistance, at least at first. But the way *Brown* went against the cultural grain proved even more decisive. In dozens of formal decisions—school disciplinary cases, teacher assignment schemes, and decisions to locate a new school or program in this part of town rather than that—as well as a myriad of informal ones, majority-race school officials interpreted their legal obligation in light of what they knew: Schools should remain as much as possible like they were before."

"Doctrinal developments didn't help, either," I added.

"No," Rodrigo replied. "Courts soon decided that segregation that results from housing patterns is unredressable.[45] Metropolitan desegregation plans are unconstitutional.[46] Education is not a fundamental interest,[47] nor poverty a suspect class,[48] so that state schemes that fund property-rich districts lavishly and property-poor ones in miserly fashion are perfectly legal."

"All this even though U.S. constitutional law remains perfectly color-blind and committed to the principle of integrated schooling. I gather you think the same applies to law reform decisions across the board."

"I do. Girardeau Spann argues that litigators should not place great faith in the Supreme Court as an instrument of social progress.[49] It, and the federal courts in general, are conservative. And even when they do hand down a ringing victory for us, as they do every decade or so, the gain is quickly cut back by foot-dragging, obstruction, narrow construction, and delay."[50]

"Sometimes the gravitational field seems to reverse itself," I said. "During the sixties, courts and the general culture were on our side. It was a period of breakthroughs."

"But it did not last long. The arrow of change is as apt to be backward as forward at any given moment. A recent poll showed that black parents think that conditions today are as bad for black families as they have been since the time of slavery."[51]

"I saw that study," I added. "It showed that homicide is the leading cause of death for black youths between ages 15 and 24. Nearly half of all black children lived under the poverty level in a recent year. Thirty-four percent of all black teenagers looking for work could not find it, a rate twice that of their white counterparts. Nearly half of all black babies were not fully immunized.

Sixty-five percent of black adults think their children will be denied jobs because of racial prejudice." [52]

"Grim statistics," Rodrigo said. "Unfortunately, this sort of thing is institutionalizing itself. Black despair is more the norm today than the exception."

"And there is little we law-types can do?" I asked. "In our role as lawyers, I mean?"

"Litigation does little good. Even when the courts do give us a rare breakthrough, it succumbs quietly to cultural weight. I used to think another route had promise for us, but now I'm not so sure."

I looked up, hoping Rodrigo would explain. But just then the waiter approached. "Would you gentlemen like something else?"

I looked at Rodrigo who uncharacteristically shook his head. "Just the bill."

As the waiter disappeared, the lights flickered briefly.

"What's that?" Rodrigo asked.

"I don't know," I said. "It happened once before. Maybe it's the kids and the video games." I indicated the teenagers tirelessly pressing buttons along the wall. "Or maybe all the professors upstairs plugged in their laptops at once."

"Maybe it's an omen," Rodrigo mused, falling silent.

"I'd love to hear your theory, though," I said. "I'm going strong, and this restaurant has plenty of empty tables. I doubt they'll rush us to leave. Do you have the time?"

"Sure," Rodrigo replied with renewed energy. "It's all related to my career decision, the one we talked about earlier. I consider you my mentor, so I'd love to run it past you. Are you sure you have the time?"

I nodded. Rodrigo was silent for a moment. Then, he began:

Exit Rodrigo: In Which My Young Friend Explains How Ontogeny Recapitulates Phylogeny and Then Goes Off to an Uncertain Fate

"Until recently, I thought that the solution to law's lockstep was storytelling," Rodrigo began.

"Storytelling?" I asked. "You mean, what we talked about before?"

"Yes. You see, Professor, storytelling has the potential to change the social background against which legal decisions are interpreted. It can make inroads into the interlocking system of meanings, cultural understandings, and interpretations that determine the 'common sense' Southern officials and other actors bring to legal and cultural decisions. It can make cases like *Brown* succeed, not fail."

"It can change the cultural weight you were talking about!" I exclaimed, sitting up in the booth cushion into which I had been progressively slumping as the evening wore on.

"Or so I used to think," Rodrigo replied. "Stories—well-told ones, at any rate—like Patricia Williams' and some of yours, Professor, can change the baseline. They can change consciousness, change the narrative stock by which we interpret new stories, like that of *Brown*. Separate is no longer equal. Clever, engaging stories can alter the way we see and interpret the world. Law fails because, as we said, 'everything must change at once.' But law cannot change everything at once. So the surprising new edict is always outnumbered. No wonder new narratives issued by a court bring about little change."

"But persistent, engaged storytelling can change everything at once," I said, leaping a little ahead of myself. I had resolved to remain quiet in order to let Rodrigo develop his case, but my excitement had gotten the better of me. "But please go on."

Rodrigo inconspicuously picked up the bill—something I remarked with surprise and a little satisfaction, akin to seeing my own children grow up. I didn't object, even though I knew his salary as a beginning professor was probably half mine.

"Let me get this. You've always paid before," Rodrigo said, as though reading my mind. "Legal storytelling is potentially the most revolutionary form of scholarship on the current scene. Which, in turn, accounts for the resistance we all see, including here at this very conference."

"How do you know it's not just old fogyism?" I asked. "Mature scholars always resist new *genres* of writing pioneered by young upstarts like you. You talk strange lingoes, use terms they don't understand like 'hegemony' and 'multiple consciousness.' And you cite authors they've never read. Gearing up to understand these new forms of scholarship takes a lot of work. I struggle with it sometimes, as you know, and I'm a friend and fellow traveler."

"We're grateful for your help, and that of others in your generation," Rodrigo replied quietly. "You give us courage to go on, and your advice has been invaluable."

"Not to mention your own native talent," I said. "But please go on. I'd love to know why stories are not the answer, either."

Rodrigo paused. "Do you remember the resistance to stories that we talked about earlier?"

"You mean the spate of recent law review articles and journalistic pieces attacking the new jurisprudence, ridiculing or trying to rein it in."

"Yes, that. Have you wondered why it exists?"

"I assume you have a theory for it—that you think that it's more than simple inertia and resistance to that which is new?"

"I think there *is* more to it than that. There's a double mechanism, which I'll explain in a minute. But underlying everything is the sense, the fear really, that stories, if well told, can become part of the narrative base, and so change the way we understand the world. That's truly subversive. And since societies, like most organic things, do not want to change, at least rapidly, we resist."

"Conservative stories seem to have real effect," I interjected. "Over the last decade or so, stories like the welfare queen, the pathogenic black family, Willie Horton, and so on, have swept the land. Maybe the political right are simply better storytellers than we are."

"I don't think they're better storytellers, although they do seem to have a knack for using the media and for coining catch-phrases, like 'political correctness.'[53] I think the real reason has to do with memory. Conservative stories recall a distant past, which we remember in a rosy glow, when everything seemed to be better. Progressives and reformers urge us to move in directions we've never been. Stories like that raise anxieties. Why abandon the safe ground we're on for an uncharted future?"

"But society sometimes listens to our stories, as it did in the sixties. And even today, some of our writers do get a favorable reception. Patricia Williams's book, for example, was well received."[54]

"Stories have to be inveigling, insinuative. Ones that are too frontal create resistance.[55] They have to engage the logic, build on the narratives of the dominant tradition. Agony tales always go over better than the other kind."

"The more hard-edged ones?"

"Yes. You've seen something like that in your own experience writing about hate speech. That first article was a classic 'agony' tale. Liberals, and even some conservatives loved it."

"The reaction was like that of some reviewers of Pat Williams's book, who praised it as so 'poignant,' so 'moving,' so poetic."

"But as happened to you when you wrote about the logic and structure of the hate speech problem, you saw that you elicited a different reaction."

"I certainly did," I admitted a little ruefully. "I stopped being a cult hero. People started inviting me to lectures in order to *debate* my views. Often they would invite a speaker from the ACLU to present 'the other side.' And then when I started writing about campus speech codes, resistance increased and the decibel level rose even higher. One columnist attacked me and my coauthor, calling us fascists, Orwellian censors, and purveyors of dangerous, un-American double-think, all in one article."[56]

"Quite an indictment," Rodrigo said, looking at me intently. "I'm glad to see you haven't begun pulling your punches. Where did the column appear?"

"A national newspaper. At least they gave me a chance to reply, even if it was several months later. But you said you had a theory to explain all this, something to do with a double axis or mechanism?"

In Which Rodrigo Explains Why Society Resists the New Storytellers and Sets Out His Double Mechanism by Which We Deploy That Resistance

"I do," Rodrigo began. "Recall two related phenomena, both having to do with stories and images." Rodrigo took a long sip of his coffee, which the waiter had obligingly refilled, even though we had paid our bill. "Not bad, for institutional coffee, I mean."

"I gather you mean ethnic imagery, whose history we discussed before. But what's the second one?" I asked.

"The other is resistance to reform in general," Rodrigo replied. "If you consider both together, you see what they have in common. And what they have in common explains our predicament and that of today's other storytellers and counterstorytellers, who are trying to get others to take a more humane approach to problems of racial justice."

"I'm not quite sure I see what they have in common. You and I recently discussed the way our culture's system of racial imagery depicts black people over the years. Early on, there were the Sambo and the Mammy images."[57]

"Which we said were necessary to reassure white society that African-Americans were content with their lot during slavery and the early Emancipation years."

"Indeed. A different image would have been too disturbing. It would have implied that the slaves wanted a normal life, had human needs, just like the rest of us. But then the image changed."

"During Reconstruction, novels, stories, and early films began depicting blacks as bestial, primitive, hypersexual, with designs on things they did not own or deserve, including white women.[58] Now, what society needed was repression. The new images served this purpose perfectly."

"The images are not always negative. Remember the Harlem Renaissance."

"Yes, society was then turning to other cultures for renewal. They adopted black music and art as a refuge from their own excesses. They found its primitivism refreshing, just as today many Americans look to Southwest culture for relief from the cares of industrialized life.[59] The images of us are never particularly flattering—beast, lackey, primitive, and so on. But they are intensely *functional* for the dominant group, changing as its needs change—now for cheap or slave labor, now for repression, now for entertainment, and so on."[60]

"A few courageous souls in every era resist those images, or write a book or play depicting us as normal—like anyone else," I pointed out.

"But they are ignored. The weight of the general system of narratives and images is too great. Harriet Beecher Stowe's novel sold well only after decades of abolitionist agitation had begun to make the American public understand that slavery might be wrong. Nadine Gordimer won the Nobel Prize only as her country was on the verge of repudiating apartheid. Or consider the recent 'rediscovery' of a generation of black novelists and writers, including Zora Neale Hurston and Charles Chesnutt. Those authors were writing many years ago, they had publishers and small audiences. Society was simply not ready to change its images of blacks. They wrote about black characters who were normal—like everyone else—who had feelings, hopes, dreams, and so on. They lacked an audience because society did not want to accept that image of blacks back then."[61]

"I'm generally familiar with that functional view of racial imagery," I replied. "But you mentioned there was another strand?"

"Yes," Rodrigo continued. "It's related to the first. Recent work has begun to focus on the problem of social reform in general. A few scholars, like Spann, have analyzed law's role."[62]

"Or lack of it," I added wryly.

"Indeed," Rodrigo went on. "Various writers are studying the natural history of social reform movements, working their way toward a general theory of reform and regression."

"And this mirrors the course of ethnic imagery which you just reviewed for me?"

"In some ways it does. At first social reform movements tend to evoke sympathy and solicitude. We consider ourselves a generous and welcoming people. So, we link arms with the newcomers, march with them, sing, 'We shall overcome.' Everyone identifies with the underdog. And so it is with most social movements—feminism, civil rights, environmentalism—at first. Then, at some point, the tide turns. The group begins to seem to us dangerous, aggressive. They are asking for things they have not earned, do not deserve, demanding concessions we cannot easily give. Now they are no longer in favor. We no longer invite them to fashionable parties. They are whiners, demanding, impossible, never satisfied. Now they are imposing on our just prerogatives. They are in the wrong, we in the right."[63]

"I've seen something like that happen with many social movements, including our own," I said. "In the sixties, they loved us. We could do no wrong. Now, we are almost completely out of favor. These days, it's almost a sick joke. When I pick up a newspaper and see a column about racism, it's almost always about Farrakhan, or some outrage a white has suffered at the hands of women or minorities."

Rodrigo nodded, and so I reminded him of the connection I hoped he would make: "And you think all of this has something to do with the resistance to legal stories and storytelling?"

"I do," Rodrigo replied. "The latest round of reaction recapitulates both of these themes. At first, society welcomed the new storytellers. We thought they were cute and endearing, like children. 'Oh, look, they're telling stories,' we said. We deemed the new stories poignant, moving, touching. At this early stage, we considered most of the stories 'agony tales,' personal accounts or journals of the writer's lives.[64] But then, we noticed that they were doing more than merely writing about their feelings, doing more than telling us how it feels to be black. They were making points about us— mainstream folks—about the ways in which we think and live.[65] And some of their points were not particularly flattering. Some were downbeat and pessimistic, like Derrick Bell's.[66] Now, we started to temper our praise, to find fault with storytelling. Reservations appeared. Writers called for criteria to evaluate, to get a handle on this new legal *genre*. Writers of color then turned to counterstories, tales and parables that mocked, jarred, displaced some comfortable majoritarian tale, myth, or narrative. Major tenets of the

majoritarian faith were now being called into question. This was disconcerting. It brought sharper attacks. Farber and Sherry appeared. Austin and
Van Alstyne began ridiculing the new narrativists openly. Austin said Crits
only cite each other."[67]

"A kind of reversal of the imperial-scholar charge," I observed wryly.

"And Van Alstyne likened us to commissars and thought police, saying
that when he read us he was reminded of the tanks clanking into Tiananmen Square."[68]

"As though we were the ones with all the power," I exclaimed.

"To him, it must actually look that way," Rodrigo replied. "It's a kind
of surplus-power phenomenon. Changes from the cultural baseline appear
unprincipled, ruthless, and wrong. Oh, and to draw out the parallel I
mentioned, it's all there. Early on, we were the Harlem Renaissance—
earthy, primitive, simple, appealing. Then, we were the simple Sambos and
Mammies, cheerfully writing in the civil rights fields but producing little of
the really important work. Then, the tide changed. Now we are the threatening, bestial, nearly out-of-control black of the late 1800s or post-civil rights
black exploitation films."

"And so they are right to resist us, have practically a moral duty to do so,
since we are the unprincipled ones, the ones on the offensive."

"True," Rodrigo replied with a slight sigh. "It's all done solemnly and for
the best of reasons—academic rigor, due process, the integrity of the personnel and promotions process."

I could sense Rodrigo was about to finish, and so decided to push for
clarification of something that had been nagging at me. "Rodrigo, you
mentioned earlier the attack on the law reviews. Did you mean to imply that
this assault has something to do with the currents we have been discussing?"

"Oh, I should have explained myself better," Rodrigo said. "I think it
does. The reviews have been publishing our stuff, that and the work of the
Crits and feminists. The old-time formalistic stuff is passing into history. All
the bright young minds in the articles departments know this, realize that
formal jurisprudence is playing itself out, has yielded all the insights it is ever
going to offer. Postmodern, Critical, feminist, and Critical Race analysis, for
now at least, offers much more—offers genuinely new and exciting ways of
understanding our social condition.[69] Many conventional scholars don't like
that. Rather than compete intellectually, which would entail retooling and
reading and learning to think differently, it's much simpler just to take over
the law reviews."

"So you think a faculty takeover really is imminent?" I asked in alarm.

"Not really a takeover, although this may happen in a few schools. What I think is much more likely is some sort of effort to increase faculty participation, certainly in the selection of articles, perhaps also in their editing once they're accepted.[70] You saw evidence of that type of discontent in the ad hoc section meeting we mentioned before. It's the first time, isn't it, Professor, that these matters have been discussed at the AALS annual meeting?"

"I'm not sure," I replied. "I don't go to all of them. But it's the first time that I can remember, although there has been the occasional article or essay in the *Journal of Legal Education* decrying the role mere students have in editing and selecting our writing."[71]

"Cultural power always reasserts itself. You make gains, then when you least expect it, there's the backlash. And those who participate in the reaction don't see themselves as counterrevolutionaries at all. Rather, they're just trying to set things right. And so when the law reviews change structure, it will just seem like a little needed infusion of rigor, of integrity. It will seem like a restoration, rather than a destructive movement aimed at aborting a host of promising social movements in the law."

Rodrigo was silent for a moment. Then, he continued as follows: "And so you can see, Professor, how the personal, the political, and the academic, even, come together. I really want to get tenure, want to live with Giannina, and yet these forces seem inexorable. They combine. Do you have any doubt that what we see with the history of ethnic depiction, with social reform generally, and with storytelling and the law reviews, is about to play itself out closer to home?"

I wasn't sure what I was hearing. "Rodrigo, you mean that you have decided not to write in the storytelling mode?"

Rodrigo nodded his head glumly. "Stories are potent—as we observed. They can change the base, and through that, law, and through that society."

"But, you're saying," I interjected, "that the base changes *us* as well. Social gravity restores itself, inevitably and always, after a few moments of exhilarating flight in which you thought you were weightless, could fly."

"It's as though society had a small, but very powerful, unseen homeostat. We replicate ourselves even when we think we are trying most sincerely to transform ourselves and each other. Social momentum is preserved. The more things change, the more they stay the same."

"And so you are forswearing stories, giving up narrative analysis?"

Rodrigo looked me straight in the eye and said nothing.

"But, Rodrigo, you can't do that. You *are* a character in a narrative. You would not continue to exist!"

"We are all characters in a narrative, Professor. We just fool ourselves into thinking that things are otherwise. Perhaps we want to escape responsibility for our own stories."

The lights flickered again. I hoped our dialog was not about to be interrupted by a blackout. But the kids over by the wall had been quiet for some time.

"Maybe you'll change your mind," I said. "I've found that when the young wax pessimistic, they never stay that way for long. What other topic were you going to write about? You mentioned there was another one," I said trying to redirect his thoughts to something less dire.

"Oh," Rodrigo said with a start. "The level playing field. Everyone wants to know whether it is or not. I was going to show exactly in what respects it is not level. I think it's an important topic. Conservatives say things are now leveled, and minorities ought to play by the same rules as everyone else.[72] Liberals and many minorities insist it is not. But everyone is vague on exactly what the concept means, and in what respects minorities are made to play an unequal game. I would have taken two or three principal playing fields as illustration, including the famous First Amendment free market of ideas, the economic marketplace of trades, exchanges, and competition, and perhaps another one. Maybe the problem of law school admissions."

"We talked about something similar to that one before," I said.

"Right," Rodrigo recalled. "The first time we met. Then, I would have employed history, cultural analysis, and close examination of the governing narratives and stories in each area to show precisely what the main disadvantaging mechanisms are that render the playing field uneven."

"Simple, brilliant, and deeply subversive," I said. I could hardly contain my enthusiasm. "What do you mean, 'you would have written'? This is a great project, Rodrigo. It's needed, it's exactly the time to do it—the cultural moment, so to speak. And you're precisely the person to carry it off."

"I wish I were as sure as you are, Professor. I just worry about the possibility that—what do you call it—that one can analyze a thing to its death?"

The lights flickered again, then went out decisively. I know they were out, perhaps for 30 seconds, because I heard voices in the hallway outside exclaiming.

I sat there quietly reflecting on our conversation. Looking back, I cannot be sure I did not drift off to sleep for a moment, worn out by the fast pace of the three days of convention and the high-pitched, although stimulating, talk with Rodrigo.

When I opened my eyes, a bare booth greeted me. Rodrigo was nowhere to be found. I was certain he had been there—his empty coffee cup remained to remind me of our conversation. But no note, then or ever, confirmed me in this. And future efforts to get in touch with him turned up blank.

After a few minutes, I got up and walked outside the hotel on the off chance he had gone there for a breath of air. No Rodrigo, indeed no one at all. I had the walkway to myself. I looked up at the night sky. A meteor flashed through the dark resort sky, and was gone.

Had Rodrigo been, as he put it, just a character in a narrative? And, if so, did he actually succumb to the critique of narrativity? What did he mean by his last lines, of being analyzed to death? Like all storytelling, had he and his lessons been lost in a cloud of abstraction, in which learned commentators paid endless attention to the form, the quality, the procedure of storytelling, and gradually lost sight of the content of the stories themselves? Was Rodrigo right that cultural momentum is preserved, while he himself turned out to be perfectly fallible, perfectly mortal?

The night was chilly. I walked back into the hotel, noticing on an easel just inside the basement door a notice about the meeting on "Publishing." I was sorry I had not attended, and wondered if I had somehow betrayed my young friend and protégé by not going.

Once before, he had returned from exile, as brash and full of life as ever. But this departure somehow to me seemed more final, more dire. I wondered if I would ever see him again.

Notes

1. DINESH D'SOUZA, ILLIBERAL EDUCATION: THE POLITICS OF RACE AND SEX ON CAMPUS (1991). The author, an Indian American, was born in Bombay. He graduated recently from Dartmouth College, where he served as editor of the *Dartmouth Review*, a conservative campus newspaper. *Illiberal Education* focuses on six universities—the University of California at Berkeley, Stanford, Howard, Michigan, Duke, and Harvard—where the author conducted interviews on affirmative action, curricular changes, teaching and scholarly styles, and the racial climate. *Id.* at 20–21. The book contains a harrowing series of stories showing the evils of affirmative action and curricular reform gone astray. At each of the campuses he visited, the author found minority students who were interested mainly in expanding their numbers and preserving their "victim" status. They were unconcerned about educational standards, unwilling to mix or compete with white students, and insistent on their right to special courses, theme houses, and professors dealing with their peculiar, Balkanized concerns. *Id.* at 46–48, 56–57, 69–70, 182–85, 239, 242–43, 248, 302. D'Souza depicts majority race professors and administrators as either spinelessly bowing to minority demands, *id.* at 52–55, 65–67, 102–103, 151, 182–85, 194–97, or actively in league with the iconoclastic newcomers. He points to this latter phenomenon at Duke University, which he charges with abandoning Shakespeare and other traditional subjects for postmodernism, semiotics, Third World literature, and other *au courant* offerings. *See id.* at 157–92. For their part, the white students are either sullenly adjusting to the radical, unprincipled leveling of their once-proud institutions, *id.* at 47, 50–51, 236–39, or bravely rebelling against the tide of revolutionists of color, *id.* at 19, 49, 224–25. At one

campus—Berkeley—D'Souza finds an even more ironic consequence of the minority revolution. There, Hispanic and black students have won concessions, but only at the expense of hardworking, high-achieving Asian students, who are beginning to fight back. *See id.* at 24–38. Using events at Michigan as his main example, D'Souza criticizes universities that have responded to the recent wave of racist incidents and name-calling by enacting hate-speech prohibitions. These prohibitions, according to D'Souza, penalize students for harmless "jokes," such as the Beethoven-Ujamaa House incident at Stanford, *id.* at 133, make faculty and students alike fearful of expressing themselves freely, chill legitimate classroom speech, and weaken the First Amendment. *Id.* at 142–48. D'Souza asserts that this approach will make matters worse by driving racism underground, where it will fester and reemerge in even more virulent forms. *Id.* at 156. Running through the book is the author's concern that each of the changes—minority admissions, curricular reform, limitations on hate speech, and changes in campus life to accommodate minority populations—are unprincipled and unjustifiable. He believes they endanger merit, self-reliance, and other tenets of Western culture. *See id.* at 56–64, 157–67. Efforts to diversify the campus culture, while laudable in intent, are often flawed in design. As such, D'Souza feels they are likely to backfire against their intended beneficiaries by inducing dependence, creating racial antagonisms where none existed before, and impairing the ability of universities to act as custodians of Western culture. *See id.* at 76–79, 82–85, 112–18, 184–90, 201–204, 230–42. These were of course just my initial reactions and notes on reading and outlining the book. As luck would have it, Rodrigo and I discussed the book more fully later in our conversation. See the middle sections of the chapter, *infra.*

2. Geneva Crenshaw is the fictional interlocutor and alter ego in a number of works, including DERRICK BELL, AND WE ARE NOT SAVED: THE ELUSIVE QUEST FOR RACIAL JUSTICE (1987); Derrick Bell, *The Supreme Court, 1984 Term—Foreword: The Civil Rights Chronicles,* 99 HARV. L. REV. 4 (1985); Richard Delgado, *Derrick Bell and the Ideology of Racial Reform: Will We Ever Be Saved?,* 97 YALE L.J. 923 (1988). Each of these works is an example of the "legal storytelling" genre employed by a number of Critical Race theorists and feminists to analyze legal thought and culture.

3. While studying in a language other than his native one, I thought. I was reminded of the many immigrants and Latino students I have known who labored under a similar handicap, yet achieved mightily in an alien system. Rodrigo disclosed the identity of his school later in the conversation: Bologna.

4. On bias in the LSAT, *see* Leslie G. Espinoza, *The LSAT: Narrative and Bias,* 1 AM. U.J. GENDER & L. (1992). On the controversy surrounding the validity and reliability of standardized tests, *see* Griggs v. Duke Power Co., 401 U.S. 424 (1971) (job setting); Sharif v. New York State Educ. Dep't, 709 F. Supp. 345 (S.D.N.Y. 1989) (educational setting).

5. I thought of the many conservative scholars who treat the SAT as a virtual measuring rod for God-given merit. *E.g.,* D'SOUZA at 44–45, 207, 265–68. On various ways of assessing test bias, *see* Espinoza, *supra.* On the test generally,

see TOWARDS A DIVERSIFIED LEGAL PROFESSION: AN INQUIRY INTO THE LAW SCHOOL ADMISSION TEST, GRADE INFLATION, AND CURRENT ADMISSIONS POLICIES (David M. White ed., 1981); LINDA F. WIGHTMAN & DAVID G. MULLER, AN ANALYSIS OF DIFFERENTIAL VALIDITY AND DIFFERENTIAL PREDICTION FOR BLACK, MEXICAN AMERICAN, HISPANIC, AND WHITE LAW SCHOOL STUDENTS (1990).

6. *See* BELL, NOT SAVED, *supra*, at 140–61 (chronicle of the "seventh candidate"). The term "tipping point" entered the lexicon from the law of housing discrimination. It refers to the phenomenon in which whites leave a neighborhood when the percentage of black families reaches a certain point. *See* Bruce L. Ackerman, *Integration for Subsidized Housing and the Question of Racial Occupancy Controls*, 26 STAN. L. REV. 245, 251–66 (1974); Boris I. Bittker, *The Case of the Checker-Board Ordinance: An Experiment in Race Relations*, 71 YALE L.J. 1387 (1962). On the validity of land use controls to promote integration, *see* Otero v. New York Hous. Auth., 484 F.2d 1122 (2d Cir. 1973); United States v. Starrett City Assoc., 660 F. Supp. 668 (E.D.N.Y. 1987), aff'd, 840 F.2d 1096 (2d Cir.), cert. denied, 488 U.S. 946 (1988).

7. For analysis of the "pool is too small" argument, *see* Richard Delgado, *Mindset and Metaphor*, 103 HARV. L. REV. 1872 (1990); *see also* D'SOUZA at 157–73 (universities said to be engaged in bidding war for minority professors). For deployment of the argument in another setting, *see* City of Richmond v. J. A. Croson Co., 488 U.S. 469, 499–503 (1988) (pool of qualified and interested minority candidates may be smaller than is thought).

8. *See* Richard Delgado, *Storytelling for Oppositionists and Others: A Plea for Narrative*, 87 MICH. L. REV. 2411, 2432–34 (1989) (ordinary hiring is deeply biased in favor of whites but not perceived as such). *See generally Symposium, Legal Storytelling*, 87 MICH. L. REV. 2073 (1989) (containing articles by Milner S. Ball, Derrick Bell, Mari J. Matsuda, Steven L. Winter, and others on use of stories and narratives to jar or displace majoritarian mindset).

9. *See* Michael A. Olivas, *Latino Faculty at the Border: Increasing Numbers Key to More Hispanic Access*, CHANGE, May–June 1988, at 6, 7.

10. The Critical Race Theory (C.R.T.) movement started in the summer of 1989 with a small workshop held outside Madison, Wisconsin. Its adherents, mostly writers of color, struggle to understand and cope with the shifting tides of racism in American society. Most are discontent with liberalism and bring insights from critical theory, deconstruction, counterstorytelling, and Third World thought to forge a new racial consciousness and program. On the C.R.T. movement, *see* Kimberlè W. Crenshaw, *Race, Reform and Retrenchment: Transformation and Legitimation in Antidiscrimination Law*, 101 HARV. L. REV. 1331 (1988); Richard Delgado, *When a Story Is Just a Story: Does Voice Really Matter?*, 76 VA. L. REV. 95 (1990); Mari J. Matsuda, *When the First Quail Calls: Multiple Consciousness as Jurisprudential Method*, 11 WOMEN'S RTS. L. REP. 7 (1989). On some of the controversy the movement has generated, *see* Charles Rothfeld, *Minority Critic Stirs Debate on Minority Writing*, N.Y. TIMES, Jan.

5, 1990, at B6; Jon Wiener, *Law Profs Fight the Power*, NATION, Sept. 4, 1989, at 246. An emerging strand in C.R.T. is cultural nationalism. Judging from his remarks thus far, Rodrigo struck me as receptive to this point of view. As it turned out, I was right.

11. See ANTONIO GRAMSCI, SELECTIONS FROM THE PRISON NOTE-BOOKS 416–18 (Quintin Hoare & Geoffrey N. Smith trans. & eds., 1971).

12. For authors deploring—in broad or narrow terms—affirmative action, *see e.g.*, D'SOUZA, *supra*; STEPHEN L. CARTER, REFLECTIONS OF AN AFFIR-MATIVE ACTION BABY 47–95 (1991); SHELBY STEELE, THE CON-TENT OF OUR CHARACTER (1990).

13. Richard Delgado, *The Imperial Scholar Revisited: How To Marginalize Outsider Writing, Ten Years Later*, 140 U. PA. L. REV. 1349 (1992); *see also* Alex M. Johnson, Jr., *The New Voice of Color*, 100 YALE L.J. 2007 (1991).

14. Richard Delgado, *The Imperial Scholar: Reflections on a Review of Civil Rights Literature*, 132 U. PA. L. REV. 561 (1984).

15. I thought of such special issues as *Symposium, Storytelling, supra*; *Symposium, The Critique of Normativity*, 139 U. PA. L. REV. 801 (1991), and the work of the many radical feminists, some of color, who are adding their voices in increasing numbers to the debate about law's role and function. But what, I wondered, about law and economics? *See, e.g.*, RICHARD POSNER, ECO-NOMIC ANALYSIS OF LAW (3d ed. 1986); Ronald H. Coase, *The Problem of Social Cost*, 3 J.L. & ECON. 1 (1960). Was that not an instrumental elaboration on legal formalism? I wondered if the irrepressible Rodrigo was familiar with this movement. *See, e.g.*, *Symposium on Law & Economics*, 85 COLUM. L. REV. 899 (1985). I wondered, too, if this brash but talented newcomer realized how the so-called "new" movements are rooted in much earlier approaches, e.g., the legal realism of Felix Cohen and Jerome Frank, or of midcentury feminists, or Simone de Beauvoir. *See, e.g.*, Elizabeth Mensch, *The History of Mainstream Legal Thought*, *in* THE POLITICS OF LAW: A PROGRESSIVE CRITIQUE 13, 24–33 (David Kairys ed., 1982); Diane Polan, *Toward a Theory of Law and Patriarchy*, *in* POLITICS OF LAW, *supra*, at 294, 295, 302 nn.4–7. Is the line between the new and the old as clear as Rodrigo seems to think?

16. *E.g.*, BELL, NOT SAVED; *Civil Rights Chronicles*, *supra*.

17. *E.g.*, *Symposium, Legal Storytelling*, *supra*.

18. *See* Delgado, *Oppositionists*, *supra*, at 2411 n.1.

19. *See Symposium, Excluded Voices: Realities in Law and Law Reform*, 42 MIAMI L. REV. 1 (1987).

20. *E.g.*, CATHARINE A. MACKINNON, FEMINISM UNMODIFIED: DIS-COURSES ON LIFE AND LAW (1987).

21. *E.g.*, Steven L. Winter, *Contingency and Community in Normative Practice*, 139 U. PA. L. REV. 963 (1989).

22. I thought of collections I had in my office, such as POLITICS OF LAW, *supra*. But, again I wondered, just how new are all these approaches with which Rodrigo seems so enamored? *See supra*.

23. *See* GRAMSCI, *supra*; *see also* ANTONIO GRAMSCI, LETTERS FROM PRISON (Lynne Lawner ed. & trans., 1973).
24. "You know, they rejected Jesus, too. I said, you're not Him." BOB DYLAN, *115th Dream*, on BRINGING IT ALL BACK HOME (Columbia/CBS Records, 1970).
25. W. E. B. DUBOIS, THE SOULS OF BLACK FOLKS 16–17 (1903); *see also* RALPH ELLISON, INVISIBLE MAN (1952). For contemporary explications of double consciousness, *see* BELL HOOKS, FEMINIST THEORY: FROM MARGIN TO CENTER (1984).
26. *E.g.*, Matsuda, *supra*.
27. *E.g.*, Derrick Bell, *The Price and Pain of Racial Perspective*, THE JOURNAL (Stanford Law School), May 9, 1986, at 5 (describing famous author's difficult experiences as a visiting professor at Stanford).
28. *See* GEORG LUKACS, HISTORY AND CLASS CONSCIOUSNESS (Rodney Livingstone trans., 1971); Duncan Kennedy, *Antonio Gramsci and the Legal System*, 6 A.L.S.A. FORUM 32 (1982).
29. On the need for self-definition among outside groups, see Crenshaw, *supra*; Richard Delgado, *Affirmative Action as a Majoritarian Device: Or, Do You Really Want to Be a Role Model?*, 89 MICH. L. REV. 1222 (1991); Derrick Bell, *What's Love of Country Got to Do With It? Hidden Messages from Two Black Women*, Keynote Address at the 1991 Award Breakfast of National Bar Association Women Lawyers' Division (Aug. 6, 1991).
30. I thought of the recent spate of writing on narrativity and the way in which law's dominant stories change very slowly. If legal culture does resist insurgent thought until it is too late—until it has lost the power to transform us—what does this bode for Rodrigo? *See, e.g.*, GRAMSCI, *supra*; Bell, *Civil Rights Chronicles*, *supra*; Delgado, *Mindset*, *supra*.
31. I thought of countless examples. Just that morning I had read about a new medical breakthrough developed at an American research university. Only two weeks ago I had my car rebuilt by a mechanic who (I hope) was well versed in linear thought. The day before I had baked a batch of brownies following a 10-step recipe.
32. Fortunately, I had the good sense to keep the printout, portions of which follow at Appendix 1A *infra*.
33. For a summary of some of these sorry chapters in Western history, *see* ROBERT A. WILLIAMS, JR., THE AMERICAN INDIAN IN WESTERN LEGAL THOUGHT (1990); Robert A. Williams, Jr., *Documents of Barbarism: The Contemporary Legacy of European Racism and Colonialism in the Narrative Traditions of Federal Indian Law*, 31 ARIZ. L. REV. 237 (1989); Delgado, *Ever Saved?*, *supra*, at 934–45.
34. The suggestion that Beethoven was a mulatto still has the power to shock. *See* PATRICIA J. WILLIAMS, THE ALCHEMY OF RACE AND RIGHTS 110–15 (1991) (discussing angry reaction of white Stanford students at being told this for the first time).

35. MARTIN BERNAL, BLACK ATHENA I (1987); MARTIN BERNAL, BLACK ATHENA II (1991). Provocative books—I resolved to press Rodrigo later if he didn't supply additional authority soon.
36. See, e.g., STEPHEN J. GOULD, THE MISMEASURE OF MAN 30–72 (1981); NANCY STEPAN, THE IDEA OF RACE IN SCIENCE (1982); Richard Delgado et al., Can Science Be Inopportune?, 31 UCLA L. REV. 128 (1983).
37. Easy? I thought: I only wish. Wait till this brash newcomer tries his hand at it.
38. ALAN BLOOM, THE CLOSING OF THE AMERICAN MIND (1987).
39. THOMAS SOWELL, CIVIL RIGHTS: RHETORIC OR REALITY? (1984).
40. Glenn Loury, Who Speaks for American Blacks?, COMMENTARY, Jan. 1987, at 34.
41. ROGER KIMBALL, TENURED RADICALS (1990).
42. STEELE, supra.
43. E. D. HIRSCH, JR., CULTURAL LITERACY (1987).
44. See D'SOUZA, supra.
45. Examples of the scapegoating phenomenon are legion: D'Souza blames minorities and their sympathizers for the academy's problems, D'SOUZA, supra, at 46–70, 142–48, 182–85, 257; the Republican Party and David Duke capitalize on Willie Horton and black crime; beleaguered American workers blame Japan for our troubles; Reconstruction-era writers blame emancipation for the Civil War's destructiveness in the South (I was pleasantly surprised that Rodrigo knew that); and so on. For discussions of racial scapegoating, see GORDON W. ALLPORT, THE NATURE OF PREJUDICE 224 (25th ed. 1979); IRWIN KATZ, STIGMA—A SOCIAL PSYCHOLOGICAL ANALYSIS 121 (1981).
46. D'SOUZA, supra, at 2–23 (listing areas of liberal excess in admissions policy, in class content, and in campus life); 94–122 (criticizing Afrocentric curricular reforms); 124–56 (decrying university restrictions on offensive speech).
47. Id. at 256–57 ("[T]he activists set the agenda and timorous administrators usually go along.").
48. Id. at 51 (white and Asian students see themselves as victims); 131 (white students feel "under attack"); 84 (reporting that academics are being intimidated by colleagues); 146, 152–56 (complaining of censorship of sensitive speech); 200 (complaining of truculent minority students).
49. See Derrick Bell, Brown v. Board of Education and the Interest-Convergence Dilemma, 93 HARV. L. REV. 518 (1980) (arguing that whites permit advances in racial justice for blacks only when doing so coincides with whites' self-interest).
50. Fortunately, I also kept this second printout, portions of which follow at Appendix 1B, infra.
51. See BELL, NOT SAVED, supra, at 26–51 (discussing original Constitution's slavery compromises); Richard Delgado & Jean Stefancic, Norms and Narratives: Can Judges Avoid Serious Moral Error?, 69 TEX. L. REV. 1929, 1934–52 (1991) (reviewing U.S. court decisions that approved slavery and "separate but

equal" laws, Indian relocation, Asian exclusion, female subordination, Japanese internment, and sterilization of persons accused of mental retardation).

52. *See* Gary Blonston, *Are Americans Really Working More Hours?*, DENVER POST, Feb. 17, 1992, at 1-A; Mary Roser, *Achievement Scores Troubling, 90% of U.S. Students Rate Among World's Worst in New Tests*, DENVER POST, Feb. 6, 1992, at 5-A; Hobart Rowen, *The Bentsen Initiative*, WASH. POST, Oct. 24, 1991, at A23 (computing six-percent drop in quality of life in America); *Top 10 Countries for Quality of Life*, WASH. POST, Nov. 5, 1991, at Z5 (ranking United States seventh, behind Japan, Canada, Iceland, Sweden, Switzerland, and Norway, on quality-of-life measurements, such as life expectancy, infant mortality, and per capita income); George Will, *Four Small Indicators of Our National Stress*, BOULDER DAILY CAMERA, Jan. 16, 1992, at 9-A.

53. *See* Eighth Chronicle, *infra* this volume, in which we return to this subject.

54. *See* DERRICK BELL, RACE, RACISM AND AMERICAN LAW 3, 40–41 (2d ed. 1980) (arguing that ideal factors play little role in racial reform); Bell, *Realism, supra*.

55. BELL, NOT SAVED, *supra*, at 250–58 (arguing that minorities should not work to replace whites at top of hierarchy, but to transform entire system in more humane directions).

56. I thought: If he doesn't frighten them all away by his cultural-supremacist ideas. But then I thought: Maybe the indignation some whites will feel on hearing Rodrigo's message will cause them to reflect on how we feel when they speak about "quality," "merit," and "standards" (with us in mind) or about not sacrificing innocent whites on the altar of affirmative action. (If whites are innocent, what does that make us?) Is that Rodrigo's plan?

57. *Compare* Robert J. Cottrol & Raymond T. Diamond, *The Second Amendment: Toward an Afro-Americanist Reconsideration*, 80 GEO. L.J. 309 (1991) (arguing that African-Americans need right to own guns as an aspect of right to resist illegitimate authority) *with Symposium, Protest and Resistance: Civil Disobedience in the 1990s*, 48 WASH. & LEE L. REV. 15 (1989) *and Symposium, On the Necessity of Violence for Any Possibility of Justice*, 13 CARDOZO L. REV. 1082 (1991) (both discussing legal and moral bases for violence as response to social inequity and injustice).

58. In retrospect, my feelings for him were complex. Part of me felt joy and hope, the first time anything in the currently dismal racial scene had inspired those feelings in quite a while. For this I was grateful. But I wondered: Would majority society heed what Rodrigo would say? And, would he himself persist in saying it—or would he soften in time, perhaps becoming seduced by the opportunities available to a high-achieving law graduate? He was certainly prepared to seek conventional indicia of success—an LL.M., a professorship, publications in respectable law reviews. And I earlier noted his pride in having attended a university (Bologna) associated with the rise of mercantilism, rationalism, and, of course, the dreaded "linear thought." Was Rodrigo likely to free himself easily

from these influences? And would his disdain for Western society survive his probable later success?

59. I immediately thought of a magazine article I had read recently. *See* Richard Lacayo, *Nowhere to Hide*, TIME, Nov. 11, 1991, at 34 (documenting huge U.S. industry devoted to electronic snooping and monitoring).

Notes to Chapter 2

1. RICHARD EPSTEIN, FORBIDDEN GROUNDS (1992). The author, professor of law at the University of Chicago and editor of the *Journal of Legal Studies*, offers an original and remorseless attack on the antidiscrimination principle in private employment and on Title VII of the 1964 Civil Rights Act in particular. For Epstein, state-enforced inhibitions against whom one may hire are costly, "imperial," inefficient, one-sided, easily sabotaged, and antithetical to the freedom of contract on which our system of liberal politics is based. Epstein argues that the only legitimate functions of government are to protect property and personal security and to enforce private contracts—in short, to protect a "zone of freedom." Such a government is principled; but when the state coerces association—as happens through Title VII and enforcement of affirmative action, its behavior is unprincipled.

2. *See* First Chronicle, *supra* this volume. (Shortly after his twentieth birthday, Rodrigo served briefly in the Italian army as a "way of paying back the Italian nation for subsidizing my education at a fine university.")

3. A foreign national who is admitted to a U.S. program of study may generally obtain a temporary U.S. visa. But this requires that the applicant disavow any intent to remain in the United States following graduation. *See* T. ALEXANDER ALEINIKOFF & DAVID A. MARTIN, IMMIGRATION: PROCESS AND POLICY 220 (2d ed. 1991).

4. On nativism and immigration policies, see Richard Delgado & Jean Stefancic, *Images of the Outsider in American Law and Culture: Can Free Expression Remedy Systemic Social Ills?*, 77 CORNELL L. REV. 1258, 1270–75 (1992); Richard Delgado & Jean Stefancic, *Norms and Narratives: Can Judges Avoid Serious Moral Error?*, 69 TEXAS L. REV. 1929, 1943–47 (1991).

5. On the use of private bills to circumvent or supplement stringent immigration laws and quotas, *see* ALEINIKOFF & MARTIN, *supra*, at 668–73.

6. On the separation-of-powers doctrine in American politics and constitutional law, *see* LAURENCE H. TRIBE, AMERICAN CONSTITUTIONAL LAW §§ 2-1 to 5-24 (2d ed. 1988) ("Model I—The Model of Separated and Divided Powers").

7. Aside from Forbidden Grounds, the titles were the following: GARY BECKER, THE ECONOMICS OF DISCRIMINATION (2d ed. 1971); CHARLES MURRAY, LOSING GROUND (1984); RICHARD A. POSNER, ECONOMIC ANALYSIS OF LAW 615 (3d ed. 1986) (I had been pondering ch. 27, "Racial Discrimination"); and THOMAS SOWELL, CIVIL RIGHTS: RHETORIC OR REALITY? (1984).

8. *See* First Chronicle, *supra* this volume, discussing the work and ideas of Dinesh D'Souza, Glenn Loury, Shelby Steele, and others writing in this general vein.

9. POSNER, ECONOMIC ANALYSIS, *supra*.

10. *See* DERRICK BELL, AND WE ARE NOT SAVED (1987); Delgado & Stefancic, *Images*, *supra*, at 1259–61, 1276–79 (both stating that racism is concerned with preserving racial advantage); *see also* Kathryn Abrams, *Hearing the Call of Stories*, 79 CAL. L. REV. 971, 975–76 (1991) (arguing that law's narrative substructure promotes advantage of the powerful but disguises its own operation).

11. *See, e.g.*, CATHARINE A. MACKINNON, FEMINISM UNMODIFIED: DISCOURSES ON LIFE AND LAW (1987); Martha Minow & Elizabeth V. Spelman, *In Context*, 63 S. CAL. L. REV. 1597 (1990).

12. Randall Kennedy, *Racial Critiques of Legal Academia*, 102 HARV. L. REV. 1745, 1770–77, 1779–87, 1794–1807 (1989).

13. *E.g.*, SOWELL, *supra*.

14. *E.g.*, FORBIDDEN GROUNDS, *supra*, at 42–47, 60; BECKER, *supra*, at 6, 16, 18, 153; POSNER, *supra*, at 615–18; SOWELL, *supra*, at 96, 112–14, 116.

15. *E.g.*, FORBIDDEN GROUNDS, *supra*, at 41–42, 265, 496; BECKER, *supra*, at 159; POSNER, *supra*, at 615 & *n.*1; SOWELL, *supra*, at 96, 112–14, 116.

16. *E.g.*, FORBIDDEN GROUNDS, *supra*, at 41–42; *see* BECKER, *supra*, at 6, 18; POSNER, *supra*, at 615–18. *But see* FORBIDDEN GROUNDS at 59–78 ("Rational Discrimination," arguing that discrimination sometimes makes sense—and confers legitimate benefits, such as greater ease, familiarity, and better communication among coworkers).

17. On the view that the essence of racism is group advantage, *see, for example*, BELL, NOT SAVED, *supra*; Derrick A. Bell, Jr., *Brown v. Board of Education and the Interest-Convergence Dilemma*, 93 HARV. L. REV. 518 (1980).

18. *See, e.g.*, Milner S. Ball, *Stories of Origin and Constitutional Possibilities*, 87 MICH. L. REV. 2280 (1989); Mari J. Matsuda, *Public Response to Racist Speech: Considering the Victim's Story*, 87 MICH. L. REV. 2320 (1989); *see also* MACKINNON, *supra* (discussing construction of women and women's role).

19. On legal storytelling as a means of jarring or displacing comfortable majoritarian beliefs, *see* BELL, NOT SAVED, *supra*; Matsuda, *supra*.

20. *See* Delgado & Stefancic, *Images*, *supra*.

21. *Id.* at 1261, 1280–82 (terming faith that we can readily escape the force of our own embedded stereotypes and cultural assumptions the "empathic fallacy").

22. I meant to remind Rodrigo of the way in which his years abroad enabled him to see U.S. culture with new eyes; *see* First Chronicle, *supra* this volume.

23. On the role of knowledge, *see* POSNER, *supra*, at 96–100, 348–50. On the view that Title VII can decrease information flow to employers and thus increase discrimination, *see* FORBIDDEN GROUNDS, *supra*, at 28–30.

24. *See* PETER L. BERGER & THOMAS LUCKMANN, THE SOCIAL CONSTRUCTION OF REALITY (1967); JOSEPH CAMPBELL, THE POWER OF MYTH (1988); MICHEL FOUCAULT, POWER/KNOWLEDGE: SELECTED INTERVIEWS AND OTHER WRITINGS 1972–1977 (Colin Gor-

don ed. & Colin Gordon et al. trans., 1980); 1 & 2 PAUL RICOUER, TIME AND NARRATIVE (Kathleen McLaughlin & David Pellauer trans., 1984–1985); *see also* JACQUES DERRIDA, OF GRAMMATOLOGY (Gayatri C. Spivak trans., 1976) (contending that words alter—do "violence" to—experience).

25. On the way narrative structures shape what we see and believe, *see* MACKINNON, *supra*; Abrams, *supra*; Charles R. Lawrence III, *The Id, The Ego, and Equal Protection: Reckoning with Unconscious Racism,* 39 STAN. L. REV. 317 (1987).

26. On women and the military, *see* Rostker v. Goldberg, 453 U.S. 57 (1981).

27. On desegregation of the Armed Forces, *see* Bell, *Interest-Convergence, supra,* at 524–25; Mary L. Dudziak, *Desegregation as a Cold War Imperative,* 41 STAN. L. REV. 61, 71–73 (1988).

28. On gays in the military, *see* Dronenberg v. Zech, 741 F.2d 1388 (D.C. Cir. 1984).

29. "Truths" that are accepted into the broader culture, that became part of received wisdom, are highly resistant to change. *See* Delgado & Stefancic, *Images, supra*; Delgado & Stefancic, *Norms and Narratives, supra*; Lawrence, *supra*.

30. FORBIDDEN GROUNDS, *supra*, at 42, 149–51.

31. MURRAY, *supra*, at 146, 224, 227–28.

32. SOWELL, *supra*, at 51–53, 77–78.

33. BECKER, *supra*, at 6, 16, 153 (describing discrimination as a "taste").

34. BELL, NOT SAVED, *supra*; Delgado & Stefancic, *Images, supra* (both characterizing racism as structural, not accidental or a matter of individual pathology).

35. For earlier views of this "optimism gap" (in which whites hold that things are getting better for blacks, while blacks think the opposite), *see* Robin D. Barnes, *An Extra-Terrestrial Trade Proposition Brings an End to the World as We Know It,* 34 ST. LOUIS U. L.J. 413 (1990); Derrick Bell, *Racial Realism,* 24 CONN. L. REV. 363 (1992); Richard Delgado, *Derrick Bell and the Ideology of Racial Reform: Will We Ever Be Saved?* 97 YALE L.J. 923 (1988).

36. *E.g.,* JOHN CALVIN, INSTITUTES OF THE CHRISTIAN RELIGION (Henry Beveridge trans., Wm. B. Eerdmans Publishing 1953); *see* DAVID HUME, DIALOGUES CONCERNING NATURAL RELIGION 51–56 (Norman K. Smith ed., 1947) (addressing "argument from design").

37. *See* Robert A. Williams, *Documents of Barbarism: The Contemporary Legacy of European Racism and Colonialism in the Narrative Traditions of Federal Indian Law,* 31 ARIZ. L. REV. 237 (1989). *See also* Ball, *supra*.

38. Delgado & Stefancic, *Norms and Narratives, supra,* at 1939–40 (on Discovery Doctrine in early U.S. law).

39. On "double consciousness," in which excluded people see themselves in two perspectives at once—that of the majority race, according to which they are demonized and despised, and their own, in which they are normal—*see* W. E. B. DU BOIS, THE SOULS OF BLACK FOLK 3–4 (Kraus-Thomson 1973) (1903); RALPH ELLISON, THE INVISIBLE MAN (1952). For contemporary explications of double or multiple consciousness, *see* BELL HOOKS, FEMI-

NIST THEORY: FROM MARGIN TO CENTER (1984); Mari J. Matsuda, *When the First Quail Calls: Multiple Consciousness as Jurisprudential Method*, 11 WOMEN'S RTS. L. REP. 7 (1989).

40. *See* SOWELL, *supra*; THOMAS SOWELL, THE ECONOMICS AND POLITICS OF RACE (1983); THOMAS SOWELL, ETHNIC AMERICA: A HISTORY (1981); THOMAS SOWELL, MARKETS AND MINORITIES (1981).

41. *See, e.g.*, SOWELL, RHETORIC, *supra*, at 20–22, 77–78, 79.

42. On the proliferation of critical writing about race and radical feminism, and its halfhearted absorption by the rest of the legal academy, see Richard Delgado, *The Imperial Scholar Revisited: How To Marginalize Outsider Writing, Ten Years Later*, 140 U. PA. L. REV. 1349 (1992). *See also* Richard Delgado, *Brewer's Plea: Critical Thoughts on Common Cause*, 44 VAND. L. REV. 1 (1991) (expressing doubt that the impasse between Critical Race scholars and mainstream civil rights scholars will soon be bridged); Richard Delgado & Jean Stefancic, *Critical Race Theory: An Annotated Bibliography*, 79 VA. L. REV. 461 (1993) (tracing development of Critical Race Theory and reviewing its major themes and writings). For criticism of the CRT movement, *see* Kennedy, *supra*.

43. Attributed to Adam Smith, the term refers to the unseen operation of the all-wise market. *See* ADAM SMITH, THE WEALTH OF NATIONS (Mod. Libr. ed. 1937).

44. On criticism of critical writing as too despairing, *see* Alan D. Freeman, *Race and Class: The Dilemma of Liberal Reform*, 90 YALE L.J. 1880 (1981); *Commentary*, 24 CONN. L. REV. 497 (1992) (including various authors' comments on Bell's realist premise); Robert M. O'Neil, *A Reaction to "The Imperial Scholar" and Professor Delgado's Proposed Solution*, 3 LAW & INEQ. J. 255 (1982).

45. *See* First Chronicle, *supra* this volume.

46. *Id.* (setting out Rodrigo's view that the West is suffering economic decline, cultural stasis, and environmental deterioration); *see also id.* Appendix 1A: Rodrigo's Printout #1; listing books and articles on the theory of cyclicity among nations and on the United States's decline in particular. I was also reminded of the United States's recent refusal to sign proposed bioprotection treaties at the Earth Summit in Rio de Janeiro. *E.g.*, Paul Raeburn, *U.S. at Loggerheads over Forests*, BOULDER (CO) DAILY CAMERA, June 11, 1992, at A1.

47. *See* Delgado & Stefancic, *Images, supra*.

48. On counterstorytelling as jurisprudential method and means for challenging, enriching, or changing the dominant culture, *see* BELL, NOT SAVED, *supra*; PATRICIA J. WILLIAMS, THE ALCHEMY OF RACE AND RIGHTS (1991); Abrams, *supra*; Matsuda, *supra*.

49. What about two well-dressed men of color put them off, I wondered briefly. Rodrigo and I had been engaged in exactly the sort of economic trading that, according to the law and economists, should reduce prejudice. Was it that we were eating in their favorite restaurant? Were of the same sex? Were engaged in intense intellectual discussion? Yet another nagging reminder of the separateness of race and economic class as disadvantaging factors, I mused. On the "hate

stare," *see* Harlon L. Dalton, *The Clouded Prism*, 22 HARV. C.R.-C.L. L. REV. 435 (1987).

Notes to Chapter 3

1. I thought of the many writers who had struggled to explain and understand "welfare capitalism," a system based on free market principles but, nevertheless, containing safety nets for the unfortunate. *E.g.*, 1 KENNETH BOULDING, ECONOMIC ANALYSIS 627–49 (4th ed. 1966) (arguing that Pareto optimality within a society must take account of certain ethical ideas of what a "better" society is); JOHN K. GALBRAITH, THE AFFLUENT SOCIETY 1–5 (3d ed. 1976) (arguing that public expenditures must increase concurrently with private production in order to redress social ills); JOHN K. GALBRAITH, THE NEW INDUSTRIAL STATE 1–10 (4th ed. 1985) (arguing that the modern economy no longer conforms to the ideal of free market capitalism). *Contra* ADAM SMITH, THE WEALTH OF NATIONS ch. 8 (Everyman's Library 1991) (1776) (expounding the traditional view—social welfare increases as a natural result of the increasing wealth of a society).
2. Rodrigo completed his degree "at a law school even older than [mine]," First Chronicle, *supra* this volume, and before that studied comparative world cultures while on scholarship at the same university.
3. *See* Richard Delgado, *Minority Law Professors' Lives: The Bell-Delgado Survey*, 24 HARV. C.R.-C.L. L. REV. 349, 367–68 (1989) (detailing problems of expected ethnic specialization and expertise).
4. ANDREW HACKER, TWO NATIONS: BLACK AND WHITE, SEPARATE, HOSTILE, UNEQUAL (1992). Hacker, a professor of political science at Queens College in New York City, is the author of numerous articles about race or American culture. In TWO NATIONS, Hacker paints a bleak portrait of the racial predicament of the United States. Drawing his title from a quotation by Benjamin Disraeli, Hacker shows, through a dazzling array of figures and statistics, that America today has in effect become a nation divided into two separate camps, white and black, one wealthy, the other poor, both hostile to one another.
5. Unfortunately, reports of such events are legion. *E.g.*, Michael Booth, *Four Deaths Probed at Bethany Care Center*, DENV. POST, July 28, 1992, at A1 (investigation into four patient deaths at a single nursing home).
6. *E.g.*, RICHARD A. EPSTEIN, FORBIDDEN GROUNDS: THE CASE AGAINST EMPLOYMENT DISCRIMINATION LAWS 15–27 (1992) (concluding that governmental coercion and interference should have little or no role in ordering the private marketplace).
7. Nancy R. Gibbs, *Grays on the Go*, TIME, Feb. 22, 1988, at 66, 70 (statistics show that an increasing percentage of Americans are over 65).
8. U.S. CONST. art. I, § 8, cl. 7.
9. *E.g.*, Zachary Margulis, *Neither Snow, nor Rain, but Huge Buildings Will Stay a Courier*, NEWSDAY, July 5, 1992, at 2 (discussing inefficient mail delivery

and overtime costs resulting from high tenant turnover in urban apartment complexes).

10. *See* HACKER, *supra*, at 105–106, 110–11 (pointing out that creation of semi-skilled jobs for black men implies racial predisposition to certain occupations and using statistics to show that a two-class job system already exists and is divided along racial lines).

11. On the stresses (and satisfactions) of life as an inner-city scholteacher, *see* JONATHAN KOZOL, DEATH AT AN EARLY AGE (1967).

12. *See* HACKER, *supra*, at 134–98.

13. *U.S. Gets Less Competitive as Japan Stays on Top, Annual Survey Indicates,* ATLANTA J. & CONST., June 22, 1992, at A10 (U.S. economy dropped to fifth-most competitive, and United States seventh in quality of workforce); *see also* First Chronicle, *supra* this volume (discussing America's economic decline and listing related resources in Appendix 1A, Part C).

14. HACKER, *supra*, at xiii; STUDS TERKEL, RACE: HOW BLACKS AND WHITES THINK AND FEEL ABOUT THE AMERICAN OBSESSION (1992) (arguing that the clock has turned back on the progress of the 1960s and that once again hostility, resentment, and racial conflict threaten to divide the nation); *see also* DERRICK BELL, AND WE ARE NOT SAVED 10 (1987) (acknowledging that the differing self-interest of blacks and whites can work to undermine already fragile legal guarantees of equality). *See generally* PATRICIA WILLIAMS, THE ALCHEMY OF RACE AND RIGHTS (1991) (detailing traditional legal thinking's inability to cope with the reality of racial relations).

15. *See generally* James M. Doyle, *"It's The Third World Down There!": The Colonialist Vocation and American Criminal Justice,* 27 HARV. C.R.-C.L. L. REV. 71 (1992) (offering harrowing description of lives of prosecutors, police, public defenders, and others charged with servicing the nation's courts).

16. On the reciprocal relation between culture and media depiction in creating "tastes," *see* Richard Delgado & Jean Stefancic, *Images of the Outsider in American Law and Culture,* 77 CORNELL L. REV. 1258 (1992).

17. ROBERT V. STOVER, MAKING IT AND BREAKING IT: THE FATE OF PUBLIC INTEREST COMMITMENT DURING LAW SCHOOL 2, 20–22, 64 (1989); Terry Carter, *Why Students Lose Their Interest in Entering Public Interest Work,* NAT'L L.J., July 31, 1989, at 4.

18. *E.g.,* Duncan Kennedy, *Legal Education as Training for Hierarchy,* in THE POLITICS OF LAW: A PROGRESSIVE CRITIQUE 40, 52 (David Kairys ed., 1982) (characterizing large-firm practice as far less interesting and demanding than public interest work).

19. *See* RICHARD POSNER, ECONOMIC ANALYSIS OF LAW 91–96 (3d ed. 1986) (discussing role of insurance in providing against future costs).

20. THE BEATLES, *Can't Buy Me Love,* on A HARD DAY'S NIGHT (Electra Records, 1964).

21. Herman Dienske & Rochelle Griffin, *Abnormal Behaviour Patterns Developing in Chimpanzee Infants During Nursery Care—A Note,* 19 J. CHILD PSYCHOL. & PSYCHIATRY 387 (1978).

22. *E.g.*, Jerry Carroll, *Your Money and Your Life*, S.F. CHRON., June 18, 1992, at D3, D6 (relating plight of patient with Lou Gehrig's disease whose family could no longer afford home care but refused to put him in a facility where, despite the good care, all the patients die within one year).

23. *See, e.g.*, CHARLES MURRAY, LOSING GROUND (1984) (arguing that social welfare programs have failed completely); THOMAS SOWELL, CIVIL RIGHTS: RHETORIC OR REALITY? 86–90 (1984) (arguing that earmarked subsidies may principally create white resentment while failing to resolve deeper problems of economic exclusion).

24. I was intrigued by Rodrigo's reversal. In supply-side economics, of course, the "trickle-down" theory was used to justify deregulation, tax incentives, and other measures the Republicans instituted to stimulate production, and to benefit capitalists and investors. In theory, the improvements such measures would bring the economy in general would filter down to the poor and underemployed.

25. I thought of the adulation and affection that Republicans and others shower on certain black "Horatio Algers," like Clarence Thomas. *See also* the sharp and sometimes poignant observations of Stephen Carter in his book, REFLECTIONS OF AN AFFIRMATIVE ACTION BABY (1991) (arguing that affirmative action must return to its simpler roots, to provide educational opportunities for those who might not have them, and that the beneficiaries of affirmative action must thereafter be held to the same standards as anyone else).

26. *See, e.g.*, EPSTEIN, *supra*, at 259–66 (arguing that the best way for less-educated blacks to compete in the job market is to offer their services at lower wages); MURRAY, *supra*, at 39–40 (arguing that white moral confusion about the course of the civil rights movement allowed the blame for poverty to shift from the poor onto the system and history).

27. *See* EPSTEIN, *supra*, at 9 (arguing that competitive markets offer better and more certain protection against invidious discrimination than any antidiscrimination law); MURRAY, *supra*, at 223 (calling for the repeal of legislation and legal precedent advocating or rewarding differential treatment according to race); SOWELL, *supra*, at 112–17 (arguing that market mechanisms will ultimately reward private parties who hire and pay for cheaper labor from underrepresented minorities or women).

28. *See* Eighth Chronicle, *supra* this volume (on black crime).

29. For examples or discussion of this anticolonialist writing, *see generally* FRANTZ FANON, THE WRETCHED OF THE EARTH (1963) (discussing decolonization and the process of national liberation); ALBERT MEMMI, THE COLONIZER AND THE COLONIZED (Howard Greenfeld trans., 1965); Doyle, *supra* (comparing role of white men in criminal justice system to that of white colonial administrators and commissioners).

30. *See, e.g.*, BELL, NOT SAVED, *supra*, at 3–7, 26–74, 123–61; Derrick A. Bell, Jr., *Brown v. Board of Education and the Interest-Convergence Dilemma*, 93 HARV. L. REV. 518, 522–28 (1980) (discussing maintenance of segregated schools as important to poorer whites who had expectation that their social status

would remain superior to blacks'); Richard Delgado, *Derrick Bell and the Ideology of Law Reform: Will We Ever Be Saved?*, 97 YALE L.J. 923 (1988) (reviewing Bell's Chronicles and the history and effects of racism through the words of Bell's alter ego, Geneva Crenshaw).

31. *See, e.g.*, BELL, NOT SAVED, *supra*, at 51–122 (discussing benefits to whites of civil rights litigation); Bell, *supra*, at 526–32 (discussing ways in which southern states and cities, as well as the Supreme Court itself, limited or impeded the implementation of the principles of Brown); Delgado, *supra*, at 925 & *n*.9, 926 (summarizing Bell's belief that "American racism is here to stay in our most prized legal institutions despite our most exalted legal rhetoric").

32. JANE GOODALL, THE CHIMPANZEES OF GOMBE: PATTERNS OF BEHAVIOR 530–34 (1986); *see also* Lionel Tiger, *Love and Murder Among the Chimps*, N.Y. TIMES, Mar. 13, 1988, § 7, at 14 (reviewing MICHAEL P. GHIGLIERI, EAST OF THE MOUNTAINS OF THE MOON (1988) and recounting Ghiglieri's observations of aggressive and often murderous behavior by male chimps asserting territorial rights or usurping the role of other male chimps).

33. *E.g.*, Jerome Grossman, *With a Demonized Enemy, Going Nuclear Seems Easy*, L.A. TIMES, Aug. 13, 1991, at B7 (citing poll in which 45% of Americans surveyed favored use of nuclear weapons against Iraq during beginning of Gulf War to save U.S. lives).

34. HACKER, *supra*, at 7, 14.

35. *E.g.*, City of Memphis v. Greene, 451 U.S. 100 (1981) (addressing a street closing that effectively curtailed traffic into an all-white community).

36. HACKER, *supra*, at 162–63. "The National School Board Association measures segregation by computing the number of Black youngsters in a state or locality who are enrolled in schools where they, or Hispanics, make up a majority of the pupils." *Id.* at 162.

37. *Id.* at 164–65.

38. *Id.* at 132.

39. *Id.* at 101.

40. *Id.* at 98–99; *see also id.* at 115 (percentage of women working is much higher among blacks than whites).

41. *Id.* at 99.

42. *Id.* at 98–99.

43. *Id.* at 110–11.

44. *E.g.*, Oscar Lewis, *The Culture of Poverty*, in ON UNDERSTANDING POVERTY: PERSPECTIVES FROM THE SOCIAL SCIENCES 187 (Daniel P. Moynihan ed., 1969) (describing the culture of poverty and its effects); *see also* NATHAN GLAZER & DANIEL P. MOYNIHAN, BEYOND THE MELTING POT: THE NEGROES, PUERTO RICANS, JEWS, ITALIANS, AND IRISH OF NEW YORK CITY lxxxvi–lxxxvii (2d ed. 1970) (discussing welfare dependency as exacerbating problems of racism); MURRAY, *supra*, at 18–20, 38–40 (discussing white resentment of the perceived permanency of welfare to

blacks and the failure of helping-hand training programs); SOWELL, *supra*, at 77–90 (arguing that cultural differences, rather than skin color, determine economic status).

45. HACKER, *supra*, at 35–38.
46. *Id*. at 14, 217 (whites continue to believe in their own superiority and suspect blacks of inferiority).
47. *Id*. at 40.
48. *Id*. at 189.
49. *Id*. at 180, 197.
50. *Id*. at 191 *n*. Moreover, even holding other factors "such as the ferocity of the crime and the social status of the victim . . . constant, the prospect for the death penalty was still four times higher when the victim was white." *Id*.
51. HACKER, *supra*, at 36.
52. *See* Richard Delgado, *Storytelling for Oppositionists and Others: A Plea for Narrative*, 87 MICH. L. REV. 2411 (1989) (arguing that the use of stories can be helpful in the struggle for racial reform because it shatters complacency and challenges the status quo); *see also* BELL, NOT SAVED, *supra* (reciting ten metaphorical tales to discuss the experiences of blacks in America and their struggle for racial equality); Kathryn Abrams, *Hearing the Call of Stories*, 79 CAL. L. REV. 971 (1992) (arguing that the emergence of feminist narrative scholarship is a distinctive form of critical legal discourse).
53. THOMAS HOBBES, LEVIATHAN 112–19, 172 (Herbert Schneider ed., The Liberal Arts Press, Inc. 1958) (1651).
54. *Id*. at 107 (life in a state of nature would be "solitary, poor, nasty, brutish and short").
55. *E.g.*, Garrett Hardin, *The Tragedy of the Commons*, 162 SCIENCE 1243 (1968) (discussing predicament of society in which a few members attempt to gain an edge by abusing the common trust).
56. Richard Delgado & Jean Stefancic, *Derrick Bell and the Chronicle of the Space Traders: Would the U.S. Sacrifice People of Color if the Price Were Right?*, 62 U. COLO. L. REV. 321 (1991) (agreeing with the plausibility of Derrick Bell's parable in which the United States sells all its African-Americans for solutions to its problems); *see also* DERRICK BELL, RACE, RACISM, AND AMERICAN LAW 1–51 (2d ed. 1980) (recounting a history of blacks in the United States in which they were given the roles of "sacrificial supergoats").
57. I thought of white colleagues and scholars who were writing helpful analyses of race. *E.g.*, T. Alexander Aleinikoff, *The Constitution in Context: The Continuing Significance of Racism*, 63 U. COLO. L. REV. 325 (1992) (arguing that race discrimination against nonwhites remains a serious problem in American society and that recognition of this bigotry has important implications for the crafting of constitutional doctrine); Alan D. Freeman, *Legitimizing Racial Discrimination Through Antidiscrimination Law: A Critical Review of Supreme Court Doctrine*, 62 MINN. L. REV. 1049 (1978) (arguing that although the law outlaws racial discrimination, it tolerates conditions that promote the lower economic status of black Americans); Duncan Kennedy, *A Cultural Pluralist Case for Affirmative*

Action in Legal Academia, 1990 DUKE L.J. 705 (arguing for a large expansion of our current commitment to cultural diversity on the ground that law schools are political institutions); Gary Peller, *Race Consciousness*, 1990 DUKE L.J. 758 (exploring the ideological roots of Critical Race Theory, its reinterpretation of race consciousness, and its break with the dominant civil rights discourse).

58. *E.g.*, HACKER, *supra*, at 35 (despite antidiscrimination housing laws, residential areas remain heavily segregated); *see also id.* at 191 (black victims of violent crime are less likely to see justice done).

59. Regarding the loopholes and exceptions that courts have created or engrafted on the civil rights laws, see Richard Delgado, *On Taking Back Our Civil Rights Promises: When Equality Doesn't Compute*, 1989 WIS. L. REV. 579, 583–84 (1989) (arguing that doctrinal retrenchment is occurring in civil rights cases just as the use of computers and sophisticated methods of statistical proof enable plaintiffs to establish discrimination); *see also* BELL, NOT SAVED, *supra*, at 51–75 (caustic critique of U.S. civil rights policy).

60. Rodrigo had blithely raised these matters before, much to my chagrin. First Chronicle, *supra* (Rodrigo discusses the use of sabotage and terrorism to quicken the pace of the dominant group's sharing power with minority groups).

61. *See* Regina Austin, *"The Black Community," Its Lawbreakers, and a Politics of Identification*, 65 S. CAL. L. REV. 1769, 1816 (1992) (if activism within the law fails to reorder priorities and change society, actions outside the law may be required); Robert J. Cottrol & Raymond T. Diamond, *The Second Amendment: Toward an Afro-Americanist Reconsideration*, 80 GEO. L.J. 309 (1991) (arguing that society's dismal record of protecting blacks ought to preclude society from disarming them).

62. I thought of the hymns of praise from the conservative white community that greeted the publication of Thomas Sowell, Stephen Carter, Clarence Thomas, and some of Randall Kennedy's works. *See also* HACKER, *supra*, at 52 (white conservatives turn to black conservatives like Sowell, Thomas, and Shelby Steele to defend and support their own positions).

63. "Spade" is a disparaging term for an African-American. 16 OXFORD ENGLISH DICTIONARY 96 (2d ed. 1989) ("A Black Person, a Negro, esp. male: freq. in White use, as a term of contempt or casual reference. Formerly among U.S. Blacks, a very dark-skinned Negro. slang [orig. U.S.].") (Definition 3a).

64. HACKER, *supra*, at 14, 26–28.

65. The term is Regina Austin's. *See* Austin, *supra*, at 1799–1800.

66. *See generally* Delgado & Stefancic, *supra* (arguing that racist images from earlier times are only viewed as racist today because consciousness has shifted and society has adopted a different narrative); Richard Delgado & Jean Stefancic, *Norms and Narratives: Can Judges Avoid Serious Moral Error?*, 69 TEX L. REV. 1929, 1930 (1991) (arguing that moral error in judging can arise from the inability to identify with the different life experiences of the judged).

67. Was I deserving of the compliment? I recalled a number of times when I had been cutting or dismissive of whites, including a number who were well-meaning. But Rodrigo was speaking with such fervor that I hesitated to interrupt.

Notes to Chapter 4

1. The first of these books, DERRICK BELL, FACES AT THE BOTTOM OF THE WELL: THE PERMANENCE OF RACISM (1992), argues that racism is likely to prove a permanent feature of America's cultural landscape. The "faces" are those of African-Americans whose existence at the bottom of society enables even the poorest whites to gain self-esteem. *Id.* at v (frontispiece). Written almost entirely in the narrative mode, FACES recounts a series of imaginary tales, each illustrating a lesson about racial justice. Although most of these lessons are bleak and severe, Bell nevertheless exhorts readers to continue the struggle for racial justice.

A second work, GERALD N. ROSENBERG, THE HOLLOW HOPE: CAN COURTS BRING ABOUT SOCIAL CHANGE? (1991), presents a critique of the role of the courts in producing social change. Although sponsored by a conservative foundation, the book purports to be an objective assessment of courts' role and function. Contrasting the view of the United States Supreme Court as dynamic in producing social change with the view that the Court is constrained in its ability to effect reform, Rosenberg concludes that the latter is a more accurate depiction. *Id.* at 10–30, 35, 157–69, 175–227. According to Rosenberg, courts produce little change that was not previously in motion and are less effective in propelling reform than other extralegal forces, such as market pressures, technological changes, political action, and legislative reform. Nevertheless, Rosenberg notes that courts are effective in blocking change.

GIRARDEAU A. SPANN, RACE AGAINST THE COURT: THE SUPREME COURT AND MINORITIES IN CONTEMPORARY AMERICA (1993), argues that the Court not only is institutionally incapable of protecting minority rights but that it serves to perpetuate majoritarian control. *Id.* at 31–59, 180–272. In Spann's view, operational and formal safeguards designed to insulate judicial decisions from political pressure are insufficient to counter the influence of majoritarian sociopolitical values. *Id.* at 22, 37–43. Indeed, often "the governing substantive principles of law themselves incorporate majoritarian values in a way that leaves the Court with no choice but to acquiesce in majority desires." *Id.* at 30. Automatically taking minority grievances to the judicial system creates a dependency relationship with an increasingly unresponsive institution. Spann believes that the use of other societal mechanisms, such as mass politics, demonstrations, and state and local governments, would be more effective in producing racial advances than judicial intervention. *Id.* at 146–75, 178–206, 219–20.

The last work, DAVID G. SAVAGE, TURNING RIGHT: THE MAKING OF THE REHNQUIST SUPREME COURT (1992), considers the Supreme Court's role in minority rights from the perspective of a *Los Angeles Times* journalist. In a discussion that contains elements of the three above-mentioned theses, Savage focuses on the changes in the Court's composition and ideology, which accompanied the emergence of the current conservative majority. Savage's book deals with the Court's treatment of civil rights, the right to die, flag desecration, the death penalty, and other notable areas. Moreover, Savage's personal interviews with the Justices enable him to give fascinating insights into the Justices' personalities and working styles. The book ends with a description of the Clarence Thomas confirmation hearings, *id.* at 423–50, and a look forward at the Court's likely quietist role in social reform.

2. Many law schools have such annual programs.

3. A similar incident happened at Harvard Law School. For a discussion of the controversy surrounding a lampoon issue of *Harvard Law Revue,* see David Margolick, *In Attacking the Work of a Slain Professor Harvard's Elite Themselves Become a Target,* N.Y. TIMES, Apr. 17, 1992, at B16, B16. This controversy concerned the following article: *Mary Doe, He-Manifesto of Post-Mortem Legal Feminism (From the Desk of Mary Doe),* 105 HARV. L. REVUE 13 (1992) (the issue subsequently was withdrawn).

4. *Compare* Margolick, *supra,* with Michele N-K Collison, *Angry Protests over Diversity and Free Speech Mark Contentious Spring Semester at Harvard,* CHRON. HIGHER EDUC., May 6, 1992, at A39, A39–40.

5. *E.g.,* Nadine Strossen, *Regulating Racist Speech on Campus: A Modest Proposal?,* 1990 DUKE L.J. 484 (The author, national president of the ACLU, contends that racial insults are protected speech.).

6. For a classic treatment of neutrality in constitutional adjudication, *see* Herbert Wechsler, *Toward Neutral Principles of Constitutional Law,* 73 HARV. L. REV. 1 (1959). For a rigorous reexamination of this position, *see* Neil Gotanda, *A Critique of "Our Constitution Is Color-Blind,"* 44 STAN. L. REV. 1 (1991).

7. *See, e.g.,* BELL, FACES, *supra,* at 2–14, 89–108; DERRICK BELL, RACE, RACISM AND AMERICAN LAW (3d ed. 1992) (arguing that neutral race-remedies law maintains white supremacy); Alan David Freeman, *Legitimizing Racial Discrimination Through Antidiscrimination Law: A Critical Review of Supreme Court Doctrine,* 62 MINN. L. REV. 1049 (1978); Gotanda, *supra.*

8. CATHARINE A. MACKINNON, FEMINISM UNMODIFIED: DISCOURSES ON LIFE AND LAW (1989); CATHARINE A. MACKINNON, TOWARD A FEMINIST THEORY OF THE STATE (1989).

9. The book was Girardeau Spann's Race Against the Court.

10. Girardeau A. Spann, *Pure Politics,* 88 MICH. L. REV. 1971 (1990).

11. *E.g.,* HOLLOW HOPE, *supra.*

12. *E.g.,* SPANN, *supra,* at iv–vi, 30–34, 180–204, 262–78, 293–97.

13. *E.g.,* SAVAGE, *supra,* at 453–58; ROSENBERG, at 10–21 (describing "Constrained Court" model of judicial function).

14. On unconscious racism, *see* Charles R. Lawrence, III, *The Id, the Ego, and Equal Protection: Reckoning with Unconscious Racism,* 39 STAN. L. REV. 317 (1987).

15. *E.g.,* T. Alexander Aleinikoff, *A Case for Race-Consciousness,* 91 COLUM. L. REV. 1060 (1991); Derrick A. Bell, Jr., *Private Clubs and Public Judges: A Nonsubstantive Debate About Symbols,* 59 TEX. L. REV. 733 (1980); Richard Delgado, *Storytelling for Oppositionists and Others: A Plea for Narrative,* 87 MICH. L. REV. 2411 (1989); Mari J. Matsuda, *When the First Quail Calls:*

Multiple Consciousness as Jurisprudential Method, 11 WOMEN'S RTS. L. REP. 7 (1989).

16. *See* Hustler Magazine, Inc. v. Falwell, 485 U.S. 46 (1988) (stating general rule that satire directed at a public figure qualifies for First Amendment protection).

17. *See* DERRICK BELL, AND WE ARE NOT SAVED: THE ELUSIVE QUEST FOR RACIAL JUSTICE, 143 (1987) (addressing alumni uneasiness with demographic shifts within contemporary law schools).

18. Most groups, of course, including the dominant one, use disparaging terms to focus anger, contempt, or dislike on members of other groups. *See* CAROL ROSEN, MAYBE HE'S JUST A JERK (1992); Peggy C. Davis, *Law as Microaggression*, 98 YALE L.J. 1559 (1989); Richard Delgado, *Words That Wound: A Tort Action for Racial Insults, Epithets, and Name-Calling*, 17 HARV. C.R.- C.L. L. REV. 133, 133–49 (1982); Richard Delgado & Jean Stefancic, *Images of the Outsider in American Law and Culture: Can Free Expression Remedy Systemic Social Ills?*, 77 CORNELL L. REV. 1258, 1282–83 (1992).

19. This concept of a "jerk" is an example of a language game. Conceived by Ludwig Wittgenstein, the notion of a language game focuses attention not on words' core or "essential" meanings or definitions but on their multiple, sometimes overlapping, uses. *See* LUDWIG WITTGENSTEIN, *TRACTATUS LOGICO-PHILOSOPHICUS* 9–25 (D. F. Pears & B. F. McGuinnes trans., 2d ed., Routledge & Kegan Paul 1974) (1921).

20. For a somewhat different depiction of a racial reversal of fortunes, *see* BELL, NOT SAVED, *supra*, at 162–77 ("Chronicle of the Amber Cloud").

21. *E.g.*, City of Richmond v. J. A. Croson Co., 488 U.S. 469 (1989) (minority set-aside held unconstitutional because city failed to show that its plan was narrowly tailored to remedy specific past discrimination that was not redressable through race-neutral means).

22. Derrick Bell has been one of the chief critics of this view. *See, e.g.*, Derrick A. Bell, Jr., *Bakke, Minority Admissions, and the Usual Price of Racial Remedies*, 67 CAL. L. REV. 3 (1979); Derrick A. Bell, Jr., *Brown v. Board of Education and the Interest-Convergence Dilemma*, 93 HARV. L. REV. 518, 523 (1979); *cf.* BELL, FACES, *supra*, at 89–108 (discussing racial realism).

23. *See* Martin v. Wilks, 490 U.S. 755, 761–62, 765, 768 (1989), superseded by statute Civil Rights Act of 1991, Pub. L. No. 102–66, 105 Stat. 1071 (codified as amended at 42 U.S.C.A. § 1981 (West Supp. 1992).

24. *See* Washington v. Davis, 426 U.S. 229, 239–40, 242, 245 (1976); Wards Cove Packing Co. v. Atonio, 490 U.S. 642 (1989), superseded by statute Civil Rights Act of 1991, Pub. L. No. 102–166, 105 Stat. 1071 (codified as amended at 42 U.S.C.A. § 1981 (West Supp. 1992)). *But see* Griggs v. Duke Power Co., 401 U.S. 424 (1971).

25. *E.g.*, Davidson v. Cannon, 474 U.S. 344, 347–48 (1986); Daniels v. Williams, 474 U.S. 327, 332–33 (1986); *see* Mark S. Brodin, *The Standard of Causation in the Mixed-Motive Title VII Action: A Social Policy Perspective*, 82 COLUM. L. REV. 292, 292–93, 304–10 (1982).

26. *See* Allen v. Wright, 468 U.S. 737, 751–61, 766 (1984).

27. *See* Richard Delgado, *Zero-Based Racial Politics: An Evaluation of Three Best-Case Arguments on Behalf of the Nonwhite Underclass*, 78 GEO. L.J. 1929, 1929–30 (1990).

28. For a description of the old regime of separate but equal schools, whites-only drinking fountains, Jim Crow laws, and of course, slavery, *see* BELL, RACE, RACISM, *supra*, at 2–63. *See generally* A. LEON HIGGINBOTHAM, JR., IN THE MATTER OF COLOR: RACE AND THE AMERICAN LEGAL PROCESS (1978); JENNIFER S. HOCHSCHILD, THE NEW AMERICAN DILEMMA (1984); KENNETH M. STAMPP, THE PECULIAR INSTITUTION: SLAVERY IN THE ANTE-BELLUM SOUTH (1956).

29. *See* Freeman, *supra*, at 1054, 1103; Richard Delgado, *Derrick Bell and the Ideology of Racial Reform: Will We Ever Be Saved?*, 97 YALE L.J. 923, 942–43 (1988) (reviewing DERRICK BELL, AND WE ARE NOT SAVED: THE ELUSIVE QUEST FOR RACIAL JUSTICE (1987)).

30. 349 U.S. 294 (1954).

31. *See* Gotanda, *supra* (discussing color blindness); Wechsler, *supra* (discussing neutrality); *see also* RICHARD EPSTEIN, FORBIDDEN GROUNDS: THE CASE AGAINST EMPLOYMENT DISCRIMINATION LAWS 147–266 (1992) (urging abandonment of race-conscious laws and programs).

32. For the view that affirmative action programs actually aid middle-class blacks instead of the more needy lower-class blacks, *see* STEPHEN L. CARTER, REFLECTIONS OF AN AFFIRMATIVE ACTION BABY 71–84, 94, 233 (1991); Delgado, *Ever Saved?, supra*.

33. CARTER, *supra*, at 230–32; SHELBY STEELE, THE CONTENT OF OUR CHARACTER: A NEW VISION OF RACE IN AMERICA 111–25 (1990) (criticizing result or quota oriented affirmative action programs).

34. On the critique of liberalism as incoherent and riddled with contradictions, *see*, for example, Jamie Boyle, *Critical Legal Studies: A Young Person's Guide* (mimeo, 1989).

35. With equality of opportunity, one never knows if one has achieved complete fairness; with equality of result, one simply notices whether one has achieved one's preselected measure or not.

36. *See* THOMAS SOWELL, CIVIL RIGHTS: RHETORIC OR REALITY? 37–60 (1984); STEELE, *supra*, at 121–22.

37. For a similar argument, *see* Richard Delgado, *Shadowboxing: An Essay on Power*, 77 CORNELL L. REV. 813, 817–21 (1992) (legal rules replicate social power, demonstrated through examples of medical informed consent, date rape, and cigarette warnings).

38. *Id.*; *see also* Richard Delgado & Jean Stefancic, *Pornography and Harm to Women: "No Empirical Evidence?"*, 53 OHIO ST. L.J. 1037 (1992) (using examples of antipornography movement).

39. For an explanation of how these factors can be manipulated into evidence justifying a "pool is so small" defense, *see* Richard Delgado, *Mindset and Metaphor*, 103 HARV. L. REV. 1872, 1876 (1990).

40. For a discussion of the role of distrust in legal theory, *see* JOHN HART ELY,

DEMOCRACY AND DISTRUST: A THEORY OF JUDICIAL REVIEW (1978); John Hart Ely, *Legislative and Administrative Motivation in Constitutional Law*, 79 YALE L.J. 1205, 1209 (1970).

41. *See* Kimberlè Williams Crenshaw, *Race, Reform and Retrenchment: Transformation and Legitimation in Antidiscrimination Law*, 101 HARV. L. REV. 1331 (1988) (describing the legitimation function of the law of race remedies); Freeman, *supra* (same).

42. For a discussion of the disparity in the quantity of racism that persons of different ethnicities perceive, *see* Delgado & Stefancic, *supra*, at 1282–84.

43. *See, e.g.*, SPANN, *supra*, at *iv–vi*, 30–34, 180–204, 269–78, 293–97.

44. *See* PATRICIA WILLIAMS, THE ALCHEMY OF RACE AND RIGHTS (1991) (arguing that racial issues must be interpreted in light of the historical and personal experiences of the oppressed); Anthony E. Cook, *Beyond Critical Legal Studies: The Reconstructive Theology of Dr. Martin Luther King, Jr.*, 103 HARV. L. REV. 985 (1990) (same).

45. *See* Luke W. Cole, *Remedies for Environmental Racism: A View From the Field*, 90 MICH. L. REV. 1991, 1992 (1992).

46. Richard Delgado, *Critical Legal Studies and the Realities of Race—Does the Fundamental Contradiction Have a Corollary?*, 23 HARV. C.R.-C.L. L. REV. 407 (1988); Delgado & Stefancic, *supra*, at 1282.

47. Delgado & Stefancic, *supra*, at 1282–83.

48. *See, e.g.*, Marjorie Heins, *Banning Words: A Comment on "Words That Wound"*, 18 HARV. C.R.-C.L. L. REV. 585 (1983) (employing the slippery-slope argument); Strossen, *supra*, at 537–39.

49. *See* BELL, NOT SAVED, *supra*, at 26–42; BELL, RACE, RACISM, *supra*, at 2–63 (providing an overview of the history of racism against African-Americans).

50. *See* Freeman, *supra*, at 1052–57 (contrasting "victim" versus "perpetrator" perspective for redressing racial wrongs, and deploring that the law almost invariably selects the latter viewpoint).

51. *See, e.g.*, ANDREW HACKER, TWO NATIONS: BLACK AND WHITE, SEPARATE, HOSTILE, UNEQUAL 94–103, 109–78 (1992); Delgado, *Ever Saved?, supra*, at 930–32.

52. ROSENBERG, *supra*, at 42–54, 175–201 (comparing pre- and post-Roe figures and trends).

53. 410 U.S. 113 (1973).

54. ROSENBERG, *supra*, at 180, tbl. 6.1 (number of abortions performed both before and after legalization); tbl. 6.2 (percentage of hospitals providing abortions); tbl. 6.4 (total number of abortion providers); 201 (concluding that *Roe v. Wade* had little effect on the availability of abortions in United States).

55. 349 U.S. 294 (1954).

56. ROSENBERG, *supra*, at 42–54 (making similar case for school desegregation and concluding that *Brown v. Board of Education* had little effect).

57. *See* United States v. Fordice, 112 S. Ct. 2727 (1992).

58. *See* Metro Broadcasting, Inc. v. FCC, 497 U.S. 547 (1990).

59. SAVAGE, *supra*, at 334–39, 346; 305–49 (chapter 9, "The Liberals' Last Surprise").

60. A contradiction-closing case is a legal decision that has the effect of closing the gap between our ideal of how law, or society, ought to be, and how it actually is.

61. ROSENBERG, *supra*, at 10–21 (explaining Court's inability to bring about social change, and labeling this the "Constrained Court" view).

Notes to Chapter 5

1. In the Third Chronicle, *supra* this volume, Rodrigo and the Professor discuss a paper Rodrigo plans to submit to a conservative writing competition. An earlier essay of his won first prize in a student writing competition.

2. See, e.g., Richard Delgado, *Enormous Anomaly? Left-Right Parallels in Recent Writing About Race*, 91 COLUM. L. REV. 1547 (1991).

3. Rodrigo's father, an African-American serviceman, served at a U.S. Army outpost in Italy, where Rodrigo attended base schools before earning a government scholarship to attend the University of Bologna. Rodrigo's late mother was an Italian citizen. His father recently retired to southern Florida.

4. CHRIS GOODRICH, ANARCHY AND ELEGANCE: CONFESSIONS OF A JOURNALIST AT YALE LAW SCHOOL (1991). Goodrich traces the personal experiences of his section-mates and himself during their first year at Yale Law School. The book details the professors' approach to teaching, the students' responses to the case method, the anxieties over moot court, the challenge of legal memo-writing, and the excesses of the fall interview season. Goodrich, a professional writer, focuses upon the personality and cognitive changes that he and his classmates underwent their first year of law school. The title of his book foreshadows the book's central theme: the dichotomy created through imposition of an elegant legal structure on an unruly world.

5. A few law schools offer one-year degrees for journalists, social scientists, and others who seek an overview of the American legal system.

6. For discussion of the republican revival in U.S. jurisprudence, *see, e.g.*, Frank I. Michelman, *Foreword: Traces of Self-Government*, 100 HARV. L. REV. 4 (1986); Frank Michelman, *Law's Republic*, 97 YALE L.J. 1493 (1988); Suzanna Sherry, *Civic Virtue and the Feminine Voice in Constitutional Adjudication*, 72 VA. L. REV. 543 (1986); Cass R. Sunstein, *Beyond the Republican Revival*, 97 YALE L.J. 1539 (1988); Cass R. Sunstein, *Interest Groups in American Public Law*, 38 STAN. L. REV. 29 (1985). The civic revival movement in law is not unique; similar revivals are taking place in a number of allied disciplines.

7. See, e.g., Derrick A. Bell & Preeta Bansal, *The Republican Revival and Racial Politics*, 97 YALE L.J. 1609 (1988); Richard Delgado, *Zero-Based Racial Politics and an Infinity-Based Response: Will Endless Talking Cure America's Racial Ills?*, 80 GEO. L.J. 1879 (1992); Richard Delgado, *Zero-Based Racial Politics: An Evaluation of Three Best-Case Arguments on Behalf of the Nonwhite Underclass*, 78 GEO. L.J. 1929 (1990). For other approaches to achieving tolerance

through communal effort, *see, for example,* Richard H. Fallon, Jr., *What Is Republicanism, and Is It Worth Reviving?,* 102 HARV. L. REV. 1695 (1989); Kenneth L. Karst, *Citizenship, Race, and Marginality,* 30 WM. & MARY L. REV. 1 (1988).

8. *Id.* at 18–19, 35–41, 62, 284.
9. Duncan Kennedy, *Legal Education as Training for Hierarchy, in* THE POLITICS OF LAW: A PROGRESSIVE CRITIQUE 40, 51–53 (David Kairys ed., 1982).
10. On the Socratic method, see LAW SCHOOL ADMISSION COUNCIL, THE OFFICIAL GUIDE TO U.S. LAW SCHOOLS 33 (1991); LAW SCHOOL ADMISSION COUNCIL, THE RIGHT LAW SCHOOL FOR YOU 101–102 (1986); JOHN JAY OSBORN, THE PAPER CHASE (1971).
11. Rodrigo loves books. Many of our conversations have begun with a discussion of recent works he and I have been reading. First Chronicle, *supra* this volume (discussing DINESH D'SOUZA, ILLIBERAL EDUCATION (1991)); Second Chronicle, *supra* this volume (discussing RICHARD A. EPSTEIN, FORBIDDEN GROUNDS: THE CASE AGAINST EMPLOYMENT DISCRIMINATION LAWS (1992)); Third Chronicle, *supra* this volume (discussing ANDREW HACKER, TWO NATIONS: BLACK AND WHITE, SEPARATE, HOSTILE, UNEQUAL (1992)); Fourth Chronicle, *supra* this volume (discussing DERRICK A. BELL, FACES AT THE BOTTOM OF THE WELL: THE PERMANENCE OF RACISM (1992); GERALD N. ROSENBERG, THE HOLLOW HOPE: CAN COURTS BRING ABOUT SOCIAL CHANGE? (1991); DAVID S. SAVAGE, TURNING RIGHT: THE MAKING OF THE REHNQUIST SUPREME COURT (1992); and GIRARDEAU A. SPANN, RACE AGAINST THE COURT: THE SUPREME COURT AND MINORITIES IN CONTEMPORARY AMERICA (1993)).
12. T. M. Knox, Translator's Foreword, *in* GEORG WILHELM FRIEDRICH HEGEL, PHILOSOPHY OF RIGHT 13 (T. M. Knox ed. & trans., 1957).
13. *See Symposium, The Critique of Normativity,* 139 U. PA. L. REV. 801 (1991).
14. On the rise of religion and other normative systems, *see* ROBERT BELLAH, HABITS OF THE HEART: INDIVIDUALISM AND COMMITMENT IN AMERICAN LIFE (1984). On the critique of normativity, *see Symposium, supra.* On normativity in law school and legal pedagogy, *see* Thomas L. Shaffer, *The Practice of Law as Moral Discourse,* 55 NOTRE DAME L. REV. 231 (1979); Michael I. Swygert, *Striving to Make Great Lawyers—Citizenship and Moral Responsibility: A Jurisprudence for Law Teaching,* 30 B.C. L. REV. 803 (1989).
15. *See, e.g.,* PHILIPPA FOOT, VIRTUES AND VICES AND OTHER ESSAYS IN MORAL PHILOSOPHY (1978); ALASDAIR C. MACINTYRE, AFTER VIRTUE: A STUDY IN MORAL THEORY (1981); MARTHA CRAVEN NUSSBAUM, LOVE'S KNOWLEDGE: ESSAYS ON PHILOSOPHY AND LITERATURE (1990); BERNARD WILLIAMS, ETHICS AND THE LIMITS OF PHILOSOPHY (1985); *see also* JOHN W. CHAPMAN & WILLIAM A. GALSTON, VIRTUE (1992) (collection of essays on politics and civic virtue).

16. *See, e.g.*, BELLAH, *supra*; PHILIP SELZNICK, THE MORAL COMMON-WEALTH: SOCIAL THEORY AND THE PROMISE OF COMMUNITY (1992).

17. *See, e.g.*, Macintyre, *supra*; Bruce A. Ackerman, *Discovering the Constitution*, 93 YALE L.J. 1013 (1984); J.G.A. Pocock, *Civic Humanism and Its Role in Anglo-American Thought, in* POLITICS, LANGUAGE AND TIME 80 (1973).

18. *See* First Chronicle, *supra* this volume, where Rodrigo and the Professor explore the declining markets of the West, the increasing incidence of crime and social disorder, and the vacuum of political leadership. They also discuss the recent decline in workers' real income, increased infant mortality among blacks, and high unemployment.

19. On the fragmentation of U.S. society, *see* First Chronicle, *supra* this volume. On its effect on communication and language paradigms, *see* Kathleen M. Sullivan, *Rainbow Republicanism*, 97 YALE L.J. 1713, 1714 (1988); Steven L. Winter, *Contingency and Community in Normative Practice*, 139 U. PA. L. REV. 963 (1991).

20. *See* First Chronicle, *supra* this volume.

21. On normative discourse as deflection and denial, *see* Richard Delgado, *Norms and Normal Science: Toward a Critique of Normativity in Legal Thought*, 139 U. PA. L. REV. 933 (1991). *See generally Symposium, supra*.

22. *See, e.g.*, MARTHA MINOW, MAKING ALL THE DIFFERENCE: INCLUSION, EXCLUSION AND AMERICAN LAW 60–70 (1990); Michelman, *Law's Republic, supra*, at 1494–95, 1530; Michelman, *Self-Government, supra*, at 74–77; Sunstein, *Republican Revival, supra*, at 1549–55, 1564–66, 1588.

23. *See* Richard A. Epstein, *Modern Republicanism—Or the Flight From Substance*, 97 YALE L.J. 1633–35 (1988); Sunstein, *Republican Revival, supra*, at 1564–66. For discussion of the concern that civic republicanism will usher in stifling conformity and group-think, *see* Steven G. Gey, *The Unfortunate Revival of Civic Republicanism*, 141 U. PA. L. REV. 801 (1993).

24. *See, e.g.*, William A. Galston, *Clinton and the Promise of Communitarianism*, CHRON. HIGHER EDUC., Dec. 2, 1992, at A52 (discussing the influence of communitarian ideas on President Clinton and Vice President Gore); Karin J. Winkler, *Finding the Moral Center: A Scholar Seeks the Multicultural Middle Ground*, CHRON. HIGHER EDUC., Dec. 9, 1992, at A6 (same); *see also* First Chronicle, *supra* this volume (discussing patriotism and revival of themes of early greatness). *But see* Michael Aaron Rockland, *Rediscovering America*, RESPONSIVE COMMUNITY, Winter 1991/1992, at 55 (decrying excesses of revivalism).

25. *See The Responsive Communitarian Platform: Rights and Responsibilities*, RESPONSIVE COMMUNITY, Winter 1991/92, at 4, 5–9 (emphasizing need for moral voice and training among communities).

26. *See, e.g.*, GOODRICH, *supra*, at 17 (citing cutthroat behavior of some law students); Mark G. Sessions, *Restore Balance to the Lives of Young Lawyers*, BARRISTER, Fall, 1992, at 2; Jenny Hontz, *How the Recession is Affecting Law*

Firms, BARRISTER, Fall, 1992, at 20; Steven Keeva, *Unequal Partners*, A.B.A. J., Feb. 1993, at 50; David Stevens, *Are You Partnership Material?*, BARRIS-TER, Fall, 1992, at 14; Richard Delgado & Jean Stefancic, *Panthers and Pin-Stripes: The Case of Ezra Pound and Archibald MacLeish*, 63 S. CAL. L. REV. 907 (1990); Nancy D. Holt, *Are Longer Hours Here to Stay?* A.B.A. J., Feb. 1993, at 62; *Stone-Age Policies Harm Morale, YLD Concludes*, BARRISTER, Fall, 1992, at 35; Derek C. Bok, *The Bok Report: A Flawed System of Law Practice and Training*, 33 J. LEGAL EDUC. 570, 583 (1983); Bates v. State Bar of Arizona, 433 U.S. 350 (1977) (dismissing challenge to state bar rule prohibiting advertising by attorneys); David A. Kaplan, *What America Really Thinks About Lawyers and What Lawyers Can Do About It*, NAT'L L.J., Aug. 18, 1986, at S-2.

27. *See* ROBERT V. STOVER, MAKING IT AND BREAKING IT: THE FATE OF PUBLIC INTEREST COMMITMENT DURING LAW SCHOOL (1989); Terry Carter, *Why Students Lose Their Interest in Entering Public Interest Work*, NAT'L L.J., July 31, 1989, at 4.

28. On the solidarity-building function of normative discourse, *see* Pierre Schlag, *Normativity and the Politics of Form*, 139 U. PA. L. REV. 801, 825–46 (1991).

29. *See, e.g.*, Richard McKeon, *General Introduction: (1) The Life and Times of Aristotle, in* INTRODUCTION TO ARISTOTLE *ix–xii* (Richard McKeon ed., 1947) ("The period of Aristotle's manhood coincided with the reduction of the Greek city-states to the hegemony of Macedonia and the twelve or thirteen years of his work in the Lyceum with the campaigns of Alexander the Great.").

30. *See id.* at *xi–xiii* (chronicling the loss of Greek liberties and decline of Greek ideals).

31. Daniel A. Farber & Philip P. Frickey, *Is Carolene Products Dead? Reflections on Affirmative Action and the Dynamics of Civil Rights Legislation*, 79 CAL. L. REV. 685, 726 (1991); Michelman, *Law's Republic, supra*, at 1494–95.

32. The doctrine holds that for individuals, "right" action will consist of moderation; that is, of avoiding the excess that tends to lie at either extreme of a particular type of behavior. *See* ARISTOTLE, *supra*, at bk. II, ch. ii.

33. *See* Michelman, *Self-Government, supra*, at 33; Kathleen M. Sullivan, *Foreword: The Justices of Rules and Standards*, 106 HARV. L. REV. 22, 22 (1992); Sunstein, *Republican Revival, supra*, at 1548–50.

34. *See, e.g.*, Bell & Bansal, *supra*, at 9; Delgado, *Zero-Based II, supra*.

35. *See* Pierre Schlag, *Normative and Nowhere to Go*, 43 STAN. L. REV. 167 (1990); Schlag, *Politics of Form, supra*.

36. GOODRICH, *supra*, at 4–5, 11–13, 17, 38–39, 61, 156, 204–206, 267 (arguing that the legal academy must cease teaching scoffing, "aggressive assurance," emphasizing competition for grades, manipulation of facts, bullying rather than cooperation, deflection, denial, and flight from the anarchy of life to simplistic rules of law, and urging an "amoral" neutrality, in which a lawyer could equally argue either side of a case).

37. For a discussion of empirical studies showing no correlation, or even a negative one, between religiosity and "helping" behavior, *see* Delgado, *Norms, supra,* at 944–45, 954. *See generally Symposium, supra,* for a discussion of the role of normativity in social and legal thought, including its legitimating functions.

38. *See, e.g.,* Charles L. Black, Jr., *Further Reflections on the Constitutional Justice of Livelihood,* 86 COLUM. L. REV. 1103 (1986). For Supreme Court decisions rejecting claims to various kinds of subsistence entitlements, *see* San Antonio Indep. Sch. Dist. v. Rodriguez, 411 U.S. 1 (1973) (holding that school funding system that favors schools in affluent districts does not violate the Equal Protection Clause); Lindsey v. Normet, 405 U.S. 56 (1972) (arguing that responsibility to address scarcity of affordable housing rests with legislatures); Dandridge v. Williams, 397 U.S. 471 (1970) (upholding constitutionality of state ceilings on AFDC grants).

39. *See, e.g.,* Black, *supra,* at 1106–11 (arguing that constitutional rights are worthless without minimum subsistence).

40. *See, e.g.,* Schlag, *Politics of Form, supra,* at 804–806, 843–84, 925–26; Schlag, *Nowhere to Go, supra,* at 183–91.

41. On the connection between normative discourse and social homeostasis, *see* Schlag, *Nowhere to Go, supra;* The term "normal science" is attributed to Thomas S. Kuhn, who used it to indicate studies carried out within the prevailing paradigm or tradition. *See* THOMAS S. KUHN, THE STRUCTURE OF SCIENTIFIC REVOLUTIONS 7 (2d ed. 1970).

42. *See, e.g.,* Michelman, *Self-Government, supra,* at 73–74; Sunstein, *Interest Groups, supra,* at 31.

43. *See, e.g.,* Epstein, *supra,* at 1642.

44. Sunstein, *Interest Groups, supra,* at 31.

45. *See* Richard Delgado, *Shadowboxing: An Essay on Power,* 77 CORNELL L. REV. 813 (1992); Richard Delgado & Jean Stefancic, *Images of the Outsider in American Law and Culture: Can Free Expression Remedy Systemic Social Ills?,* 77 CORNELL L. REV. 1258 (1992); Pierre Schlag, *Pre-figuration and Evaluation,* 80 CAL. L. REV. 965 (1992).

46. *See, e.g.,* Bell & Bansal, *supra;* Delgado, *Zero-Based II, supra;* Delgado, *Zero-Based I, supra;* Delgado & Stefancic, *supra.*

47. *See* Fourth Chronicle, *supra* this volume.

48. *Images, supra; see also* Richard Delgado, *Campus Antiracism Rules: Constitutional Narratives in Collision,* 85 Nw. U. L. REV. 343, 384–86 (1991).

49. *See* JOANNA RUSS, HOW TO SUPPRESS WOMEN'S WRITING (1983); *cf.* Richard Delgado, *The Imperial Scholar Revisited: How To Marginalize Outsider Writing, Ten Years Later,* 140 U. PA. L. REV. 1349, 1364–65 (1992) (similar analysis of treatment accorded "outsider scholarship" in law).

50. *See* JACK BASS, UNLIKELY HEROES (1981); Mari J. Matsuda, *When the First Quail Calls: Multiple Consciousness as Jurisprudential Method,* 11 WOMEN'S RTS. L. REP. 7 (1989); First Chronicle, *supra* this volume.

51. HARRY KALVEN, JR., THE NEGRO AND THE FIRST AMENDMENT

(1965) (describing the way abuses stand out in the glare of racial injustice, enabling correction, often to the betterment of all, and citing New York Times v. Sullivan, 376 U.S. 254 (1964), as one example).

52. See, e.g., Goss v. Lopez, 419 U.S. 565 (1975) (holding that the Due Process Clause requires that a student facing disciplinary action be given oral or written notice of the charges and an explanation of the evidence against him or her, as well as an opportunity to present his or her version of the facts).

53. For instance, the affirmative action policy requirement that job openings be posted and advertised, rather than dispensed through "old-boy networks," makes the hiring market more accessible to all job seekers, not just minorities.

54. See, e.g., BELL, NOT SAVED, supra, at 239–58 (concluding that no single civil rights strategy will succeed in bringing justice for blacks, and urging broad-based programs aimed at remedying class-based, as well as racial, inequalities); see also ROY L. BROOKS, RETHINKING THE AMERICAN RACE PROBLEM (1990) (urging a similar course).

55. For a critique of affirmative action, see BELL, NOT SAVED, supra, at 140–61; Richard Delgado, Affirmative Action as a Majoritarian Device: Or, Do You Really Want to Be a Role Model?, 89 MICH. L. REV. 1222 (1991).

56. See generally Delgado & Stefancic, supra.

57. ARISTOTLE, supra, at bk. VIII, bk. IX (discussing duties to one's friends and what makes a person a good friend).

Notes to Chapter 6

1. On essentialism, see generally BELL HOOKS, AIN'T I A WOMAN? BLACK WOMEN AND FEMINISM (1981) (discussing inseparability of race and sex for black women); BELL HOOKS, YEARNING: RACE, GENDER AND CULTURAL POLITICS (1991); BELL HOOKS & CORNEL WEST, BREAKING BREAD: INSURGENT BLACK INTELLECTUAL LIFE (1991); ELIZABETH V. SPELMAN, INESSENTIAL WOMAN: PROBLEMS OF EXCLUSION IN FEMINIST THOUGHT (1988) (showing how essentialism denies significance of heterogeneity for feminist theory and political activity); Trina Grillo & Stephanie M. Wildman, Obscuring the Importance of Race: The Implications of Making Comparisons Between Racism and Sexism or Other -Isms, 1991 DUKE L.J. 397 (discussing dangers of analogizing other phenomena to racism); Angela P. Harris, Race and Essentialism in Feminist Legal Theory, 42 STAN L. REV. 581 (1990) (criticizing gender essentialism for failing to take into account black women's experiences). As Rodrigo and the professor use the term, essentialism consists of treating as unitary a concept or group that, to some at least, contains diversity. On essentialism as the selective ignoring of difference, see text infra.

2. See Richard Delgado, The Imperial Scholar: Reflections on a Review of Civil Rights Literature, 132 U. PA. L. REV. 561 (1984) (discussing mechanisms by which mainstream scholars marginalize contribution of civil rights scholars of color); Richard Delgado, The Imperial Scholar Revisited: How to Marginalize Outsider Writing, Ten Years Later, 140 U. PA. L. REV. 1349 (1992) (same).

3. *See* LUDWIG WITTGENSTEIN, *TRACTATUS LOGICO-PHILOSOPH-ICUS* 9–25 (D. F. Pears & B. F. McGuiness trans., 2d ed. 1974) (1921) (developing idea that meaning of term or symbol lies in its use).

4. The antinominalist argument holds, in short, that words and terms do not correspond to permanent essences or things existing in a realm outside time. *See, e.g.*, 3 ENCYCLOPEDIA OF PHILOSOPHY 59–60 (P. Edwards ed., 1967) (Essence and Existence); 8 ENCYCLOPEDIA OF PHILOSOPHY, *supra*, at 199–204 (on conceptualism, nominalism, and resemblance theories).

5. *See generally* Kimberlè Crenshaw, *Demarginalizing the Intersection of Race and Sex: A Black Feminist Critique of Antidiscrimination Doctrine, Feminist Theory and Antiracist Politics*, 1989 U. CHI. LEGAL F. 139 (examining how tendency to treat race and gender as mutually exclusive categories of experience and analysis is perpetuated by a single-axis framework that is dominant in antidiscrimination law, feminist theory, and antiracist politics); Harris, *supra*.

6. *See* Martha L. Fineman, *Challenging Law, Establishing Differences: The Future of Feminist Legal Scholarship*, 42 U. FLA. L. REV. 25, 36 (1990) (advocating unified stand by all women against patriarchy).

7. *See* Harris, *supra*.

8. *See* Harris, *supra*, at 585–604.

9. *Id.* at 585–90, 595–605, 612–13. *See also* Crenshaw, *supra*, at 139–40.

10. *See, e.g.*, DINESH D'SOUZA, ILLIBERAL EDUCATION (1991); RICHARD RODRIGUEZ, HUNGER OF MEMORY (1982); SHELBY STEELE, THE CONTENT OF OUR CHARACTER (1990); *see also* STEPHEN L. CARTER, REFLECTIONS OF AN AFFIRMATIVE ACTION BABY (1991). *See also* Randall L. Kennedy, *Racial Critiques of Legal Academia*, 102 HARV. L. REV. 1745 (1989) (analyzing writings that examine effect of racial difference on distribution of prestige in legal academia).

11. *See* Kennedy, *supra* (taking various members of Critical Race Theory school to task for various overstatements and omissions).

12. *Colloquy, Responses to Randall Kennedy's Racial Critiques of Legal Academia*, 103 HARV. L. REV. 1844 (1990).

13. Fineman, *supra*, at 39–43.

14. *See, e.g.*, ALLAN BLOOM, THE CLOSING OF THE AMERICAN MIND (1987) (arguing that great and esteemed Western classics must be preserved at all costs); HENRY LOUIS GATES, JR., LOOSE CANONS: NOTES ON THE CULTURE WARS (1992) (arguing that battles over canon are overblown).

15. *See, e.g.*, Jack Miles, *Blacks v. Browns: The Struggle for the Bottom Rung*, ATLANTIC MONTHLY, Oct. 1992, at 41 (discussing economic competition between Latinos and African-Americans). *See Symposium, Los Angeles, April 29, 1992 and Beyond: The Law, Issues, and Perspectives*, 66 S. CAL. L. REV. 133 (1993) (detailing role of interethnic rivalries in Los Angeles Uprising).

16. *See* First Chronicle, *supra* this volume.

17. On the role of stories and "counterstories" in confining or broadening a culture's store of narratives, *see Symposium, Legal Storytelling*, 87 MICH. L. REV. 2073 (1989) (containing articles by Milner S. Ball, Mari J. Matsuda, Steven L.

Winter, Patricia Williams, and Richard Delgado on use of stories to enforce or challenge consensus, to advance or retard progress of outsider groups, and to mediate between legal power (as expressed in general rules) and individual action). On the critique of legal storytelling, *see* Daniel A. Farber & Suzanna Sherry, *Telling Stories Out of School: An Essay on Legal Narratives,* 45 STAN. L. REV. 807 (1993).

18. *Viz.,* include the meaning of words, the theory of coalitions, and the debate about the canon of cultural knowledge, *see* text *immediately supra* this chapter.

19. *See* Crenshaw, *supra,* at 141–46.

20. *See id.* at 139–52.

21. Marching in the right direction, of course, does not guarantee that one will arrive there. *See, e.g.,* ALEX HALEY, THE AUTOBIOGRAPHY OF MALCOLM X (1964).

22. Attributed to Antonio Gramsci, the term refers to the way some oppressed people come to identify with their oppressors, internalize their views, and thus appear to consent to their own subordination. *See* ANTONIO GRAMSCI, LETTERS FROM PRISON (Lynne Lawner, ed. & trans., 1973); SELECTIONS FROM THE PRISON NOTEBOOKS 416–18 (Quintin Hoare & Geoffrey N. Smith eds. & trans., 1971).

23. *See, e.g.,* EMIL DURKHEIM, THE DIVISION OF LABOR IN SOCIETY (George Simpson trans., 1933); TALCOTT PARSONS, INTRODUCTION TO MAX WEBER, THE SOCIOLOGY OF RELIGION *xxxviii–xxxix* (1971).

24. *See, e.g.,* Derrick A. Bell, Jr., *Brown v. Board of Education and the Interest-Convergence Dilemma,* 93 HARV. L. REV. 518 (1980); *see also* Lani Guinier, *The Triumph of Tokenism: The Voting Rights Act and the Theory of Black Electoral Success,* 89 MICH. L. REV. 1077 (1991) (criticizing overreliance on judicial remedies as unlikely to challenge white interest and hegemony); Girardeau A. Spann, *Pure Politics,* 88 MICH. L. REV. 1971 (1990) (same).

25. 347 U.S. 483 (1954).

26. *See* Bell, *supra,* at 524–25, 532 (white groups allow civil rights breakthroughs, such as *Brown v. Board of Education,* not out of altruism, but sporadically to promote their own self-interest); DERRICK A. BELL, JR., RACE, RACISM, AND AMERICAN LAW 1–70 (2d ed. 1980).

27. *See* ANDREW HACKER, TWO NATIONS: BLACK AND WHITE, SEPARATE, HOSTILE, UNEQUAL 147–63 (1992), discussed in Third Chronicle, *supra* this volume.

28. *See, e.g.,* Webster v. Reproductive Health Servs., Inc., 492 U.S. 490 (1989) (construing right to abortion narrowly, as subject to reasonable limitations responsive to state interests); Maher v. Roe, 432 U.S. 464 (1977) (construing right to abortion narrowly, and stating that right is not absolute and states need not fund abortions even if they do fund natural childbirth). *See also* Sara Rimer, *Abortion Foes in Boot Camp Mull Doctor's Killing,* N.Y. TIMES, Mar. 19, 1993, at A12; Larry Rohter, *Doctor Is Slain During Protest Over Abortions,* N.Y. TIMES, Mar. 11, 1993, at A1, B10.

29. *See Symposium, The Critique of Normativity,* 139 U. PA. L. REV. 801 (1991) (containing articles by Pierre Schlag, Steven L. Winter, Frederick Schauer, and Richard Delgado). "Normativity" refers to normative discourse—that is to say, discourse concerning values, about good and evil, and about ethics. "Prescription" refers to uttering *prescripts,* that is, moral statements about what should be done. *See also* Fifth Chronicle, *supra* this volume.

30. For a discussion of the way that the costs of racial reform are always placed on blacks or lower-class whites, *see* DERRICK A. BELL, JR., FACES AT THE BOTTOM OF THE WELL: THE PERMANENCE OF RACISM (1992) (putting forward an economic-determinist view of American legal history); Derrick A. Bell, Jr., *Bakke, Minority Admissions, and the Usual Price of Racial Remedies,* 67 CAL. L. REV. 3 (1979).

31. On the role of the "new communitarians" and their emphasis on social responsibilities as correlatives of rights, *see* Robin West, *Foreword: Taking Freedom Seriously,* 104 HARV. L. REV. 43 (1990); William A. Galston, *Clinton and the Promise of Communitarianism,* CHRON. HIGHER EDUC., Dec. 2, 1992, at A52; Denise K. Magner, *Probing the Imbalance Betweeen Individual Rights, Community Needs,* CHRON. HIGHER EDUC., Feb. 13, 1991, at A3; Michael A. Rockland, *Rediscovering America,* RESPONSIVE COMMUNITY, Winter 1991/1992, at 55; *The Responsive Communitarian Platform: Rights and Responsibilities,* RESPONSIVE COMMUNITY, Winter 1991/1992, at 4.

32. *See, e.g.,* Robin West, *supra,* at 67–68, 79–85 (deriving ethic of responsibility from general feminist principles of caring for others).

33. *See* Bell, *Bakke, supra,* at 14–16.

34. *See* West, *supra,* at 81–82; Richard Delgado, *Pep Talks for the Poor: A Reply and Remonstrance on the Evils of Scapegoating,* 70 B.U. L. REV. 525, 527–29 (1991) (commenting on West's approach).

35. That is to say, the fairness norm is understood to mean that white men get jobs; normative terms like "merit" and "fair" derive their principal meanings in relation to empowered actors and their viewpoints. *See* Fifth Chronicle, *supra* this volume; *see also* S. Steele, *supra,* at 120–21.

36. This is especially true for women. On the social construction of women and women's roles, *see generally* CAROL GILLIGAN, IN A DIFFERENT VOICE (1982); CATHARINE A. MACKINNON, FEMINISM UNMODIFIED (1987).

37. *See* Gary Peller, *Race Consciousness,* 1990 DUKE L.J. 758; Delgado & Stefancic, *supra,* at 463 (on cultural nationalism).

38. On double consciousness generally, *see* W. E. BURGHARDT DU BOIS, THE SOULS OF BLACK FOLK 3–4, 16–17 (1903); *see also* RALPH ELLISON, INVISIBLE MAN 7–17 (Signet ed. 1952); BELL HOOKS, AIN'T I A WOMAN, *supra;* BELL HOOKS, FEMINIST THEORY: FROM MARGIN TO CENTER (1991).

39. *See generally* Robin D. Barnes, *Black Women Law Professors and Critical Self-Consciousness: A Tribute to Professor Denise S. Carty-Bennia,* 6 BERKELEY WOMEN'S L.J. 57, 61–62 (1990–91); Mari Matsuda, *When the First Quail*

Calls: Multiple Consciousness as Jurisprudential Method, 11 WOMEN'S RTS. L. REP. 7 (1989). For a collection of writings on the distinct experiences of women of color vis-à-vis each other and men, *see* THIS BRIDGE CALLED MY BACK: WRITINGS BY RADICAL WOMEN OF COLOR (2d ed. 1983); of black women, *see* PAULA GIDDINGS, WHEN AND WHERE I ENTER: THE IMPACT OF BLACK WOMEN ON RACE AND SEX IN AMERICA (1984).

40. *See* G. W. F. HEGEL, THE PHENOMENOLOGY OF MIND 229–40 (J. B. Baillie trans., 1967). On the difference in the ways that slaves and masters knew one another, *see* JAMES BALDWIN, THE PRICE OF THE TICKET 554 (1985); STANLEY ROSEN, G. W. F. HEGEL 162–64 (1974).

41. *See generally* Delgado & Stefancic, *Images, supra* (drawing on linguistic theory to explain invisibility of ethnic depiction, and drawing on history to show how harms of such ethnic depiction operate effectively but below consciousness).

42. On the canon generally, *see* text *supra* this chapter; *see also* STANLEY FISH, IS THERE A TEXT IN THIS CLASS? (1980) (discussing role of conventional meanings in facilitating and confining discourse). On the role of majoritarian mindset in controlling the course of racial reform, *see* DERRICK BELL, AND WE ARE NOT SAVED: THE ELUSIVE QUEST FOR RACIAL JUSTICE 95–96, 140–61 (1987); BELL, FACES, *supra*, at 2–9, 109–26, 158–94; Kimberlè Crenshaw, *Race, Reform, and Retrenchment: Transformation and Legitimation in Antidiscrimination Law*, 101 HARV. L. REV. 1331, 1350–52, 1370–76 (1988).

43. On the role of majoritarian narratives in enabling society to exclude outsider stories, *see* Jerome Culp, *Firing Legal Canons and Shooting Blanks: Finding a Neutral Way in the Law*, 10 ST. LOUIS U. PUB. L. REV. 185, 191–95 (1991) Delgado & Stefancic, *Images, supra*, at 1284–88.

44. *See* Second Chronicle, *supra* this volume.

45. *See* Delgado & Stefancic, *Images, supra*, at 1261, 1281–82. "Empathic fallacy" refers to the exaggerated faith to achieve new levels of sensitivity through free expression in the marketplace of ideas, and subsequently to dispel broadscale cultural evils, such as racism.

46. *See id.* at 1259–61, 1277–82 (examining history of ethnic depiction of people of color and its purpose for majority culture); *see also* Richard Delgado & Jean Stefancic, *Hateful Speech, Loving Communities: Why Our Notion of "A Just Balance" Changes So Slowly*, 82 CALIF. L. REV. (1994); Milner S. Ball, *Stories of Origin and Constitutional Possibilities*, 87 MICH. L. REV. 2280, 2296–2300 (1989) (discussing difficulty of re-adopting original stories and need for multiple voices to be realized in one story). *See also* Charles Lawrence, *The Id, The Ego, and Equal Protection: Reckoning with Unconscious Racism*, 39 STAN. L. REV. 317, 321–24 (1987) (perpetrators of racism rarely see their behavior as racist).

47. That is, white authors who have written work supportive of Critical Race scholarship. *See generally* Alan D. Freeman, *Legitimizing Racial Discrimination through Antidiscrimination Law: A Critical Review of Supreme Court Doctrine,*

62 MINN. L. REV. 1049 (1978); Alan D. Freeman, *Racism, Rights, and the Quest for Equality of Opportunity: A Critical Legal Essay*, 23 HARV. C.R.-C.L. L. REV. 295 (1988).

48. *See, e.g.*, FEMINISM AND POLITICAL THEORY (Cass R. Sunstein ed., 1990) (providing a representative, wide-ranging, yet unified, set of readings on feminist political thought); Cass R. Sunstein, *Pornography and the First Amendment*, 1986 DUKE L.J. 589 (arguing that pornography is low-value speech that can be regulated consistently with First Amendment).

49. *See* MICHEL FOUCAULT, POWER/KNOWLEDGE: SELECTED INTERVIEWS AND OTHER WRITINGS 1972–77 (Colin Gordon ed. & Colin Gordon et al. trans., 1980). Michel Foucault wrote about the relation between structures of social control and what is regarded as knowledge. He believed that knowledge is often socially constructed—that is, a matter of consensus—and that what is regarded as true is as much a function of power and influence as objective truth.

50. "Interpretive community" refers to the manner in which texts and words acquire meaning in reference to a community of speakers who agree tacitly to employ them in particular ways. *See* FISH, *supra*, at 8–17. As Rodrigo employs it, he means that large numbers of people can sometimes change the way we see things, deploy words, and ascribe meanings to concepts such as *woman*.

51. *See* FOUCAULT, *supra*.

52. JOHN DEWEY, EXPERIENCE AND EDUCATION (First Collier Books ed. 1963) (classic statement of progressive education, which includes theory of inquiry learning, freedom, and learning through experiences); *see also* JOHN DEWEY, HOW WE THINK (1933) (articulating philosopher's approach to thought and action in relation to his program of American pragmatism).

53. On the notion that reforms born of the struggle for racial justice often end up benefiting all, not just blacks, *see generally* HARRY KALVEN, THE NEGRO AND THE FIRST AMENDMENT (1965) (focusing on impact of the civil rights movement on First Amendment); *see also* Second Chronicle, *supra* this volume.

54. On the idea that small is better *see, e.g.*, KENNETH E. BOULDING *et al.*, ENVIRONMENTAL QUALITY IN A GROWING ECONOMY 3–14 (Henry Jarrett ed., 1966) (criticizing society's obsession with production and consumption and its lack of concern for future ramifications); ALDO LEOPOLD, A SAND COUNTY ALMANAC AND SKETCHES HERE AND THERE *viii*, *ix*, 199–226 (1949) (arguing for a land ethic which examines land use questions in terms of ethics and esthetics, and not just as economic problems).

55. On the idea that government should be as small and nonintrusive as possible, *see generally* RICHARD A. EPSTEIN, FORBIDDEN GROUNDS: THE CASE AGAINST EMPLOYMENT DISCRIMINATION LAWS (1992) (arguing that economic and social consequences of antidiscrimination laws in employment should be focused on more than historical injustices).

56. *See* Ralph Blumenthal, *Trade Center Bombing Suspect Not a Patsy, Officials Conclude*, N.Y. TIMES, Mar. 9, 1993, at A1 (describing suspected terrorist

group conspirator in bombing of New York office building); Chris Hedges, *Bomb Suspect's Path to Piety and Elusive Dreams*, N.Y. TIMES, Mar. 8, 1993, at A1.

57. *See generally* BOULDING, *supra* (arguing for long-term vision of environment in dealing with present problems); REWEAVING THE WORLD: THE EMERGENCE OF ECOFEMINISM (Irene Diamond & Gloria F. Orenstein eds., 1990) (presenting multicultural, global vision of reform in response to current environmental, political, and social crises).

Notes to Chapter 7

1. For the variety found within just one of the approaches Rodrigo mentions, see Richard Delgado & Jean Stefancic, *Critical Race Theory: An Annotated Bibliography*, 79 VA. L. REV. 461 (1993).
2. For examples of work advocating an expansive role for government, *see, e.g.*, JOHN K. GALBRAITH, THE AFFLUENT SOCIETY (3d ed. 1976); MARIAN WRIGHT EDELMAN, FAMILIES IN PERIL: AN AGENDA FOR SOCIAL CHANGE (1987); JOEL F. HANDLER & ELLEN J. HOLLINGSWORTH, THE "DESERVING POOR": A STUDY OF WELFARE ADMINISTRATION (1971).
3. For works in this other vein, *see, e.g.*, RICHARD A. EPSTEIN, FORBIDDEN GROUNDS: THE CASE AGAINST EMPLOYMENT DISCRIMINATION LAWS (1992); THOMAS SOWELL, CIVIL RIGHTS: RHETORIC OR REALITY? (1984).
4. *E.g.*, Frank I. Michelman, *Foreword: Traces of Self-Government*, 100 HARV. L. REV. 4 (1986); Frank I. Michelman, *Law's Republic*, 97 YALE L.J. 1493 (1988); Suzanna Sherry, *Civic Virtue and the Feminine Voice in Constitutional Adjudication*, 72 VA. L. REV. 543 (1986); Cass R. Sunstein, *Beyond the Republican Revival*, 97 YALE L.J. 1539 (1988); Cass R. Sunstein, *Interest Groups in American Public Law*, 38 STAN. L. REV. 29 (1985).
5. *See* Richard Delgado, *Zero-Based Racial Politics: An Evaluation of Three Best-Case Arguments on Behalf of the Nonwhite Underclass*, 78 GEO. L.J. 1929 (1990).
6. On U.S. slavery and the "separate but equal" regime, *see, e.g.*, DERRICK A. BELL, JR., RACE, RACISM AND AMERICAN LAW 15–46 (3d ed. 1992); A. LEON HIGGINBOTHAM, IN THE MATTER OF COLOR: RACE AND THE AMERICAN LEGAL PROCESS (1978); LEON F. LITWACK, NORTH OF SLAVERY: THE NEGRO IN THE FREE STATES, 1790–1860 (1961). On America's comparative lateness in repudiating slavery, *see* JOHN HOPE FRANKLIN, FROM SLAVERY TO FREEDOM 344–45 (3d ed. 1967); on our systematic mistreatment of Native Americans, *see* Robert A. Williams, Jr., *The Algebra of Federal Indian Law: The Hard Trail of Recolonizing and Americanizing the White Man's Indian Jurisprudence*, 1986 WIS. L. REV. 219; Robert A. Williams, Jr., *Documents of Barbarism: The Contemporary Legacy of European Racism and Colonialism in the Narrative Traditions of Federal Indian Law*, 31 ARIZ. L. REV. 237 (1989).

7. On this problem and that of judicial review generally, *see* LAURENCE H. TRIBE, AMERICAN CONSTITUTIONAL LAW § 16 (2d ed. 1988) (Model VI—Model of Equal Protection); ALEXANDER M. BICKEL, THE LEAST DANGEROUS BRANCH: THE SUPREME COURT AT THE BAR OF POLITICS (2d ed. 1986); John H. Ely, *Toward a Representation-Reinforcing Mode of Judicial Review*, 37 MD. L. REV. 451 (1978); JOHN H. ELY, DEMOCRACY AND DISTRUST: A THEORY OF JUDICIAL REVIEW (1980).

8. On some of these formal values, *see* Richard Delgado, et al., *Fairness and Formality: Minimizing the Risk of Prejudice in Alternative Dispute Resolution*, 1985 WIS. L. REV. 1359, 1383–84, 1400–1401. On the gap between the official values and the informal ones, *see id.* at 1383–84; ALEXIS DE TOCQUEVILLE, DEMOCRACY IN AMERICA (Henry Reeve trans., 1946) (1835); GUNNAR MYRDAL, AN AMERICAN DILEMMA: THE NEGRO PROBLEM AND MODERN DEMOCRACY 23–24 (20th anniversary ed. 1962) (dichotomy persists 100 years later).

9. *Fairness and Formality, supra*, at 1384–85; *see* Richard Delgado, *Words That Wound: A Tort Action for Racial Insults, Epithets, and Name-Calling*, 17 HARV. C.R.-C.L. L. REV. 133 (1982).

10. *Fairness and Formality, supra*, at 1385–86 (on situational dependency of much race-based behavior). That formality is a better guarantee of fairness is only contingently, not necessarily, true. In particular, *see text* immediately following (describing a different situation in South Africa).

11. *See Zero-Based, supra*, at 1930.

12. *E.g.*, CATHARINE A. MACKINNON, SEXUAL HARASSMENT OF WORKING WOMEN: A CASE OF SEX DISCRIMINATION (1979).

13. *E.g.*, Catharine A. MacKinnon, *Pornography, Civil Rights, and Speech* (Biddle Lecture), 20 HARV. C.R.-C.L. L. REV. 1 (1985); CATHARINE A. MACKINNON & ANDREA DWORKIN, PORNOGRAPHY AND CIVIL RIGHTS: A NEW DAY FOR WOMEN'S EQUALITY (1988).

14. CATHARINE A. MACKINNON, FEMINISM UNMODIFIED: DISCOURSES ON LIFE AND LAW (1987).

15. *E.g.*, NEW DAY, *supra*, at 24; FEMINISM UNMODIFIED, *supra*.

16. MALCOLM X (Forty Acres and a Mule Productions, 1992); ALEX HALEY, THE AUTOBIOGRAPHY OF MALCOLM X 175–86 (1965) (on the "whitening" of history); *see also* Trina Grillo & Stephanie M. Wildman, *Obscuring the Importance of Race: The Implication of Making Comparisons Between Racism and Sexism (Or Other -Isms)*, 1991 DUKE L.J. 397, 412 (description of Jewish service in which the Rabbi explained that the covering of the dais was white "to symbolize atonement and cleanliness").

17. JOHN LOCKE, TWO TREATISES OF GOVERNMENT, Ch. 4, §§ 23–24 (Peter Laslett ed., 2d ed. 1970). *See* SEYMOUR DRESCHER, CAPITALISM AND ANTISLAVERY 23–24 and nn.69–70 (1986) (Locke ambivalent, at times supported slavery, other times declared it foul and evil); RUTH W. GRANT, JOHN LOCKE'S LIBERALISM 67 (1987); *see also* FRANKLIN, *supra*, at 78

(Locke wrote that free men of Carolina were entitled to absolute power and authority over Negro slaves, "of what opinion or religion soever").

18. *E.g.,* THOMAS HOBBES, LEVIATHAN, pt. II, ch. 21 (Richard Tuck ed., 1991) ("Of the Liberty of Subjects"); DEBORAH BAUMGOLD, HOBBES' POLITICAL THEORY 93–97 (1988). On the complex relationship of these and other Enlightenment figures to the institution of slavery, *see* ALAN RYAN, PROPERTY 58, 85, 94–100 (1987). *See also* DRESCHER, *supra.*

19. The Framers, like others of this period, often equated light (both the skin color and energy source) with civilization, and darkness with savagery and superstition, *see, e.g.,* Thomas Jefferson, *Notes on the State of Virginia in* 2 WRITINGS OF THOMAS JEFFERSON 192–98, 201 (Definitive Ed., Thomas Jefferson Mem. Assoc. 1905); RACE, RACISM, *supra,* § 1.9, at 29; *see also* J. H. PARRY, THE AGE OF RECONNAISSANCE 281–82 (1963) (Native Americans seen as primitive, savage, endearing, and repulsive, all at same time); HENRY F. MAY, THE ENLIGHTENMENT IN AMERICA 215–17 (1976) (equation of light with knowledge, science, reason, and order). These views were not universal or characteristic of every period—at earlier times, Africans were looked on with curiosity and interest, not repulsion. *See* FRANK M. SNOWDEN, JR., BEFORE COLOR PREJUDICE: THE ANCIENT VIEW OF BLACKS (1983). On the early Elizabethan reception, *see* JAMES WALVIN, BLACK AND WHITE: THE NEGRO IN ENGLISH SOCIETY, 1555–1945, at 19 (1973).

20. *E.g.,* EDMOND S. MORGAN, AMERICAN SLAVERY, AMERICAN FREEDOM: THE ORDEAL OF COLONIAL VIRGINIA (1975) (U.S. presidents were slaveholders during 32 of first 36 years of new republic) (summary, back cover); *accord,* MAY, THE ENLIGHTENMENT, *supra,* at 300–301; RUSSEL B. NYE & J. E. MORPURGO, I HISTORY OF THE UNITED STATES 200 (2d ed. 1964).

21. RACE, RACISM, *supra,* § 1.9, at 26, § 1.16, at 56. Jefferson and even Abraham Lincoln shared these sentiments. *See* THOMAS JEFFERSON, NOTES ON THE STATE OF VIRGINIA 201 (William Peden ed. 1955) (Jefferson advanced "as a suspicion only, that the blacks, whether originally a distinct race, or made distinct by time and circumstances, are inferior to the whites in the endowments both of mind and body. . . . This unfortunate difference of colour, and perhaps of faculty, is a powerful obstacle to the emancipation of these people. . . . When freed he is to be removed beyond the reach of mixture"). *See also* MAY, THE ENLIGHTENMENT, *supra,* at 100 (on Madison); PETER N. CAROLL & DAVID W. NOBLE, THE FREE AND THE UNFREE: A NEW HISTORY OF THE UNITED STATES 138–39 2d ed. 1988); JOHN C. MILLER, THE WOLF BY THE EARS: THOMAS JEFFERSON AND SLAVERY (1977). On Lincoln's view that freeing the slaves was less important than saving the Republic, *see* RACE, RACISM, *supra,* at 9–10, 36.

22. *E.g.,* JAMES G. CROWTHER, FAMOUS AMERICAN MEN OF SCIENCE 138, 141, 148–49 (1937) (Madison thought of Constitution in rationalistic and

Newtonian terms, as a system of devices and balances to maintain equilibrium); *id.* at 135–37 (same: Adams and Taylor); A. KOCH, MADISON'S "ADVICE TO MY COUNTRY" 35 (1966) (Madison and Jefferson collaborated in establishing University of Virginia out of belief that science and liberty would reinforce each other); CALEB P. PATTERSON, THE CONSTITUTIONAL PRINCIPLES OF THOMAS JEFFERSON 188–89 (1953); MARK H. WADDICOR, MONTESQUIEU AND THE PHILOSOPHY OF NATURAL LAW 46–65, 182–92 (1970); THOMAS L. PANGLE, MONTESQUIEU'S PHILOSOPHY OF LIBERALISM (1973); EDWARD M. BURNS, JAMES MADISON: PHILOSOPHER OF THE CONSTITUTION 24–25, 63, 125, 175–84 (1938). On the scientific spirit of early colonial leaders and their enthusiasm for the way that education and science could serve as an antidote for superstition, religious tyranny, and other forms of authoritarianism, *see* BROOKE HINDLE, THE PURSUIT OF SCIENCE IN REVOLUTIONARY AMERICA, 1735–1789 (1956); DON K. PRICE, THE SCIENTIFIC ESTATE 86–88 (1965). On the view that the Constitution was also designed to serve as a perfect countermajoritarian machine—viz., protecting the interests of the white male, propertied class, *see, e.g.,* DERRICK BELL, AND WE ARE NOT SAVED: THE ELUSIVE QUEST FOR RACIAL JUSTICE 26–50 (1987); CHARLES A. BEARD, AN ECONOMIC INTERPRETATION OF THE CONSTITUTION OF THE UNITED STATES (1941).

23. CROWTHER, *supra*, at 141; BURNS, *supra*, at 24–25; WADDICOR, *supra*, at 46–65, 192.
24. On this common insistence that "things are getting better," *see* Richard Delgado, *Derrick A. Bell and the Ideology of Racial Reform: Will We Ever Be Saved?*, 97 YALE L.J. 923, 931–32 (1988); Derrick A. Bell, *Racial Realism*, 24 CONN. L. REV. 363 (1992); DERRICK A. BELL, FACES AT THE BOTTOM OF THE WELL: THE PERMANENCE OF RACISM (1992) (essays showing ineradicability of U.S. racism, but arguing that reformers should nevertheless persist).
25. *See, e.g.,* LEWIS HANKE, BARTOLOME DE LAS CASAS HISTORIADOR (1951) (on the missionary's life and works); AGE OF RECONNAISSANCE, *supra*, at 307–19 (on role of de las Casas in defending the Native American).
26. *See* BELL, FACES, *supra*; MATTER OF COLOR, *supra*; *Algebra, supra*. *See also* First Chronicle, *supra* this volume, on the West's history of colonialism and empire.
27. *See* LITWACK, NORTH, *supra*.
28. On the European Community's relaxation of restrictions on workers' movements, *see* BASIC COMMUNITY LAWS 39–44 (Title III. Free Movement of Persons, Service and Capital), 228–45 (Freedom of Movement for Workers) (Bernard Rudden & Derrick Wyatt eds., 2d ed. 1986).
29. *See* Robert A. Williams, Jr., *The Medieval and Renaissance Origins of the Status of the American Indian in Western Legal Thought*, 57 S. CAL. L. REV. 1 (1983); *Algebra, supra*; *Documents of Barbarism, supra*. *See also* ROBERT

A. WILLIAMS, JR., THE AMERICAN INDIAN IN WESTERN LEGAL THOUGHT: THE DISCOURSES OF CONQUEST (1990) (tracing notions of European superiority in self-justificatory myths used to permit plunder of Native American lands).

30. On this system of imagery and its relation to the First Amendment "marketplace of ideas," see Richard Delgado & Jean Stefancic, *Images of the Outsider in American Law and Culture: Can Free Expression Remedy Systemic Social Ills?*, 77 CORNELL L. REV. 1258 (1992).

31. *E.g.*, RICHARD POSNER, ECONOMIC ANALYSIS OF LAW (4th ed. 1992); *see* Second Chronicle, *supra* this volume.

32. *See* STEPHEN JAY GOULD, THE MISMEASURE OF MAN 30–72 (1981); STEPHEN JAY GOULD, THE FLAMINGO'S SMILE: REFLECTIONS IN NATURAL HISTORY 290–318 (1985) (detailing exaggerations and misstatements of early eugenicists and race-I.Q. theorists bent on proving theories of innate superiority and inferiority); Annette B. Weiner, *Anthropology's Lessons for Cultural Diversity*, CHRON. HIGHER EDUC., July 22, 1992, at B1 (on the way early anthropology played into the hands of racism).

33. Garret Hardin, *Carrying Capacity as an Ethical Concept*, in LIFEBOAT ETHICS: THE MORAL DILEMMA OF WORLD HUNGER 120 (George R. Lucas, Jr. & Thomas W. Ogletree eds., 1976); Garret Hardin, *The Tragedy of the Commons*, 162 SCIENCE 1243 (1968).

34. *Id.* at 1244.

35. Rodrigo and I had discussed this weakness of the law-and-economics approach in Second Chronicle, *supra* this volume. *See also* FORBIDDEN GROUNDS, *supra*, at 26–27 (racial "tastes" or preferences are natural, sometimes rational, and not to be deplored or criminalized).

36. *See, e.g.*, FORBIDDEN GROUNDS, *supra*, at 130–43 (urging that proper role of government is limited to providing for safety against crime, policing against flagrant misrepresentation, and a few other functions).

37. *Id. See also* POSNER, *supra*, § 13.4 ("there is a respectable case for regulation of activities that can cause death"); *id.* § 17.2 (discussing conscription into the military); *id.* §13.1, at 369 (discussing government's role in punishing drunk drivers).

38. I recalled certain hair-raising moments I recently had driving the *autostradas* of Rodrigo's old country, but resolved to hold my tongue.

39. *See* ROBERT V. STOVER, MAKING IT AND BREAKING IT: THE FATE OF PUBLIC INTEREST COMMITMENT DURING LAW SCHOOL (Howard S. Erlanger ed., 1989); Terry Carter, *Why Students Lose Their Interest in Entering Public Interest Work*, NAT'L L.J., July 31, 1989, at 4.

40. On this theory of judicial review (namely that judges should intervene, when necessary, to protect the minority from domination by the majority), *see* THE LEAST DANGEROUS BRANCH, *supra*; DEMOCRACY AND DISTRUST, *supra*; TRIBE, *supra*, at 61–66. Rodrigo seemed to be implying that tyranny of the minority by the majority is virtually a normal state, not a rare miscarriage which alert judges might correct.

41. I had in mind, of course, the period just after *Brown v. Board of Educ.*, 347 U.S. 483 (1954), and later the heady 1960s.
42. On the cyclical nature of racial reform, *see Racial Realism, supra; Interest-Convergence Dilemma, supra; Renaissance Origins, supra;* PATRICIA J. WILLIAMS, THE ALCHEMY OF RACE AND RIGHTS (1991) (showing race's imprint in our history and very thoughts).
43. *See, e.g., Interest-Convergence Dilemma, supra; Ever Saved?, supra;* Gary Peller, *Race Consciousness,* 1990 DUKE L.J. 758.
44. GIRARDEAU A. SPANN, RACE AGAINST THE COURT: THE SUPREME COURT AND MINORITIES IN CONTEMPORARY AMERICA (1993) (putting forward the view that the Supreme Court is unlikely to advance minorities' interests, and that faith in the Court as an instrument of social reform is seriously misplaced).
45. On these constitutional and prudential doctrines that confine the judiciary's reach, *see* TRIBE, *supra,* at 77–82, 82–93, 107–11.
46. *See Images of the Outsider, supra;* Richard Delgado, *Recasting the American Race Problem,* 79 CAL. L. REV. 1389 (1991); Charles Lawrence, *The Id, the Ego, and Equal Protection: Reckoning with Unconscious Racism,* 39 STAN. L. REV. 317 (1987).
47. *Recasting, supra.*
48. Lani Guinier, *No Two Seats: The Elusive Quest for Political Equality,* 77 VA. L. REV. 1413 (1991); Lani Guinier, *The Triumph of Tokenism: The Voting Rights Act and the Theory of Black Electoral Success,* 89 MICH. L. REV. 1077 (1991).
49. *E.g.,* HOLLOW HOPE, *supra;* Duncan Kennedy, *A Cultural Pluralist Case for Affirmative Action in Legal Academia,* 1990 DUKE L.J. 705.
50. On the role of liberation theology on behalf of the poor in Latin America and elsewhere, *see* Claude Pomerleau, *The Christian Left in Latin America, in* III LATIN AMERICA AND CARIBBEAN CONTEMPORARY RECORD 246 (Jack W. Hopkins ed., 1985); Claude Pomerleau, *Changing Roles in Latin American Catholicism, in id.* vol. IV, at 95.
51. *See, e.g.,* Colo. Const. art. II, § 30(b) ("Amendment 2," enacted in 1992 by initiative and providing that no subdivision of the state may enact a gay-rights law or ordinance; enforcement currently prohibited by judicial injunction); *see* Evans v. Romer, 854 P.2d 1270, petition for cert. filed (Sept. 21, 1993); *see* Reitman v. Mulkey, 387 U.S. 369 (1967) (invalidating California proposition that prohibited local measures to integrate housing).
52. *See* note immediately *supra; see also* Derrick A. Bell, Jr., *The Referendum: Democracy's Barrier to Racial Equality,* 54 WASH. L. REV. 1 (1978) (calling attention to way that the referendum process can give effect to racist sentiments).
53. United States v. Carolene Prod. Co., 304 U.S. 144, 152 n.4 (1938); *see Toward Representation, supra;* DEMOCRACY AND DISTRUST, *supra.*
54. On the way that the careers of even eminent justices are sometimes marred by anomalous opinions, *see* Richard Delgado & Jean Stefancic, *Norms and Narratives: Can Judges Avoid Serious Moral Error?,* 69 TEX. L. REV. 1929 (1991).

55. Much earlier Rodrigo had alerted me to the possibility that this might be so. *See* First Chronicle, Third Chronicle, both *supra* this volume.

56. On the way that perspectivism, semantics, narrative theory, and other aspects of poststructuralist thought came late to legal academia—and are still resisted by many judges—*see* Pierre Schlag, *Normative and Nowhere to Go*, 43 STAN. L. REV. 167 (1990). On the critique of legal formalism, *see generally* THE POLITICS OF LAW: A PROGRESSIVE CRITIQUE (David Kairys ed., rev. ed. 1992); on that of the current school of normative analysis as empty, self-referential, and inscribed, *see Symposium: The Critique of Normativity*, 139 U. PA. L. REV. 801 (1991).

57. RHETORIC OR REALITY?, *supra*, at 77–79.

58. On the relaxed, reassuring cardigan-wearing TV black, *see* Shelby Steele, *I'm Black, You're White—Who's Innocent?*, HARPERS' MAGAZINE, June 1988, at 45.

59. I could not help contrasting our reception here with that which we received at the hands of fellow diners in another restaurant, *see* Second Chronicle, *supra* this volume.

60. *E.g., Ever Saved?, supra.*

61. First Chronicle, *supra* this volume.

62. *E.g.,* AMERICAN INDIAN ENVIRONMENTS: ECOLOGICAL ISSUES IN NATIVE AMERICAN HISTORY (Christopher Vecsey & Robert W. Venables eds., 1980); Rennard Strickland, *The Idea of Environment and the Ideal of the Indian*, 10 J. AM. INDIAN EDUC. 8 (1970); N. Scott Momaday, *An American Land Ethic, in* ECOTACTICS: THE SIERRA CLUB HANDBOOK FOR ENVIRONMENTAL ACTIVISTS 97 (John G. Mitchell & Constance L. Stallings eds., 1970); David H. Getches, *A Philosophy of Permanence: The Indians' Legacy for the West*, J. OF THE WEST, July 1990, at 54–55, 64, 67.

63. I was reminded of the vitality I had observed in the American Southwest on a recent trip. Many well-known painters and writers have sought refuge and refreshment there over the years, including D. H. Lawrence, Georgia O'Keefe, Carol Griggs, and Natalie Goldberg.

64. On the Harlem Renaissance, *see* CATHERINE SILK & JOHN SILK, RACISM AND ANTI-RACISM IN AMERICAN POPULAR CULTURE 63 (1990); WILLIAM L. VAN DEBURG, SLAVERY AND RACE IN AMERICAN POPULAR CULTURE 120–21, 202–203, 211 (1984).

65. *See, e.g.,* Stanley Fish, *There's No Such Thing as Free Speech*, BOSTON REV., Feb. 1992, at 3; Schlag, *supra*; Winter, *Cognitive Stakes, supra*.

66. On Critical Race Theory, *see* Alan D. Freeman, *Legitimizing Racial Discrimination Through Antidiscrimination Law: A Critical Review of Supreme Court Doctrine*, 62 MINN. L. REV. 1049 (1978); Kimberlè W. Crenshaw, *Race, Reform, and Retrenchment: Transformation and Legitimation in Antidiscrimination Law*, 101 HARV. L. REV. 1331 (1988); *Annotated Bibliography, supra*.

67. *E.g.,* FEMINISM UNMODIFIED, *supra* (employing perspectivism, textual analysis, and other techniques associated with postmodern thought in developing a critique of law centered on women and women's role).

68. I winced, once again, at Rodrigo's casual mention of the possibility of violence. *See* First Chronicle, Third Chronicle, *supra* this volume.
69. *See* RACE, RACISM, *supra*, § 1.9 at 27–30 (identifying clauses in original document that implicitly or explicitly provided for the continuation of slavery).
70. *Id*. at 27–29; *see also* BEARD, *supra*.
71. RACE, RACISM, *supra*, at 26.
72. *See* Jack Kisling, *No . . . Uh . . . Men Need Apply*, DENVER POST, May 4, 1993, at 7B (lamenting that most advice columnists are women, writing for women); *see also* Michael Levin, *Book Review*, 5 CONST. COMMENTARY 201 (1988) (attributing women authors' success to a kind of "intellectual affirmative action," in which their work is published and reviewed under more relaxed standards than those applied to men).

Notes to Chapter 8

1. Regina Austin, *"The Black Community," Its Lawbreakers, and a Politics of Identification*, 65 S. CAL. L. REV. 1769 (1992) (discussing relation of black community to its offenders).
2. DERRICK BELL, AND WE ARE NOT SAVED: THE ELUSIVE QUEST FOR RACIAL JUSTICE 162–77 (the Chronicle of the Amber Cloud), 215–35 (Chronicle of the Slave Scrolls), 245–58 (the Chronicle of the Black Crime Cure) (1987).
3. *See* Memphis v. Greene, 451 U.S. 100 (1981) (concerning litigation over an affluent white community that built a wall to discourage the entry of cars from a nearby lower-class black area).
4. *E.g.*, CRIMINAL CAREERS AND "CAREER CRIMINALS" (Alfred Blumstein, Jacqueline Cohen, Jeffrey A. Roth, & Christy A. Visher eds., 1986); MARVIN WOLFGANG, DELINQUENCY CAREERS IN TWO BIRTH CO-HORTS 99–174, 271–72 (1992); MARVIN WOLFGANG, DELINQUENCY IN A BIRTH COHORT 65–74, 89–99, 269–71 (1972).
5. *See e.g.*, MARC MAUER, YOUNG BLACK MEN AND THE CRIMINAL JUSTICE SYSTEM (1992).
6. ANDREW HACKER, TWO NATIONS: BLACK AND WHITE, SEPARATE, HOSTILE, UNEQUAL 180, 188 (1992); U.S. DEP'T OF COMMERCE, BUREAU OF THE CENSUS, STATISTICAL ABSTRACT OF THE UNITED STATES 1992 83, 197; *see also* SOCIETY, Jan./Feb. 1992, at 3.
7. REPORT OF THE NATIONAL ADVISORY COMMISSION ON CIVIL DISORDERS (1968) ("Kerner Commission Report"); NATIONAL COMMIS-SION ON THE CAUSES AND PREVENTION OF VIOLENCE, TO ES-TABLISH JUSTICE, TO INSURE DOMESTIC TRANQUILLITY (1969); PRESIDENT'S COMMISSION ON LAW ENFORCEMENT AND THE AD-MINISTRATION OF JUSTICE, THE CHALLENGE OF CRIME IN A FREE SOCIETY (1967).
8. U.S. DEP'T OF LABOR, OFFICE OF POLICY PLANNING AND RE-

SEARCH, THE NEGRO FAMILY: THE CASE FOR NATIONAL ACTION (1965).

9. Alfred Blumstein, *On the Racial Disproportionality of United States' Prison Populations*, 73 J. CRIM. L. AND CRIMINOLOGY 1259 (1982) (arguing that high black crime rate is real and not the product of discriminatory enforcement).

10. *E.g.*, MICKEY KAUS, THE END OF EQUALITY (1992); DANIEL PATRICK MOYNIHAN, FAMILY AND NATION (1986); CHARLES MURRAY, LOSING GROUND: AMERICAN SOCIAL POLICY, 1950–1980 (1984); WILLIAM JULIUS WILSON, THE TRULY DISADVANTAGED: THE INNER CITY, THE UNDERCLASS, AND PUBLIC POLICY (1987).

11. Richard Delgado & Jean Stefancic, *Images of the Outsider in American Law and Culture: Can Free Expression Remedy Systemic Social Ills?*, 77 CORNELL L. REV. 1258, 1261–75 (1992); Adeno Addis, *"Hell, Man, They Did Invent Us": The Mass Media, Law, and African Americans*, 41 BUFF. L. REV. 523, 553–58 (1993).

12. *Images, supra*, at 1275–77.

13. *Images, supra*, at 1262–67 (describing the Tom, the Coon, the Jemima, and the superstud images that proliferated at various periods).

14. For an account of this period, *see, e.g.*, RICHARD KLUGER, SIMPLE JUSTICE: THE HISTORY OF BROWN V. BOARD OF EDUCATION AND BLACK AMERICA'S STRUGGLE FOR EQUALITY (1976); JUAN WILLIAMS, EYES ON THE PRIZE: AMERICA'S CIVIL RIGHTS YEARS, 1954–1965 (1987).

15. For a description of the ebb and flow of America's racist depictions of blacks, *see Images, supra*, at 1266–67.

16. *Images, supra*, at 1264–65, 1267.

17. The author collects racial grotesquerie. Rodrigo is referring to a state fair poster with a grinning stereotype of an Asian. The poster was withdrawn because of the activism of a group of law students and faculty in the region.

18. U.S. DEPARTMENT OF JUSTICE, UNIFORM CRIME REPORTS FOR THE UNITED STATES 1991, at 27, 39, 44 (1992) (listing disaggregated statistics for robbery, burglary, and larceny-theft); Russell Mokhiber, *Invisible, Expensive Crime*, WASH. POST, Nov. 18, 1991, at A-20; *see also* RUSSELL MOKHIBER, CORPORATE CRIME AND VIOLENCE 3 (1988) (comparing losses due to burglary, street murder, and manslaughter with those due to corporate crime and violence).

19. *See The Bill for Graffiti Is Past Due*, L.A. TIMES, Aug. 8, 1993, at B12 (California Dep't of Transportation estimates overall private and public cost of removing graffiti is $66 million for California). California has approximately one-ninth of the United States total population. Extrapolation from these two figures gives an estimated national bill of $600 million for removing graffiti.

20. *See infra*, Appendix 8A (setting out Rodrigo's calculation). On white-collar crime in general, *see* Robert S. Bennett, *Eighth Survey of White Collar Crime*, 30 AM. CRIM. L. REV. 441 (1993).

21. There is no commonly accepted definition of white-collar crime, but most writers consider that it includes bribery, embezzlement, fraud (other than welfare fraud), price-fixing, and insider trading—in general, nonviolent economic crimes that include some degree of fraud, collusion, or deception and that lack an element of face-to-face interpersonal force. *See* STANTON WHEELER, KENNETH MANN, & AUSTIN SARAT, SITTING IN JUDGMENT: THE SENTENCING OF WHITE-COLLAR CRIMINALS 5 (1988); DAVID WEISBURD, STANTON WHEELER, ELIN WARING, & NANCY BODE, CRIMES OF THE MIDDLE CLASS: WHITE-COLLAR OFFENDERS IN THE FEDERAL COURTS 9–11 (1991). A few authorities, such as Russell Mokhiber, *supra*, and Ralph Nader include the marketing of known dangerous products, toxic dumping, and other acts of corporate irresponsibility as white-collar crimes. On annual losses from white-collar crime, see Appendix 8A.

22. UNIFORM, *supra*, at 231; MIDDLE CLASS, *supra*, at 50; *see also Invisible*, *supra* (noting that all 46 of the individuals convicted of Operation Ill-Wind defense procurement fraud were white males); *infra* this section (observing that no CEO of a Fortune 500 corporation is black). For a narrative discussion of each of the scandals Rodrigo mentions, *see* CORPORATE CRIME, *supra*. For a discussion of the role of "opportunity" in white-collar crime, *see* MIDDLE CLASS, *supra*, at 74–99.

23. On the recoveries of some of the losses from defense procurement fraud, *see* William Barr, *Foreword, Seventh Survey of White Collar Crime*, 29 AM. CRIM. L. REV. 169, 171–72 (1992); Appendix 8A, *infra*. On bribery, *see* CORPO-RATE CRIME, *supra*, at 258–66 (describing the Lockheed bribery scandal). On PACs, honoraria, and other forms of "legal bribery," *see* 1992 FACTS ON FILE 673, 681 at B3, 682 at B1 (reporting yearly figures close to $75 million). *See also* Russell Mokhiber, *Corporate Crime and Violence in Review: The 10 Worst Corporations of 1991*, MULTINATIONAL MONITOR, Dec. 1991, at 10 (noting that the individuals convicted in operation Ill-Wind and the vast majority of those convicted in the recent Wall Street insider trade scandals were white males).

24. *See* CORPORATE CRIME, *supra*, at 15 (estimating that corporate illegal trade practices cost $174 to $231 billion a year); *see also id.* at 16, 213–27 (discussing the approximately $2 billion costs of the General Electric price-fixing conspiracy and analyzing the General Motors predatory conspiracy).

25. *See Invisible, supra* (estimating cost to consumers at $300 to $500 billion). On mortgage and escrow-company abuses, totaling as much as $5 to $10 billion/year, *see* Victoria Reid, *Homeowners Challenging Mortgage Escrow Abuses*, DENVER POST, Aug. 10, 1993, at 3C, col. 1; Kenneth Harney, *Mortgage Includes 'Junk' Fees, id.*

26. *See infra*, Appendix 8A (setting out this calculation); *Ten Worst, supra*, at 9 (stating that "corporation crime and violence combined inflicts far greater damage on society than all street crime combined").

27. *See* Victoria Slind-Flor, *A City's Week of Darkness: Legal Community Mourns Its Dead and Redirects Its Rage*, NAT'L L.J., July 19, 1993, at 1.

28. *See* HARRY KALVEN, THE NEGRO AND THE FIRST AMENDMENT (1965) (arguing that reforms born of the cauldron of social injustice often end up benefiting all of society, not just blacks).

29. *See Developments in the Law—Corporate Crime: Regulating Corporate Behavior Through Criminal Sanctions*, 92 HARV. L. REV. 1227, 1368 (1979) (noting and partially endorsing the use of criminal sanctions, although confessing that fines will often be most effective as punishments); CORPORATE CRIME, *supra*, at 6.

30. Gady A. Epstein, *Judge Cuts Milken Jail Time: Ex-Junk Bond King's Term in Prison Ends in March*, THE BOSTON GLOBE, Aug. 6, 1992, at 53; Larry Reibstein, *Wall Street's Cons Paid Their Debt to Society—But Have Plenty to Spare*, NEWSWEEK, Oct. 7, 1991, at 44; CORPORATE CRIME, *supra*, at 1–10, 23, 25–38, 220; CHRISTOPHER STONE, WHERE THE LAW ENDS 57 (1975). On the theory of corporate punishment, *see* John C. Coffee, Jr., *"No Soul to Damn: No Body to Kick": An Unscandalized Inquiry into the Problem of Corporate Punishment*, 79 MICH. L. REV. 386 (1981).

31. *See* JUDGMENT, *supra*, at 15–16 (Table 1), 16–22, 46–50; CORPORATE CRIME, *supra*, at 20–21, 26–29, 32, 35 (explaining that judges are apt to consider white-collar criminals more sensitive and redeemable than other offenders, hence less appropriate candidates for harsh punishment). *See also* Russell Mokhiber, *George Bush: White-Collar Criminal Coddler*, N.J.L.J., Sept. 14, 1992, at 15.

32. Lisa C. Ikemoto, *The Code of Perfect Pregnancy: At the Intersection of the Ideology of Motherhood, the Practice of Defaulting to Science, and the Interventionist Mindset of Law*, 53 OHIO ST. L.J. 1205, 1244 n.186 (1992). *See also id.* at 1248–49; In re Jamaica Hospital, 491 N.Y.S.2d 898 (N.Y. Sup. Ct. 1985) (requiring pregnant woman to undergo unwanted blood transfusion in order to save the life of a midterm fetus).

33. Steven Findlay, *Medicine by the Book*, U.S. NEWS AND WORLD REP., July 6, 1992, at 68 ("About 20 percent of hysterectomies and coronary bypass, back and prostate surgery, as well as dozens of other medical procedures, are done unnecessarily, often before trying more conservative measures."); *Wasted Health Care Dollars*, CONSUMER REPORTS, July, 1992, at 435, 440 (citing study which found that 27% of hysterectomies were unnecessary); Judith Randal, *Mammoscam*, NEW REPUB., Oct. 12, 1992, at 13.

34. Jenni Bergal, *How Self-Referral Gives Physicians a License to Steal*, CHICAGO TRIBUNE, Dec. 16, 1992, at 27 (citing study showing that in Florida in 1991, cancer patients were overcharged about $12 million because of physician self-referral); David Brown, *When Healing, Investing Overlap: "Physician Self-Referral" Divides Medical Community*, WASH. POST, Dec. 6, 1992, at A1 (1989 study showed that Medicare patients whose doctors had financial interest in laboratories received 45% more lab tests than did Medicare patients as a group); THE MACNEIL/LEHRER NEWSHOUR: OPTIONS FOR CHANGE (PBS television broadcast, May 25, 1993) (discussing medical malpractice, including

abuse of physician self-referral); Francis J. Serbaroli, *New York's Tough New Anti-Referral Law*, N.Y.L.J., Jan. 5, 1993, at 1 (discussing law recently signed by Governor Cuomo which prohibits and restricts referrals to labs in which the doctor has a financial interest).

35. CORPORATE CRIME, *supra*, at 307–17.
36. *See id.* at 6, 267–75 (noting the 22 suicide deaths and numerous injuries caused by Love Canal); *id.* at 6, 87 (observing the 2,000 to 5,000 deaths and 200,000 injuries resulting from deadly gas escapes at the Union Carbide plant in Bhopal, India); *id.* at 383–90 (discussing Reserve Mining dumping of toxic mining waste that endangered the lives of over 150,000 local residents). *See also* WHO'S POISONING AMERICA (R. Nader, et al. eds., 1981); Michael Weissklopf, *Particles in Air Help Kill 60,000 a Year, Study Says*, WASH. POST, May 13, 1991, at A-13; Spencer Heinz, *The Glossary of Ecospeak: A Language of Losses and Lessons*, OREGONIAN, Apr. 22, 1990, § 4, at 10 (reporting that U.S. industry put 22 billion pounds of chemicals into U.S. air, water, and ground in a recent year).
37. 588 F. Supp. 247 (D. Utah 1984), reversed 816 F.2d 1417 (10th Cir. 1987), cert. denied, 484 U.S. 1004 (1988).
38. *See Deaths Associated with Infant Carriers*, 267 J. AM. MED. ASSN. 2586 (May 20, 1992).
39. War Powers Resolution, P.L. 93–148, 87 Stat. 555 (1973) (H.J. Res. 542, adopted over presidential veto on November 7, 1973; codified as 50 U.S.C. § 1541 (1988).
40. U.S. Const. art. 1, § 8, cl. 11. For a discussion of the constitutionality of undeclared wars, *see* John Hart Ely, *The American War in Indochina, Part I: The (Troubled) Constitutionality of the War They Told Us About*, 42 STAN. L. REV. 877 (1990); *id. Part II: The Unconstitutionality of the War They Didn't Tell Us About*, 42 STAN. L. REV. 1093 (1990).
41. On limitations to warmaking, *see, e.g.*, T. O. ELIAS, THE MODERN LAW OF TREATIES 114–18, 138–42 (1974).
42. ZBIGNIEW BRZEZINSKI, OUT OF CONTROL: GLOBAL TURMOIL ON THE EVE OF THE TWENTY-FIRST CENTURY 9 (1993) (citing total number of deaths from wars and other aggressions during twentieth century).
43. *Id.* at 9–10. *See* Appendix 8B, *infra*, giving statistics for more recent wars.
44. *See infra*, Appendix 8B.
45. On the small number of African-American chief executive officers, *see* Shelly Branch, *America's Most Powerful Black Executives*, BLACK ENTERPRISES, Feb. 1993, at 78, 92 (not a single black CEO in any of nation's top 500 industrial corporations).
46. For various estimates of the number of deaths resulting from slavery, *see, e.g.*, HOWARD ZINN, A PEOPLE'S HISTORY OF THE UNITED STATES 29 (1980) (50 million deaths from the institution as a whole); Donna Britt, *The Dimensions of a Number*, WASH. POST, May 28, 1993, at D1 (discussing the controversy over the number of deaths from crossing the Atlantic on their way to

slavery in the Americas and concluding that estimates range from 7 to 40 million); TONI MORRISON, BELOVED (1987) (dedication page, citing the figure of "60 million and more").

47. *Amnesty Cites Rising U.S. Executions*, DENVER POST, July 9, 1993, at 10-1.

48. *Id.*; Stanford v. Kentucky, 492 U.S. 361 (1989) (approving execution of children aged 16 and 17); Penry v. Linaugh, 492 U.S. 392 (1989) (of the mentally retarded). *See generally* VICTOR L. STREIB, DEATH PENALTY FOR JUVENILES (1987) (discussing the American criminal justice system and its current and historical willingness to execute juveniles).

49. McCleskey v. Kemp, 481 U.S. 279, 286–87 (1987). *See also* DAVID C. BALDUS & JAMES W.L. COLE, STATISTICAL PROOF OF DISCRIMINATION (1980 and Supp. 1987); TWO NATIONS, *supra*, at 183 (most crime is *intra*-racial—that is, whites tend to be victims of other whites).

50. STATISTICAL, *supra*; 481 U.S. at 287.

51. TWO NATIONS, *supra*, at 180, 197.

52. YOUNG BLACK MEN, *supra*, at 8. *See also Developments, supra.*

53. On the impact of race on the treatment of offenders, *see Developments in the Law—Race and the Criminal Process*, 101 HARV. L. REV. 1472 (1988). On sentencing, *see id.* at 1603–40; *cf.* Sheri L. Johnson, *Unconscious Racism and the Criminal Law*, 73 CORNELL L. REV. 1016 (1988) (discussing the role of racism and unconscious racism in the criminal law).

54. Rodrigo's Printout, *infra*, at Appendix 8A.

55. I was astonished by Rodrigo's effrontery, but immediately thought of the spate of books that had focused on the allegedly dysfunctional black family. Rodrigo's suggestion was sure to spark controversy—I thought of the many white folks I knew who were certain that their own family structure was the best in the world and the model for others. But, then it struck me—was that Rodrigo's point, namely to show his readers how blacks feel when their family is depicted as socially pathological?

56. On Italy's approach to child-raising and early education, *see, e.g.*, E. M. STANDING, MARIA MONTESSORI: HER LIFE AND WORK (1957); CAROLYN EDWARDS, LELLA GANDINI, & GEORGE FORMAN, THE HUNDRED LANGUAGES OF CHILDREN: THE REGGIO EMILIA APPROACH TO EARLY CHILDHOOD EDUCATION (1993).

57. KEVIN PHILLIPS, THE POLITICS OF RICH AND POOR: WEALTH AND THE AMERICAN ELECTORATE IN THE REAGAN AFTERMATH 96, 114, 217 (1990).

58. *U.S. Gets Less Competitive as Japan Stays on Top, Annual Survey Indicates*, ATLANTA J. AND CONST., June 22, 1992, at A10 (asserting that the American economy is now fifth in world, and its workforce only seventh best). *See also Top 10 Countries for Quality of Life*, WASH. POST, Nov. 5, 1991, at 25 (placing the United States in seventh place, behind Japan, Canada, Iceland, Sweden, Switzerland, and Norway, on quality-of-life measurements such as life expectancy, income, and infant mortality).

59. On the problems of today's middle class, *see, e.g.*, Stephen Koepp, *Is the Middle Class Shrinking?*, TIME, Nov. 3, 1986, at 54; Lance Morrow, *Voters Are Mad as Hell*, TIME, March 2, 1992, at 16, 19–20.

60. *See infra* Appendix 8A (calculating losses due to white-collar crime to be $411 to $806 per U.S. citizen, considerably more if corporate misconduct is added to the total).

61. *See, e.g.*, Robert A. Williams, Jr., *The Algebra of Federal Indian Law: The Hard Trail of Decolonizing and Americanizing the White Man's Indian Jurisprudence*, 1986 WIS. L. REV. 219; Robert A. Williams, Jr., *Documents of Barbarism: The Contemporary Legacy of European Racism and Colonialism in the Narrative Traditions of Federal Indian Law*, 31 ARIZ. L. REV. 237 (1989).

62. *See, e.g.*, U.S. DEP'T OF COMMERCE, WORKERS WITH LOW EARNINGS: 1964 TO 1990, P-60, No. 178 (Mar. 1992) (reporting that between 1979 and 1990 proportion of full-time workers who earned less than poverty-level wages increased from 12.1 to 18 percent, resulting in a total of 14.4 million workers in 1990); THE REAGAN YEARS (J. Palmer & I. Sawhill eds. 1986) (analyzing effects of recent trend to emphasize the business sector at expense of social spending); POLITICS OF RICH AND POOR, *supra* (discussing concentration of wealth and power at expense of poor and middle class).

63. *E.g.*, Lillie Fong, *Flood Victims Get a Colorado Hand: TV Stations, Charities Accepting Donations of Money, Food and Other Supplies for Midwest*, ROCKY MT. NEWS, July 16, 1993, at 6-A; Liz Spayd, *For Volunteers from D.C. Area, Flood Means a Working Vacation*, WASH. POST, July 29, 1993, at A4.

64. *Around the Nation: Rescued Girl's Circulation Improves; Reagans Send Cheer*, WASH. POST, Oct. 19, 1987, at A-10.

65. *See supra* this chapter (discussing Harry Kalven's The Negro and the First Amendment).

Notes to Chapter 9

1. The Association of American Law Schools (AALS) is the semiofficial organization of U.S. law schools and professors, with a membership of about 159 schools and 7,446 professors and administrators. It holds an annual meeting and many regional workshops. The annual meeting, held in different cities every year, spans several days, draws over a thousand professors, and includes 50 to 100 section meetings, workshops, and plenary sessions, all held in one or more large, conference-type hotels. *See* Assoc. Amer. Law Schools, 1994 Annual Meeting Program.

2. On legal storytelling, *see generally* Symposium: *Legal Storytelling*, 87 MICH. L. REV. 2073 (1989); Richard Delgado, *Brewer's Plea: Critical Thoughts on Common Cause*, 44 VAND. L. REV. 1 (1991). For critiques of legal storytelling, *see, e.g.*, Randall Kennedy, *Racial Critiques of Legal Academia*, 102 HARV. L. REV. 1745 (1989); Daniel Farber & Suzanna Sherry, *Telling Stories Out of School: An Essay on Legal Narratives*, 45 STAN. L. REV. 807 (1993); Arthur

Austin, *Storytelling Deconstructed by Double Session*, 46 U. MIAMI L. REV. 1155 (1992); *Deconstructing Voice Scholarship*, 30 HOUSTON L. REV. 1671 (1993); Mark Tushnet, *The Degradation of Constitutional Discourse*, 81 GEO. L.J. 251 (1992). *See also* William van Alstyne, *The University in the Manner of Tiananmen Square*, 21 HAST. CON. L.Q. 1 (1993) (employing storytelling to criticize diversity movement in university governance).

3. On the critique of storytelling (narrative jurisprudence), *see* Farber & Sherry, *supra*; Arthur Austin, *Double Session, Deconstructing, supra*; Randall Kennedy, *supra*; William van Alstyne, *supra*. *See also* Daniel Farber & Suzanna Sherry, *The 200,000 Cards of Dimitri Yurasov: Further Reflections on Scholarship and Truth*, 46 STAN. L. REV. 647 (1994).

4. *Out of School, supra*, at 809–19.

5. *See, e.g.*, Richard Delgado, *On Telling Stories in School: A Reply to Farber and Sherry*, 46 VAND. L. REV. 665, 668–69 (1993), making this point.

6. Derrick Bell, *Serving Two Masters: Integration Ideals and Client Interests*, 85 YALE L.J. 470 (1976).

7. On the use of stories to accomplish these purposes, *see, e.g.*, Milner Ball, *Stories of Origin and Constitutional Possibilities*, 87 MICH. L. REV. 2280 (1989); Richard Delgado, *Storytelling for Oppositionists and Others: A Plea for Narrative*, 87 MICH. L. REV. 2411 (1989).

8. *Out of School, supra*, at 809, 830–54 & n.244 (citing Stone and Rubin).

9. Tushnet, *Degradation, supra*, at 251, 260–77.

10. *Id.* at 260–77 (distortions and exaggerations).

11. *Id.* at 263–76.

12. For examples of Professor Ross's writings in the narrative-analysis vein, *see, e.g.*, *Innocence and Affirmative Action*, 43 VAND. L. REV. 297 (1990); *The Rhetorical Tapestry of Race: White Innocence and Black Abstraction*, 32 WM. & MARY L. REV. 1 (1990); *The Richmond Narratives*, 68 TEX. L. REV. 381 (1989); *The Rhetoric of Poverty: Their Immorality, Our Helplessness*, 79 GEO. L.J. 1499 (1991); *Metaphor and Paradox*, 23 GA. L. REV. 1053 (1989).

13. *The Discourse of Constitutional Degradation*, 81 GEO. L.J. 313 (1992).

14. *Resistance to Stories*, 67 S. CAL. L. REV. 255 (1994).

15. *Hearing the Call of Stories*, 79 CAL. L. REV. 971 (1991).

16. Edward L. Rubin, *Beyond Truth: A Theory for Evaluating Legal Scholarship*, 80 CAL. L. REV. 889 (1993).

17. *Outsider Scholarship: The Law Review Stories*, 63 U. COLO. L. REV. 683 (1992).

18. *See* DERRICK BELL, FACES AT THE BOTTOM OF THE WELL: THE PERMANENCE OF RACISM 158–194 (1992).

19. PATRICIA WILLIAMS, THE ALCHEMY OF RACE AND RIGHTS: DIARY OF A LAW PROFESSOR 44–51 (1991).

20. *ZigZag Stitching and the Seamless Web: Thoughts on "Reproduction" and the Law*, 13 NOVA L. REV. 355 (1989).

21. President Clinton nominated Professor Guinier for the position of Assistant Attorney General but withdrew the nomination when it became controversial.

See Clint Bolick, *Clinton's Quota Queens*, WALL ST. J., April 30, 1993, at A12; Alexander Aleinikoff & Richard H. Pildes, *In Defense of Lani Guinier*, WALL ST. J., May 13, 1993, at A15.

22. *Derrick Bell Leaving Harvard*, N.Y. TIMES, Oct. 28, 1992, at C-1; *Harvard Law Notifies Bell of Dismissal*, N.Y. TIMES, Jul. 1, 1992, at A-19.

23. *See, e.g.*, *Out of School, supra*, at 835–38 (applying the term).

24. On counterstories, *see* Delgado, *Plea for Narrative, supra*, at 2412–18, 2429–35.

25. On this and similar responses to the new Critical Race Theory generation of narrativists, *see, e.g.*, Richard Delgado, *The Imperial Scholar Revisited: How to Marginalize Outsider Writing, Ten Years Later*, 140 U. PA. L. REV. 1349 (1992).

26. On the romanticization of all things black during this period, *see* Richard Delgado & Jean Stefancic, *Images of the Outsider in American Law and Culture: Can Free Expression Remedy Systemic Social Ills?* 77 CORNELL L. REV. 1258, 1266 (1992).

27. On the "small pool" argument, *see, e.g.*, Kennedy, *Critiques, supra*, at 1762–65. For responses to this argument, *see* Richard Delgado, *Mindset and Metaphor*, 103 HARV. L. REV. 1872, 1875–76 (1990); Ross, *Richmond Narratives, supra*.

28. *See* Richard Delgado, *The Imperial Scholar: Reflections on a Review of Civil Rights Literature*, 132 U. PA. L. REV. 561, 561 (1984).

29. First Chronicle, *supra* this volume.

30. *See* Seventh Chronicle, *supra* this volume.

31. AALS Annual Meeting: Struggle Between Author/Editor—Control of Text (Tapes 160–161, on file with author). *See also* 1994 Annual Meeting Program, *supra*, at 94–95, describing Open Program on Scholarship and Law Reviews: The Struggle Between Author and Editor for Control of the Text and Gathering to Consider Formation as an AALS Section. ("In the organizational meeting to determine if a Section on Scholarship and Law Reviews should be formed, we will discuss the struggle between author and editor for control of the text").

32. *Struggle, supra*; *Law Reviews: A Waste of Time and Money?* (round table), AMER. LAWYER, April 1994, at 50.

33. *See* Seventh Chronicle, *supra* this volume (discussing similar point).

34. On the discontent of many young lawyers, *see* Stephanie Goldberg, *Quality of Life Trade-Offs*, A.B.A. J., Apr. 1989, at 38; *Satisfaction*, A.B.A. J., Apr. 1989, at 40; John Halstuk, *Rising Tide of Lawyers Who Quit*, S.F. CHRON., Oct. 2, 1989, at A-1, col. 1.

35. *See, e.g.*, Girardeau Spann, *Pure Politics*, 88 MICH. L. REV. 1971 (1990) (on the difficulties of effecting racial reform through litigation); DERRICK BELL, AND WE ARE NOT SAVED: THE ELUSIVE QUEST FOR RACIAL JUSTICE (1991) (on the failures of various civil rights strategies); RICHARD DELGADO & JEAN STEFANCIC, FAILED REVOLUTIONS: SOCIAL REFORM AND THE LIMITS OF LEGAL IMAGINATION (Westview Press 1994) (same).

36. Spann, *Pure Politics*, *supra*; Richard Delgado & Jean Stefancic, *The Social Construction of* Brown v. Board of Education: *Law Reform and the Reconstructive Paradox*, 36 WM. & MARY L. REV. (forthcoming 1994).
37. *Social Construction of Brown*, *supra*.
38. Michael Klarman, Brown, *Racial Change and the Civil Rights Movement*, 80 VA. L. REV. 7, 11–12, 76–86 (1994).
39. *Id.* at 8, 11–12.
40. On the plight of black schoolchildren today, *see*, *e.g.*, *id.* at 11–12, 76–86; ANDREW HACKER, TWO NATIONS: BLACK AND WHITE, SEPARATE, HOSTILE, UNEQUAL (1992); Jerome Culp, *Water Buffaloes and Diversity: Naming Names and Reclaiming the Racial Discourse*, 26 CONN. L. REV. 209, 246–47 (1993) (on situation in law schools).
41. For a similar argument, *see*, *e.g.*, Richard Delgado, *Shadowboxing: An Essay on Power*, 77 CORNELL L. REV. 813 (1992). *See also* Fourth Chronicle, *supra*.
42. Sources cited immediately *supra*; *see also* Social Construction of Brown, *supra*; CATHARINE MACKINNON, FEMINISM UNMODIFIED (1987) (on the way cultural practices and meanings impede reform).
43. *Social Construction of* Brown, *supra*.
44. *Id.*; Klarman, *supra*, at 11–12, 76–86.
45. Milliken v. Bradley, 433 U.S. 267 (1977).
46. Metropolitan desegregation plans are permissible only if segregation is found to have resulted from official discrimination, not individual decisions of white families to flee from black areas. *Id.*
47. San Antonio Indep. School Dist. v. Rodriguez, 411 U.S. 1 (1973).
48. *Id.*; James v. Valtiera, 402 U.S. 137 (1971).
49. RACE AGAINST THE COURT: THE SUPREME COURT AND MINORITIES IN CONTEMPORARY AMERICA (1993).
50. *Id.* (on instability of court-won gains). *See also* BELL, NOT SAVED, *supra*, at 26–74 (same).
51. Richard Whitmire, *Adults in Poll: It's Worst Time Since Slavery*, DENVER POST, May 27, 1994, at 2-A, col. 2.
52. *Id.* For further statistics on the black condition, *see* ANDREW HACKER, TWO NATIONS, *supra*.
53. For the development of the *imposition* trope, *see* Richard Delgado & Jean Stefancic, *Imposition*, 35 WM. & MARY L. REV. 1025 (1994).
54. ALCHEMY, *supra*.
55. *Plea for Narrative*, *supra*, at 2415, 2434–35.
56. *Compare* Jonathan Yardley, *The Code Word: Alarming*, WASH. POST, Aug. 16, 1993, at B2 (Style).
57. *Images*, *supra*, at 1262–64.
58. *Id.* at 1264–66.
59. *Id.* at 1275.
60. *Id.* at 1275–76.
61. *Id.* at 1281–82.
62. AGAINST THE COURT, *supra*.

63. *Imposition, supra*, at 1025–26.
64. *Out of School, supra*, at 835–38; *Ten Years Later, supra*, at 1366–67.
65. *E.g.*, Kimberlè Crenshaw, *Foreword: Toward a Race-Conscious Pedagogy in Legal Education*, 11 NAT. BLACK L.J. 1 (1989).
66. *E.g.*, BELL, NOT SAVED, *supra*; DERRICK BELL, FACES AT THE BOT-TOM OF THE WELL (1994).
67. Arthur Austin, *Political Correctness Is a Footnote*, 71 OR. L. REV. 543, 548–51, 554 *n.*81, 555 (1992).
68. *Tiananmen Square, supra.*
69. First Chronicle, Seventh Chronicle, *supra* this volume. *See also* Pierre Schlag, *Normative and Nowhere To Go*, 43 STAN. L. REV. 167 (1990); *Symposium, The Critique of Normativity*, 139 U. PA. L. REV. 801–1075 (1991) (all on the changing legal paradigm).
70. *See Waste of Time, supra.*
71. *See, e.g.*, Cramton, *"The Most Remarkable Institution:" The American Law Review*, 36 J. LEGAL ED. 1 (1986); John Kester, *Faculty Participation in Student-Edited Law Reviews*, 36 J. LEGAL ED. 14 (1986); Richard A. Posner, *Legal Scholarship Today*, 45 STAN. L. REV. 1647, 1656 (1993); *Waste, supra.*
72. *E.g.*, Lino Graglia, *Race Conscious Remedies*, 9 HARV. J.L. & PUB. POL'Y 83 (1986); Suzanna Sherry, *The Forgotten Victims*, 63 U. COLO. L. REV. 375, 376–80 (1993).

Appendix 1A

Rodrigo's Printout #1: The West's Predicament

A. *Essays and Books on the Theory of Cyclicity in Nations and Cultures*

ROBERT M. ADAMS, DECADENT SOCIETIES (1983).

THE BREAKDOWN OF DEMOCRATIC REGIMES (Joan J. Linz & Alfred Stepan eds., 1978)

DANIEL BELL, THE CULTURAL CONTRADICTIONS OF CAPITALISM (1975).

GEORG W. F. HEGEL, PHILOSOPHY OF RIGHT 13 (T. M. Knox trans., 1967).

DAVID HUME, POLITICAL ESSAYS 120 (Charles W. Hendel ed., 1953).

MANCUR OLSON, THE RISE AND DECLINE OF NATIONS: ECONOMIC GROWTH, STAGFLATION, AND SOCIAL RIGIDITIES (1982).

PITIRIM A. SIROKIN, THE CRISIS OF OUR AGE (1942).

OSWALD SPENGLER, DECLINE OF THE WEST (Helmut Werner ed., 1991).

ARNOLD TOYNBEE, CIVILIZATION ON TRIAL (1948).

B. *Essays and Articles on the General Decline of the West*

BELL, *supra.*

ALLAN BLOOM, THE CLOSING OF THE AMERICAN MIND (1987).

LAWRENCE HAWORTH, DECADENCE AND OBJECTIVITY (1977).

CHRISTOPHER LASCH, THE CULTURE OF NARCISSISM: AMERICAN LIFE IN AN AGE OF DIMINISHING EXPECTATIONS (1978).

ALASDAIR C. MACINTYRE, AFTER VIRTUE: A STUDY IN MORAL THEORY (2d ed. 1984).

SPENGLER, *supra.*

Israel Shanker, *Solzhenitsyn, in Harvard Speech, Terms West Weak and Cowardly,* N.Y. TIMES, June 9, 1978, at A8.

Michael Loewe, *Decline and Fall in East and West,* 19 EUR. J. SOC. 168 (1978).

C. Essays and Books on the United States's and West's Economic Decline

AMERICAN ENTERPRISE INSTITUTE FOR PUBLIC POLICY RESEARCH,
SHARING WORLD LEADERSHIP?: A NEW ERA FOR AMERICA & JAPAN
(John H. Makin & Donald C. Hellmann eds., 1989).

BARRY BLUESTONE & BENNETT HARRISON, THE GREAT AMERICAN
JOB MACHINE: THE PROLIFERATION OF LOW-WAGE EMPLOYMENT
IN THE U.S. ECONOMY (1986).

PEARL M. KAMER, THE U.S. ECONOMY IN CRISIS: ADJUSTING TO THE
NEW REALITIES (1988).

TOM KEMP, CLIMAX OF CAPITALISM: THE U.S. ECONOMY IN THE
TWENTIETH CENTURY (1990).

JAMES LAXER, DECLINE OF THE SUPERPOWERS: WINNERS AND LOS-
ERS IN TODAY'S GLOBAL ECONOMY (1987).

FRANK S. LEVY & RICHARD C. MICHEL, THE ECONOMIC FUTURE OF
AMERICAN FAMILIES: INCOME AND WEALTH TRENDS (1941).

PAUL A. TIFFANY, THE DECLINE OF AMERICAN STEEL: HOW MAN-
AGEMENT, LABOR, AND GOVERNMENT WENT WRONG (1988).

DAVID M. TUCKER, THE DECLINE OF THRIFT IN AMERICA (1990).

America's Wasting Disease, ECONOMIST, Mar. 25, 1989, at 95.

Charles A. Ferguson, *America's High-Tech Decline*, FOREIGN POL'Y, Spring
1989, at 123.

Samuel P. Huntington, *The U.S. —Decline or Renewal?*, FOREIGN AFF., Winter
1988/89, at 76.

Paul Kennedy, *The U.S. as World Leader: The (Relative) Decline of America*, CUR-
RENT, Dec. 1987, at 30.

Robert Kuttner, *The Abyss: Does America Have a Parachute?*, NEW REPUBLIC,
Oct. 29, 1990, at 21.

Werner Meyer-Larsen, *America's Century Will End with a Whimper: A German
Forecasts the Decline of a Superpower*, WORLD PRESS REV., Jan. 1991, at 24.

Alicia H. Munnell, *Why Have Productivity and Growth Declined?*, NEW EN-
GLAND ECON. REV., Jan. 1, 1990, at 3.

Ben Stein, *The Decline and Fall of the American Empire*, BUS. MONTHLY, May
1990, at 60.

Suffering from Decline? Try the Consortium Cure, ECONOMIST, Mar. 25, 1989,
at 45.

D. Essays and Books on Problems of the Cities and the Underclass

REYNOLDS FARLEY & WALTER ALLEN, THE COLOR LINE AND THE
QUALITY OF LIFE IN AMERICA (1987).

WILLIAM J. WILSON, THE TRULY DISADVANTAGED: THE INNER CITY,
THE UNDERCLASS, AND PUBLIC POLICY (1987).

Jose E. Becerra et al., *Infant Mortality Among Hispanics*, 265 JAMA 217 (1991).

Council on Ethical and Judicial Affairs, *Black-White Disparities in Health Care*, 263 JAMA 2344 (1990).

Sarah Glazer, *Crime and Punishment: A Tenuous Link*, EDITORIAL RES. REP. 586, 596 (1989).

Ezra E. H. Griffin & Carl C. Bell, *Recent Trends in Suicide and Homicides Among Blacks*, 262 JAMA 2265 (1989).

Gene Koretz, *A Disturbing Decline in Black Life Expectancy*, BUS. WEEK, Feb. 27, 1989, at 28.

Study Finds High Death-Sentencing Rate Among Blacks, NAT'L CATH. REP., Apr. 20, 1990, at 5.

Philip Yam, *Grim Expectations: Life Expectancy of Blacks Is Sliding*, SCI. AM., Mar. 1991, at 33.

Allan C. Hutchinson, *Indiana Dworkin and Law's Empire*, 96 YALE L.J. 637 (1987) (book review).

This last source offered a dazzling array of statistics:

Percentage of black children who live below the poverty line: 47.3.

Percentage of nonblack Americans who say that there should be a law against interracial marriage: 28.

Percentage of nonblack Americans who say that blacks "should not push themselves where they are not wanted": 58.

Chance that a white male in the United States will be murdered in a given year: 1 in 9927.

Chance that a black male in the United States will be murdered in a given year: 1 in 1539.

Percentage of black high school graduates over 16 who are unemployed: 18.3.

Percentage of white high school dropouts under 25 who are unemployed: 15.2.

Percentage of blacks unemployed in 1984: 17.2.

Percentage of whites unemployed in 1984: 7.2.

Percentage increase in ratio of black to white unemployment rates between 1965 and 1984: 20.

Percentage of elected officials who were black in 1985: 1.2.

Percentage of black families below poverty level: 32.4.

Percentage of white families at poverty level: 9.7.

Ratio of male black children dying in first year of life to male white children dying in first year of life: 1.8 to 1.

Percentage of persons in New Orleans who are black: 50.

Percentage of qualified applicants for police in New Orleans who are black: 40.

Percentage of police officers in New Orleans who are black: 2.

Chance of an American being in state prison on any given day: 1 in 800.

Chance of a black male American being in state prison on any given day: 1 in 33.

Median income for all black families in 1983: $14,506.

Median income for all white families in 1983: $25,757.

Median income of black families as a percentage of that of white families in 1970: 61.

Median income of black families as a percentage of that of white families in 1983: 56.

Percentage increase in black unemployment rate from 1972–82: 82.

Percentage increase in white unemployment rate from 1972–82: 69.

Id. at 662–64.

When I queried him about the relevance of these statistics, Rodrigo explained that great disparity in wealth and well-being is a standard index of social malaise and a barometer indicating possible trouble for a society. It later struck me that slavery and other forms of group exploitation may be fully compatible with stability and a flourishing of the arts.

E. Books and Articles on the United States's and West's Environmental Predicament and Exhaustion of Natural Resources

RACHEL CARSON, SILENT SPRING (1963).
ALDO LEOPOLD, SAND COUNTY ALMANAC (1972).
REWEAVING THE WORLD: EMERGENCE OF ECOFEMINISM (Irene Diamond & Gloria F. Orenstein eds., 1990).
WILLIAM H. RODGERS, NATURAL RESOURCES LAW: CASES AND MATERIALS (2d ed. 1983).

Derrick Bell, *After We're Gone: Prudent Speculations on America in a Post-Racial Epoch*, 34 ST. LOUIS U. L.J. 393 (1990).

See also sources cited *supra* (United States's high rates of incarceration, white-collar and ordinary crime, law school test scores, declining quality of life, lengthening work week, and increasing indicators of stress).

Appendix 1B

Rodrigo's Printout #2: Non-Western Sources

A. *Essays and Books on Non-Western Business Organization and Management*

WILLIAM G. OUCHI, THEORY Z: HOW AMERICAN BUSINESS CAN MEET THE JAPANESE CHALLENGE (1981).

YOSHITAKA SUZUKI, JAPANESE MANAGEMENT STRUCTURES 1920–80 (1991).

Alan S. Blinder, *How Japan Puts the "Human" in Human Capital*, BUS. WK., Nov. 11, 1991, at 22.

The Evolving Mind of Global Management: An Inside View of Japan in a Changing Business Environment, FORTUNE, July 29, 1991, at S1.

Neil Gross, *Rails That Run on Software*, BUS. WK., Oct. 25, 1991, at 84.

B. *Essays and Books on Japanese Educational Systems*

JAMES J. SHIELDS, JAPANESE SCHOOLING: PATTERNS OF SOCIALIZATION, EQUALITY, AND POLITICAL CONTROL (1989).

David Seligman, *Is America Smart Enough? IQ and National Productivity*, 43 NAT'L REV., Apr. 15, 1991, at 24.

Alison L. Sprout, *Do U.S. Schools Make the Grade?*, FORTUNE, Spring 1991, at 50.

C. *Essays and Books on Eastern Religious and Mystical Thought and Its Relation to Modern Physics*

ROBERT AITKIN, TAKING THE PATH OF ZEN (1982).

FRITJOF CAPRA, THE TAO OF PHYSICS (2d ed. 1983).

ALAN W. WATTS, THE WAY OF ZEN (1957).

GARY ZUKAV, THE DANCING WU LI MASTERS: AN OVERVIEW OF THE NEW PHYSICS (1979).

D. Books on Hispanic Families and Caregiving

ESSAYS ON MEXICAN KINSHIP (Hugo G. Nutini et al. eds., 1976).

OSCAR LEWIS, FIVE FAMILIES (1965).

EDWARD RIVERA, FAMILY INSTALLMENTS: MEMORIES OF GROWING UP HISPANIC (1982).

RICHARD RODRIGUEZ, HUNGER OF MEMORY: THE EDUCATION OF RICHARD RODRIGUEZ (1981).

E. Essays and Books on the Influence of Black Composers and Musicians on American Popular Music

BLACK MUSIC IN THE HARLEM RENAISSANCE: A COLLECTION OF ES-SAYS (Samuel A. Floyd, Jr. ed., 1991).

JAMES H. CONE, THE SPIRITUALS AND THE BLUES: AN INTERPRETA-TION (1991).

ARNOLD SHAW, BLACK POPULAR MUSIC: FROM THE SPIRITUALS, MIN-STRELS, AND RAGTIME TO SOUL, DISCO, AND HIP-HOP (1986).

DAVID TOOP, THE RAP ATTACK: AFRICAN JIVE TO NEW YORK HIP HOP (1984).

Mark Moses, *Aretha*, NEW YORKER, Feb. 1, 1988, at 84.

Lynn Norment, *Music*, EBONY, Aug. 1991, at 42.

Ed Ward, *Generation Rap*, MOTHER JONES, Oct. 1988, at 48.

F. Essays and Books on the Influence of American Indian Ideas on the U.S. Constitution

BRUCE JOHANSEN, FORGOTTEN FOUNDERS: BENJAMIN FRANKLIN, THE IROQUOIS, AND THE RATIONALE FOR THE AMERICAN REVO-LUTION (1982).

NATIVE ROOTS: HOW THE INDIANS NOURISHED AMERICA (1991).

J. MCIVER WEATHERFORD, INDIAN GIVERS: HOW THE INDIANS OF THE AMERICAS TRANSFORMED THE WORLD (1988).

Felix Cohen, *Americanizing the White Man*, in THE LEGAL CONSCIENCE: SELECTED PAPERS OF FELIX COHEN 315 (Lucy K. Cohen ed., 1960).

Rodrigo's Printout #3: White-Collar and Street Crime, Property Losses

I. Costs of Street Crime per Year
   Robberies: $562 million (UNIFORM, *supra,* at 27)
   Burglary: $3.9 billion (*id.* at 39)
   Larceny-theft: $3.9 billion (*id.* at 44) (category includes picking pockets, purse-snatching, theft from cars, bicycle theft, etc.)
   Graffiti: $600 million (*Bill for Graffiti, supra;* STATISTICAL AB-STRACT, *supra,* at 22) (figure reached through rough calculation of multiplying the figure for California by its proportion of the U.S. population)
   TOTAL: $9 billion
II. Costs of White-Collar/Corporate Crime per Year (*see supra* for a description of white-collar crime)
   A. Individual
      Tax fraud: $100–200 billion. (Michael Kinsley, *TRB: From Washington: Accounts Receivable,* NEW REPUBLIC, June 8, 1992, at 6)
      Embezzlement and banking fraud (other than S & L scandal): $800 million (Efforts to Combat Criminal Financial Institution Fraud, Hearings before the Subcommittee on Consumer and Regulatory Affairs of the Senate Committee on Banking, Housing, and Urban Affairs, 102d Cong., 2d Sess. 537, at 53 (1992))
      Insider trading, antitrust violations, and securities fraud: $2 billion (CORPORATE CRIME, *supra,* at 3; *see also Invisible Crime, supra;* MIDDLE CLASS, *supra,* at 24–28; *Drexel Burnham Lambert Files for Bankruptcy, Facts on File,* WORLD NEWS DIGEST, Feb. 16, 1990, at 102)

Bribery: $20 million (CORPORATE CRIME, *supra,* at 264)
TOTAL: $100–200 billion

B. Corporate Crime/Corruption
Defense procurement fraud: $230 million (Barr, *supra,* at 172)
Consumer fraud: $174–231 billion (CORPORATE CRIME, *supra,* at 15)
Savings and loan scandal: $30–50 billion (*Invisible Crime, supra,* at A20)
Toxic dumping: $15–25 billion/year ($300–500 billion over a 20-year period) (Adriel Bettelheim, *Munitions Mess on Public Lands,* DENVER POST, July 9, 1993, at A1. *See Ten Worst, supra,* at 14-15, 17)
Nuclear cleanup: $13 billion/year ($400 billion over a 30-year period) (*Washington Whispers,* U.S. NEWS AND WORLD REP., July 12, 1993, at 24)
TOTAL: $228–$319 billion

C. Total White-Collar Crime: $328–519 billion

III. Comparisons
Population of the United States: 253 million (STATISTICAL ABSTRACT, *supra,* at 1) 84% is white (*id.* at 16) 12% is black (*id.*)
Ratio of white to black population: approximately 7:1
Costs of street crime per U.S. citizen/year: $35
Costs of individual white-collar crime per U.S. citizen/year: $395–790
Costs of individual white-collar plus corporate crime per U.S. citizen/year: $1252–1952
Ratio of cost of individual white-collar to street crime: 11:1 to 22:1
Ratio of cost of individual white-collar plus corporate crime to street crime: 36:1 to 55:1

Appendix 8B

Rodrigo's Printout #4: Annual Deaths from Street Crime, Corporate Crime and Misconduct, and Wars and Military Actions, Compared

I. Deaths Resulting Annually from Street Crime
Murder and nonnegligent manslaughter: 24,703 (UNIFORM, *supra,* at 13)

II. Deaths Resulting Annually from Corporate Actions
Cigarettes: 350,000 (Frank J. Vandall, *Reallocating the Costs of Smoking: The Application of Absolute Liability to Cigarette Manufacturers,* 52 OHIO ST. L.J. 504 (1991))
Asbestos-related cancer: 8,000 (CORPORATE CRIME, *supra,* at 284)
Dangerous products: 28,000 (*id.* at 16)
The use of infant formula rather than breast-feeding, worldwide: 1,000,000 (*id.* at 4, 307–17)
*Employee exposure to dangerous chemicals and other safety hazards:*100,000 (*id.* at 16)
TOTAL: 1,486,000 deaths per year

III. Military Actions
U.S. military deaths resulting from undeclared wars since 1950: an average of 2,250/year (90,000 total deaths) (JAMES STOKESBURY, A SHORT HISTORY OF THE KOREAN WAR 254 (1988); GUENTHER LEWY, AMERICA IN VIETNAM 451 (1978). *See also* this appendix, *supra,* giving totals including deaths of enemy soldiers and noncombatants.)

IV. Comparisons of Annual Death Statistics
Corporate and military actions combined: 1,488,250 deaths
Ratio of deaths resulting from corporate crimes and undeclared wars to ones resulting from street crime: 60:1

Causes of deaths: One out of 518 Americans will die because of corporate actions. One out of 10,242 Americans will die because of street crime.

The bottom of Rodrigo's printout contained the following handwritten note:

Dear Professor:

Much white-collar crime by nature is surrounded by stealth and not discovered, if at all, until much later. Many of my figures are only for successful prosecutions— the actual amount of crime is probably much higher. In a few cases, the figures I've brought up result from a years-long investigation and, in that sense, may be atypically large—*i.e.*, greater than those for surrounding years. (*E.g.*, Barr, *supra*, describing successful investigation of defense procurement fraud, Operation Ill-Wind). Not all my figures are for the same year, although I've tried to make them both as recent and as typical as possible. New information is coming out all the time. I can show you how to program your computer to update automatically, if you like.

Best of luck at the panel discussion, and let me know if I can help.